THE MAKING OF ENGLISH LITERATURE

The Making of English Literature

By

Abraham Mathew

CYBER TECH PUBLICATIONS
4264/3, Ansari Road, Daryaganj, New Delhi-110002 (India)
Ph.: 011-23244078, 011-43559448 Fax: 011-23280028
E-Mail: cyberpublicationsdelhi@yahoo.com
Website: www.cybertechpublications.com

The Making of English Literature

Abraham Mathew

First Edition 2011

Asian Offset Printers

Published by
G.S. Rawat for Cyber Tech Publications
4264/3, Ansari Road, Daryaganj, New Delhi-110002 (India)
Ph.: 011-23244078, 011-43559448 Fax: 011-23280028
E-Mail: cyberpublicationsdelhi@yahoo.com
cyberpublications@gmail.com
Website: www.cybertechpublications.com

Contents

Preface

> "It may easily come to pass that a vain man may become proud and imagine himself pleasing to all when he is in reality a universal nuisance."
>
> —*Benedict Spinoza*

No exaggeration, English is the largest spoken language of the world, moreso in the modern times. English literature is widely read throughtout the world and it serves as global lingua franca. In the strict sense, by English literature we mean the literature produced by English speaking Britishers (i.e. UK nationals). Though as of now this is loosened as very good literature that too voluuminously is being produced in English all over the world.

The Making of English Literature presents a vivid account of it from beginning to the present times. Since it is impossible to deal with such an vast topic in single volume, we have touched some topics spherically while all others are dealt with elaborately. The judiciously selected readings are grouped under the following chapters—Introduction; Early English Literature; Major Trends in Medieval Literature; Seventeenth Century Literature: A Survey; Elizabethan Literature and Ben Jonson; A Survey of Augustan Literature; Eighteenth Century Literature: An Overview; Later Eighteenth Century Literature; The Nineteenth Century English Literature; Modern Phase and Bibliography etc.

Certainly, students, researchers, teachers of English literature besides all inquisitive readers will find this volume informative and useful.

For furnishing authentic information, we have drawn upon authoritative works of many scholars in the field. We have tried to acknowledge them amply in references and bibliography. If any name is left, it is unintentional. We express our gratefulness to these scholars.

My teachers, colleagues and friends have contributed a lot in completing this work by way of guidance, inspiration and assistance. I am extremely grateful to them also. Last but not the least I am thankful to my publishers for publishing this work in superb way.

—Abraham Mathew

1

Introduction

"No literature is complete until the language in which it is written is dead."

—*H.W. Longfellow*

English as of now can be rightly considered as global lingua franca. Evolved in Great Britain, it has traversed a long path to reach global dimensions. Every student of English literature must know how English language came to being.

Here in this chapter we will describe the long journey of English during different epochs of history.

It is pertinent to note that present English race has gradually shaped itself out of several distinct peoples which successively occupied or conquered the island of Great Britain. The earliest one of these peoples which need here be mentioned belonged to the Celtic family and was itself divided into two branches. The Goidels or Gaels were settled in the northern part of the island, which is now Scotland, and were the ancestors of the present Highland Scots.

On English literature they exerted little or no influence until a late period. The Britons, from whom the present Welsh are descended, inhabited what is now England and

Wales; and they were still further subdivided, like most barbarous peoples, into many tribes which were often at war with one another.

Though the Britons were conquered and chiefly supplanted later on by the Anglo-Saxons, enough of them, were spared and intermarried with the victors to transmit something of their racial qualities to the English nation and literature. The characteristics of the Britons, which are those of the Celtic family as a whole, appear in their history and in the scanty late remains of their literature.

Two main traits include or suggest all the others: first, a vigorous but fitful emotionalism which rendered them vivacious, lovers of novelty, and brave, but ineffective in practical affairs; second, a somewhat fantastic but sincere and delicate sensitiveness to beauty. Into impetuous action they were easily hurried; but their momentary ardor easily cooled into fatalistic despondency.

To the mysterious charm of Nature—of hills and forests and pleasant breezes; to the loveliness and grace of meadow-flowers or of a young man or a girl; to the varied sheen of rich colors—to all attractive objects of sight and sound and motion their fancy responded keenly and joyfully; but they preferred chiefly to weave these things into stories and verse of supernatural romance or vague suggestiveness; for substantial work of solider structure either in life or in literature they possessed comparatively little faculty. Of the Roman conquest and occupation of Britain (England and Wales) we need only make brief mention, since it produced virtually no effect on English literature. The fact should not be forgotten that for over three hundred years, from the first century A.D. to the beginning of the fifth, the island was a Roman province, with Latin as the language of the ruling class of Roman immigrants, who introduced

Roman civilization and later on Christianity, to the Britons of the towns and plains. But the interest of the Romans in the island was centered on other things than writing, and the great bulk of the Britons themselves seem to have been only superficially affected by the Roman supremacy. At the end of the Roman rule, as at its beginning, they appear divided into mutually jealous tribes, still largely barbarous and primitive.

The Anglo-Saxons

Meanwhile across the North Sea the three Germanic tribes which were destined to form the main element in the English race were multiplying and unconsciously preparing to swarm to their new home. The Angles, Saxons, and Jutes occupied territories in the region which includes parts of the present Holland, of Germany about the mouth of the Elbe, and of Denmark. They were barbarians, living partly from piratical expeditions against the northern and eastern coasts of Europe, partly from their flocks and herds, and partly from a rude sort of agriculture.

At home they seem to have sheltered themselves chiefly in unsubstantial wooden villages, easily destroyed and easily abandoned; For the able-bodied freemen among them the chief occupation, as a matter of course, was war. Strength, courage, and loyalty to king and comrades were the chief virtues that they admired; ferocity and cruelty, especially to other peoples, were necessarily among their prominent traits when their blood was up; though among themselves there was no doubt plenty of rough and ready companionable good-humor.

Their bleak country, where the foggy and unhealthy marshes of the coast gave way further inland to vast and somber forests, developed in them during their long inactive winters a sluggish and gloomy mood, in which, however, the alternating spirit of aggressive enterprise was never quenched. In religion they had reached a moderately advanced state of heathenism, worshipping especially, it seems, Woden, a 'furious' god as well as a wise and crafty one; the warrior Tiu; and the strong-armed Thunor (the Scandinavian Thor); but together with these some milder deities like the goddess of spring, Eostre, from whom our Easter is named.

For the people on whom they fell these barbarians were a pitiless and terrible scourge; yet they possessed in undeveloped form the intelligence, the energy, the strength—most of the qualities of head and heart and body—which were to make of them one of the world-races of renown.

In fact, the process by which Britain became England was a part of the long agony which transformed the Roman Empire into modern Europe. In the fourth century A. D. the Angles, Saxons, and Jutes began to harry the southern and eastern shores of Britain, where the Romans were obliged to maintain a special military establishment against them. But early in the fifth century the Romans, hard-pressed even in Italy by other barbarian invaders, withdrew all their troops and completely abandoned Britain. Not long thereafter, and probably before the traditional date of 449, the Jutes, Angles, and Saxons began to come in large bands with the deliberate purpose of permanent settlement. Their conquest, very different in its methods and results from that of the Romans, may roughly be said to have occupied a hundred and fifty or two hundred years.

The earlier invading hordes fixed themselves at various points on the eastern and southern shore and gradually fought their way inland, and they were constantly augmented by new arrivals. In general the Angles settled in the east and north and the Saxons in the south, while the less numerous Jutes, the first to come, in Kent, soon ceased to count in the movement. In this way there naturally came into existence a group of separate and rival kingdoms, which when they were not busy with the Britons were often at war with each other. Their number varied somewhat from time to time as they were united or divided; but on the whole, seven figured most prominently, whence comes the traditional name 'The Saxon Heptarchy' (Seven Kingdoms).

The resistance of the Britons to the Anglo-Saxon advance was often brave and sometimes temporarily successful. Early in the sixth century, for example, they won at Mount Badon in the south a great victory, later connected in tradition with the legendary name of King Arthur, which for many years gave them security from further aggressions. But in the long run their racial defects proved fatal; they were unable to combine in permanent and steady union, and tribe by tribe the newcomers drove them slowly back; until early in the seventh century the Anglo-Saxons were in possession of nearly all of what is now England, the exceptions being the regions all along the west coast, including what has ever since been, known as Wales. Of the Roman and British civilization the Anglo-Saxons were ruthless destroyers, exulting, like other barbarians, in the wanton annihilation of things which they did not understand. Every city, or nearly every one, which they took, they burned, slaughtering the inhabitants. They themselves occupied the land chiefly as masters of scattered farms, each warrior established in a large rude house surrounded by its various outbuildings and the huts of the British slaves and the Saxon and British bondmen.

Just how largely the Britons were exterminated and how largely they were kept alive as slaves and wives, is uncertain; but it is evident that at least a considerable number were spared; to this the British names of many of our objects of humble use, for example *mattoc* and *basket*, testify. In the natural course of events, however, no sooner had the Anglo-Saxons destroyed the (imperfect and partial) civilization of their predecessors than they began to rebuild one for themselves; possessors of a fertile land, they settled down to develop it, and from tribes of lawless fighters were before long transformed into a race of farmer-citizens.

Gradually trade with the Continent, also, was reestablished and grew; but perhaps the most important humanizing influence was the reintroduction of Christianity. The story is famous of how Pope Gregory the Great, struck by the beauty of certain Angle slave-boys at Rome, declared that they ought to be called not *Angli* but *Angeli* (angels) and forthwith, in 597, sent to Britain St. Augustine (not the famous African saint of that name), who landed in Kent and converted that kingdom. Within the next two generations, and after much fierce fighting between the adherents of the two religions, all the other kingdoms as well had been christianized.

It was only the southern half of the island, however, that was won by the Roman missionaries; in the north the work was done independently by preachers from Ireland, where, in spite of much anarchy, a certain degree of civilization had been preserved. These two types of Christianity, those of Ireland and of Rome, were largely different in spirit. The Irish missionaries were simple and loving men and won converts by the beauty of their lives; the Romans brought with them the architecture, music, and learning of their imperial city and the aggressive energy which in the following centuries was to make their Church supreme throughout the Western world.

When the inevitable clash for supremacy came, the king of the then-dominant Anglian kingdom, Northumbria, made choice of the Roman as against the Irish Church, a choice which proved decisive for the entire island. And though our personal sympathies may well go to the finer-spirited Irish, this outcome was on the whole fortunate; for only through religious union with Rome during the slow centuries of medieval rebirth could England be bound to the rest of Europe as one of the family of cooperating Christian states; and outside that family she would have been isolated and spiritually starved. One of the greatest gifts of Christianity, it should be observed, and one of the most important influences in medieval civilization, was the network of monasteries which were now gradually established and became centers of active hospitality and the chief homes of such learning as was possible to the time.

Evolution of Early Literature

The Anglo-Saxons doubtless brought with them from the Continent the rude beginnings of poetry, such as come first in the literature of every people and consist largely of brief magical charms and of rough 'popular ballads' (ballads of the people). The charms explain themselves as an inevitable product of primitive superstition; the ballads probably first sprang up and developed, among all races, in much the following way. At the very beginning of human society, long before the commencement of history, the primitive groups of savages who then constituted mankind were instinctively led to express their emotions together, communally, in rhythmical fashion. Perhaps after an achievement in hunting or war the village-group would mechanically fall into a dance, sometimes, it might be, about their village fire. Suddenly from among the inarticulate cries of the crowd some one excited individual would shout

out a fairly distinct rhythmical expression. This expression, which may be called a line, was taken up and repeated by the crowd; others might be added to it, and thus gradually, in the course of generations, arose the regular habit of communal composition, composition of something like complete ballads by the throng as a whole.

This procedure ceased to be important everywhere long before the literary period, but it led to the frequent composition by humble versifiers of more deliberate poems which were still 'popular' because they circulated by word of mouth, only, from generation to generation, among the common people, and formed one of the best expressions of their feeling. At an early period also professional minstrels, called by the Anglo-Saxons scops or gleemen, disengaged themselves from the crowd and began to gain their living by wandering from village to village or tribe to tribe chanting to the harp either the popular ballads or more formal poetry of their own composition.

Among all races when a certain stage of social development is reached at least one such minstrel is to be found as a regular retainer at the court of every barbarous chief or king, ready to entertain the warriors at their feasts, with chants of heroes and battles and of the exploits of their present lord. All the earliest products of these processes of 'popular' and minstrel composition are everywhere lost long before recorded literature begins, but the processes themselves in their less formal stages continue among uneducated people (whose mental life always remains more or less primitive) even down to the present time.

Out of the popular ballads, or, chiefly, of the minstrel poetry which is partly based on them, regularly develops epic poetry. Perhaps a minstrel finds a number of ballads which deal with the exploits of a single hero or with a single event. He combines them as best he can into a unified story and recites this on important and stately occasions. As his work passes into general circulation other minstrels add other ballads, until at last, very likely after many generations, a complete epic is formed, outwardly continuous and whole, but generally more or less clearly separable on analysis into its original parts. Or, on the other hand, the combination may be mostly performed all at once at a comparatively late period by a single great poet, who with conscious art weaves together a great mass of separate materials into the nearly finished epic. Not much Anglo-Saxon poetry of the pagan period has come down to us. By far the most important remaining example is the epic 'Beowulf,' of about three thousand lines.

This poem seems to have originated on the Continent, but when and where are not now to be known. It may have been carried to England in the form of ballads by the Anglo-Saxons; or it may be Scandinavian material, later brought in by Danish or Norwegian pirates. At any rate it seems to have taken on its present form in England during the seventh and eighth centuries. It relates, with the usual terse and unadorned power of really primitive poetry, how the hero Beowulf, coming over the sea to the relief of King Hrothgar, delivers him from a monster, Grendel, and then from the vengeance of Grendel's only less formidable mother. Returned home in triumph, Beowulf much later receives the due reward of his valor by being made king of his own tribe, and meets his death while killing a fire-breathing dragon which has become a scourge to his people. As he appears in the poem, Beowulf is an idealized Anglo-Saxon hero, but in origin he may have been any one of several other different things. Perhaps he was the old Germanic god Beowa, and his exploits originally allegories, like some of those in the Greek mythology, of his services to man; he may, for instance, first have been the sun, driving away the mists and cold of winter and of the swamps, hostile forces personified in Grendel and his mother.

Or, Beowulf may really have been a great human fighter who actually killed some especially formidable wild beasts, and whose superhuman strength in the poem results, through the similarity of names, from his being confused with Beowa.

In fact, 'Beowulf' presents an interesting though very incomplete picture of the life of the upper, warrior, caste among the northern Germanic tribes during their later period of barbarism on the Continent and in England, a life more highly developed than that of the Anglo-Saxons before their conquest of the island. About King Hrothgar are grouped his immediate retainers, the warriors, with whom he shares his wealth; it is a part of the character, of a good king to be generous in the distribution of gifts of gold and weapons.

Somewhere in the background there must be a village, where the bondmen and slaves provide the daily necessaries of life and where some of the warriors may have houses and families; but all this is beneath the notice of the courtly poet. The center of the warriors' life is the great hall of the king, built chiefly of timber. Inside, there are benches and tables for feasting, and the walls are perhaps adorned with tapestries. Near the center is the hearth, whence the smoke must escape, if it escapes at all, through a hole in the roof.

In the hall the warriors banquet, sometimes in the company of their wives, but the women retire before the later revelry which often leaves the men drunk on the floor. Sometimes, it seems, there are sleeping-rooms or niches about the sides of the hall, but in 'Beowulf' Hrothgar and his followers retire to other quarters. War, feasting, and hunting are the only occupations in which the warriors care to be thought to take an interest. The spirit of the poem is somber and grim.

There is no unqualified happiness of mood, and only brief hints of delight in the beauty and joy of the world. Rather, there is stern satisfaction in the performance of the warrior's and the sea-king's task, the determination of a strong-willed race to assert itself, and do, with much barbarian boasting, what its hand finds to do in the midst of a difficult life and a hostile nature. For the ultimate force in the universe of these fighters and their poets (in spite of certain Christian touches inserted by later poetic editors before the poem crystallized into its present form) is Wyrd, the Fate of the Germanic peoples, cold as their own winters and the bleak northern sea, irresistible, despotic, and unmoved by sympathy for man.

Great as the differences are, very much of this Anglo-Saxon pagan spirit persists centuries later in the English Puritans. For the finer artistic graces, also, and the structural subtilties of a more developed literary period, we must not, of course, look in 'Beowulf.'

The narrative is often more dramatic than clear, and there is no thought of any minuteness of characterization. A few typical characters stand out clearly, and they were all that the poet's turbulent and not very attentive audience could understand. But the barbaric vividness and power of the poem give it much more than a merely historical interest; and the careful reader cannot fail to realize that it is after all the product of a long period of poetic development.

The Prose

It is pertinent to note that poetic form of 'Beowulf' is

that of virtually all Anglo-Saxon poetry down to the tenth century, or indeed to the end, a form which is roughly represented in the present book in a passage of imitative translation two pages below. The verse is unrimed, not arranged in stanzas, and with lines more commonly end-stopped (with distinct pauses at the ends) than is true in good modern poetry. Each line is divided into halves and each half contains two stressed syllables, generally long in quantity. The number of unstressed syllables appears to a modern eye or ear irregular and actually is very unequal, but they are really combined with the stressed ones into 'feet' in accordance with certain definite principles.

At least one of the stressed syllables in each half-line must be in alliteration with one in the other half-line; and most often the alliteration includes both stressed syllables in the first halfline and the first stressed syllable in the second, occasionally all four stressed syllables. It will be seen therefore that (1) emphatic stress and (2) alliteration are the basal principles of the system. To a present-day reader the verse sounds crude, the more so because of the harshly consonantal character of the Anglo-Saxon language; and in comparison with modern poetry it is undoubtedly unmelodious.

But it was worked out on conscious artistic principles, carefully followed; and when chanted, as it was meant to be, to the harp it possessed much power and even beauty of a vigorous sort, to which the pictorial and metaphorical wealth of the Anglo-Saxon poetic vocabulary largely contributed. The use of metaphors is perhaps the most conspicuous one in the style of the Anglo-Saxon poetry. The language, compared to that of our own vastly more complex time, was undeveloped; but for use in poetry, especially, there were a great number of periphrastic but vividly picturesque metaphorical synonyms (technically called kennings).

Thus the spear becomes 'the slaughter-shaft'; fighting 'hand-play'; the sword 'the leavings of the hammer' (or 'of the anvil'); and a ship 'the foamy-necked floater.' These kennings add much imaginative suggestiveness to the otherwise over-terse style, and often contribute to the grim irony which is another outstanding trait.

Anglo-Sexon Poetry

Remarkably, the Anglo-Saxons were for a long time fully occupied with the work of conquest and settlement, and their first literature of any importance, aside from 'Beowulf,' appears at about the time when 'Beowulf' was being put into its present form, namely in the seventh century. This was in the Northern, Anglian, kingdom of Northumbria (Yorkshire and Southern Scotland), which, as we have already said, had then won the political supremacy, and whose monasteries and capital city, York, thanks to the Irish missionaries, had become the chief centers of learning and culture in Western Christian Europe.

Still pagan in spirit are certain obscure but, ingenious and skillfully developed riddles in verse, representatives of one form of popular literature only less early than the ballads and charms. There remain also a few pagan lyric poems, which are all not only somber like 'Beowulf' but distinctly elegiac, that is pensively melancholy. They deal with the hard and tragic things in life, the terrible power of ocean and storm, or the inexorableness and dreariness of death, banishment, and the separation of friends.

In their frequent tender notes of pathos there may be some influence from the Celtic spirit. The greater part of the literature of the period, however, was Christian, produced in the monasteries or under their influence. The first Christian writer was Caedmon (pronounced Kadmon), who toward the end of the seventh century paraphrased in Anglo-Saxon verse some portions of the Bible. The legend of his divine call is famous. After Caedmon comes Bede, not a poet but a monk of strong and beautiful character, a profound scholar who in nearly forty Latin prose works summarized most of the knowledge of his time. The other name to be remembered is that of Cynewulf (pronounced Kinnywulf), the author of some noble religious poetry (in Anglo-Saxon), especially narratives dealing with Christ and Christian Apostles and heroes.

There is still other Anglo-Saxon Christian poetry, generally akin in subjects to Cynewulf's, but in most of the poetry of the whole period the excellence results chiefly from the survival of the old pagan spirit which distinguishes 'Beowulf'. Where the poet writes for edification he is likely to be dull, but when his story provides him with sea-voyages, with battles, chances for dramatic dialogue, or any incidents of vigorous action or of passion, the zest for adventure and war rekindles, and we have descriptions and narratives of picturesque color and stern force.

Sometimes there is real religious yearning, and indeed the heroes of these poems are partly medieval hermits and ascetics as well as quick-striking fighters; but for the most part the Christian Providence is really only the heathen Wyrd under another name, and God and Christ are viewed in much the same way as the Anglo-Saxon kings, the objects of feudal allegiance which is sincere but rather self-assertive and worldly than humble or consecrated.

Briefly, Anglo-Saxon poetry exhibits the limitations of a culturally early age, but it manifests also a degree of power which gives to Anglo-Saxon literature unquestionable superiority over that of any other European country of that time.

Further, it is pertinent to note that the horrors which the Anglo-Saxons had inflicted on the Britons they themselves were now to suffer from their still heathen and piratical kinsmen the 'Danes' or Northmen, inhabitants or the Scandinavian peninsula and the neighboring coasts. For a hundred years, throughout the ninth century, the Danes, appearing with unwearied persistence, repeatedly ravaged and plundered England, and they finally made complete conquest of Northumbria, destroyed all the churches and monasteries, and almost completely extinguished learning. It is a familiar story how Alfred, king from 871 to 901 of the southern kingdom of Wessex (the land of the West Saxons), which had now taken first place among the Anglo-Saxon states, stemmed the tide of invasion and by ceding to the 'Danes' the whole northeastern half of the island obtained for the remainder the peace which was the first essential for the reestablishment of civilization.

Peace secured, Alfred, who was one of the greatest of all English kings, labored unremittingly for learning, as for everything else that was useful, and he himself translated from Latin into Anglo-Saxon half a dozen of the best informational manuals of his time, manuals of history, philosophy, and religion. His most enduring literary work, however, was the inspiration and possibly partial authorship of the *'Anglo-Saxon Chronicle,'* a series of annals beginning with the Christian era, kept at various monasteries, and recording year by year (down to two centuries and a half after Alfred's own death), the most important events of history, chiefly that of England. Most of the entries in the 'Chronicle' are bare and brief, but sometimes, especially in the accounts of Alfred's own splendid exploits, a writer is roused to spirited narrative, occasionally in verse; and in the tenth century two great battles against invading Northmen, at Brunanburh and Maldon, produced the only important extant pieces of Anglo-Saxon poetry which certainly belong to the West Saxon time. For literature, indeed, the West-Saxon period has very little permanent significance.

Plenty of its other writing remains in the shape of religious prose—sermons, lives and legends of saints, biblical paraphrases, and similar work in which the monastic and priestly spirit took delight, but which is generally dull with the dulness of medieval commonplace didacticism and fantastic symbolism. The country, too, was still distracted with wars. Within fifty years after Alfred's death, to be sure, his descendants had won back the whole of England from 'Danish' rule.

But near the end of the tenth century new swarms of 'Danes' reappeared from the Baltic lands, once more slaughtering and devastating, until at last in the eleventh century the 'Danish' though Christian Canute ruled for twenty years over all England. In such a time there could be little intellectual or literary life. But the decline of the Anglo-Saxon literature speaks also partly of stagnation in the race itself. The people, though still sturdy, seem to have become somewhat dull from inbreeding and to have required an infusion of altogether different blood from without. This necessary renovation was to be violently forced upon them, for in 1066 Duke William of Normandy landed at Pevensey with his army of adventurers and his ill-founded claim to the crown, and before him at Hastings fell the gallant Harold and his nobles.

By the fortune of this single fight, followed only by

stern suppression of spasmodic outbreaks, William established himself and his vassals as masters of the land.

The Norman -French Period

The Normans who conquered England were originally members of the same stock as the 'Danes' who had harried and conquered it in the preceding centuries—the ancestors of both were bands of Baltic and North Sea pirates who merely happened to emigrate in different directions; and a little farther back the Normans were close cousins, in the general Germanic family, of the Anglo-Saxons themselves. The exploits of this whole race of Norse sea-kings make one of the most remarkable chapters in the history of medieval Europe. In the ninth and tenth centuries they mercilessly ravaged all the coasts not only of the West but of all Europe from the Rhine to the Adriatic. 'From the fury of the Norsemen, good Lord, deliver us!' was a regular part of the litany of the unhappy French.

They settled Iceland and Greenland and prematurely discovered America; they established themselves as the ruling aristocracy in Russia, and as the imperial body-guard and chief bulwark of the Byzantine empire at Constantinople; and in the eleventh century they conquered southern Italy and Sicily, whence in the first crusade they pressed on with unabated vigor to Asia Minor. Those bands of them with whom we are here concerned, and who became known distinctively as Normans, fastened themselves as settlers, early in the eleventh century, on the northern shore of France, and in return for their acceptance of Christianity and acknowledgment of the nominal feudal sovereignty of the French king were recognized as rightful possessors of the large province which thus came to bear the name of Normandy.

Here by intermarriage with the native women they rapidly developed into a race which while retaining all their original courage and enterprise took on also, together with the French language, the French intellectual brilliancy and flexibility and in manners became the chief exponent of medieval chivalry.

The different elements contributed to the modern English character by the latest stocks which have been united in it have been indicated by Matthew Arnold in a famous passage ('On the Study of Celtic Literature'): 'The Germanic [Anglo-Saxon and 'Danish'] genius has steadiness as its main basis, with commonness and humdrum for its defect, fidelity to nature for its excellence. The Norman genius, talent for affairs as its main basis, with strenuousness and clear rapidity for its excellence, hardness and insolence for its defect.'

The Germanic (Anglo-Saxon and 'Danish') element explains, then, why uneducated Englishmen of all times have been thick-headed, unpleasantly self-assertive, and unimaginative, but sturdy fighters; and the Norman strain why upper-class Englishmen have been self-contained, inclined to snobbishness, but vigorously aggressive and persevering, among the best conquerors, organizers, and administrators in the history of the world. In most respects, or all, the Norman conquest accomplished precisely that racial rejuvenation of which, as we have seen, Anglo-Saxon England stood in need. For the Normans brought with them from France the zest for joy and beauty and dignified and stately ceremony in which the Anglo-Saxon temperament was poor—they brought the love of light-hearted song and chivalrous sports, of rich clothing, of finely-painted manuscripts, of noble architecture in cathedrals and palaces, of formal religious ritual, and of the pomp and display of all elaborate pageantry.

In the outcome they largely reshaped the heavy mass of Anglo-Saxon life into forms of grace and beauty and brightened its duller surface with varied and brilliant colors. For the Anglo-Saxons themselves, however, the Conquest meant at first little else than that bitterest and most complete of all national disasters, hopeless subjection to a tyrannical and contemptuous foe. The Normans were not heathen, as the 'Danes' had been, and they were too few in number to wish to supplant the conquered people; but they imposed themselves, both politically and socially, as stern and absolute masters.

King William confirmed in their possessions the few Saxon nobles and lesser land-owners who accepted his rule and did not later revolt; but both pledges and interest compelled him to bestow most of the estates of the kingdom, together with the widows of their former holders, on his own nobles and the great motley throng of turbulent fighters who had made up his invading army. In the lordships and manors, therefore, and likewise in the great places of the Church, were established knights and nobles, the secular ones holding in feudal tenure from the king or his immediate great vassals, and each supported in turn by Norman men-at-arms; and to them were subjected as serfs, workers bound to the land, the greater part of the Saxon population.

As visible signs of the changed order appeared here and there throughout the country massive and gloomy castles of stone, and in the larger cities, in place of the simple Anglo-Saxon churches, cathedrals lofty and magnificent beyond all Anglo-Saxon dreams.

It is pertinent to note that in language and literature

the most general immediate result of the Conquest was to make of England a trilingual country, where Latin, French, and Anglo-Saxon were spoken separately side by side. With Latin, the tongue of the Church and of scholars, the Norman clergy were much more thoroughly familiar than the Saxon priests had been; and the introduction of the richer Latin culture resulted, in the latter half of the twelfth century, at the court of Henry II, in a brilliant outburst of Latin literature. In England, as well as in the rest of Western Europe, Latin long continued to be the language of religious and learned writing—down to the sixteenth century or even later.

French, that dialect of it which was spoken by the Normans—Anglo-French (English-French) it has naturally come to be called—was of course introduced by the Conquest as the language of the governing and upper social class, and in it also during the next three or four centuries a considerable body of literature was produced. Anglo-Saxon, which we may now term English, remained inevitably as the language of the subject race, but their literature was at first crushed down into insignificance. Ballads celebrating the resistance of scattered Saxons to their oppressors no doubt circulated widely on the lips of the people, but English writing of the more formal sorts, almost absolutely ceased for more than a century, to make a new beginning about the year 1200.

In the interval the 'Anglo-Saxon Chronicle' is the only important document, and even this, continued at the monastery of Peterboro, comes to an end in 1154, in the midst of the terrible anarchy of Stephen's reign. It must not be supposed, notwithstanding, that the Normans, however much they despised the English language and literature, made any effort to destroy it. On the other hand, gradual union of the two languages was no less inevitable than that of the races themselves.

From, the very first the need of communication, with their subjects must have rendered it necessary for the Normans to acquire some knowledge of the English language; and the children of mixed parentage of course learned it from their mothers. The use of French continued in the upper strata of society, in the few children's schools that existed, and in the law courts, for something like three centuries, maintaining itself so long partly because French was then the polite language of Western Europe. But the dead pressure of English was increasingly strong, and by the end of the fourteenth century and of Chaucer's life French had chiefly given way to it even at Court.

As we have already implied, however, the English which triumphed was in fact English-French—English was enabled to triumph partly because it had now largely absorbed the French. For the first one hundred or one hundred and fifty years, it seems, the two languages remained for the most part pretty clearly distinct, but in the thirteenth and fourteenth centuries English, abandoning its first aloofness, rapidly took into itself a large part of the French (originally Latin) vocabulary; and under the influence of the French it carried much farther the process of dropping its own comparatively complicated grammatical inflections—a process which had already gained much momentum even before the Conquest. This absorption of the French was most fortunate for English.

To the Anglo-Saxon vocabulary—vigorous, but harsh, limited in extent, and lacking in fine discriminations and power of abstract expression, was now added nearly the whole wealth of French, with its fullness, flexibility, and grace. As a direct consequence the resulting language, modern English, is the richest and most varied instrument of expression ever developed at any time by any race. For poetry the fusion meant even more than for prose. The metrical system, which begins to appear in the thirteenth century and comes to perfection a century and a half later in Chaucer's poems combined what may fairly be called the better features of both the systems from which it was compounded. We have seen that Anglo-Saxon verse depended on regular stress of a definite number of quantitatively long syllables in each line and on alliteration; that it allowed much variation in the number of unstressed syllables; and that it was without rime.

French verse, on the other hand, had rime (or assonance) and carefully preserved identity in the total number of syllables in corresponding lines, but it was uncertain as regarded the number of clearly stressed ones. The derived English system adopted from the French (1) rime and (2) identical line-length, and retained from the Anglo-Saxon (3) regularity of stress. (4) It largely abandoned the Anglo-Saxon regard for quantity and (5) it retained alliteration not as a basic principle but as an (extremely useful) subordinate device.

This metrical system, thus shaped, has provided the indispensable formal basis for making English poetry admittedly the greatest in the modern world. The study of the literature of the period is further complicated by the division of English into dialects. The Norman Conquest put a stop to the progress of the West-Saxon dialect toward complete supremacy, restoring the dialects of the other parts of the island to their former positions of equal authority. The actual result was the development of three groups of dialects, the Southern, Midland (divided into East and

West) and Northern, all differing among themselves in forms and even in vocabulary.

Literary activity when it recommenced was about equally distributed among the three, and for three centuries it was doubtful which of them would finally win the first place. In the outcome success fell to the East Midland dialect, partly through the influence of London, which under the Norman kings replaced Winchester as the capital city and seat of the Court and Parliament, and partly through the influence of the two Universities, Oxford and Cambridge, which gradually grew up during the twelfth and thirteenth centuries and attracted students from all parts of the country. This victory of the East Midland form was marked by, though it was not in any large degree due to, the appearance in the fourteenth century of the first great modern English poet, Chaucer.

To the present day, however, the three dialects, and subdivisions of them, are easily distinguishable in colloquial use; the common idiom of such regions as Yorkshire and Cornwall is decidedly different from that of London or indeed any other part of the country.

One of the most striking general facts in the later Middle Ages is the uniformity of life in many of its aspects throughout all Western Europe. It was only during this period that the modern nations, acquiring national consciousness, began definitely to shape themselves out of the chaos which had followed the fall of the Roman Empire. The Roman Church, firmly established in every corner of every land, was the actual inheritor of much of the unifying power of the Roman government, and the feudal system everywhere gave to society the same political organization and ideals.

In a truer sense, perhaps, than at any later time, Western Europe was one great brotherhood, thinking much the same thoughts, speaking in part the same speech, and actuated by the same beliefs. At least, the literature of the period, largely composed and copied by the great army of monks, exhibits everywhere a thorough uniformity in types and ideas. We of the 21st century should not allow ourselves to think vaguely of the Middle Ages as a benighted or shadowy period when life and the people who constituted it had scarcely anything in common with ourselves. In reality the men of the Middle Ages were moved by the same emotions and impulses as our own, and their lives presented the same incongruous mixture of nobility and baseness.

Yet it is true that the externals of their existence were strikingly different from those of more recent times. In society the feudal system—lords with their serfs, towns struggling for municipal independence, kings and nobles doing, peaceably or with violence, very much what they pleased; a constant condition of public or private war; cities walled as a matter of course for protection against bands of robbers or hostile armies; the country still largely covered with forests, wildernesses, and fens; roads infested with brigands and so bad that travel was scarcely possible except on horseback; in private life, most of the modern comforts unknown, and the houses, even of the wealthy, so filthy and uncomfortable that all classes regularly, almost necessarily, spent most of the daylight hours in the open air; in industry no coal, factories, or large machinery, but in the towns guilds of workmen each turning out by hand his slow product of single articles; almost no education except for priests and monks, almost no conceptions of genuine science or history, but instead the abstract system of scholastic logic and philosophy, highly ingenious but highly fantastic; in religion no outward freedom of thought except for a few courageous spirits, but the arbitrary dictates of a despotic hierarchy, insisting on an ironbound creed which the remorseless process of time was steadily rendering more and more inadequate—this offers some slight suggestion of the conditions of life for several centuries, ending with the period with which we are now concerned. In medieval literature likewise the modern student encounters much which seems at first sight grotesque. One of the most conspicuous examples is the pervasive use of allegory.

The men of the Middle Ages often wrote, as we do, in direct terms and of simple things, but when they wished to rise above the commonplace they turned with a frequency which to-day appears astonishing to the devices of abstract personification and veiled meanings. No doubt this tendency was due in part to an idealizing dissatisfaction with the crudeness of their actual life (as well as to frequent inability to enter into the realm of deeper and finer thought without the aid of somewhat mechanical imagery); and no doubt it was greatly furthered also by the medieval passion for translating into elaborate and fantastic symbolism all the details of the Bible narratives. But from whatever cause, the tendency hardened into a ruling convention; thousands upon thousands of medieval manuscripts seem to declare that the world is a mirage of shadowy forms, or that it exists merely to body forth remote and highly surprising ideas.

Of all these countless allegories none was reiterated with more unwearied persistence than that of the Seven Deadly Sins (those sins which in the doctrine of the Church lead to spiritual death because they are wilfully committed). These sins are: Covetousness, Unchastity, Anger, Gluttony, Envy, Sloth, and, chief of all, Pride, the earliest of all, through which Lucifer was moved to his fatal rebellion against God, whence spring all human ills. Each of the seven, however, was interpreted as including so many related offences that among them they embraced nearly the whole range of possible wickedness.

Personified, the Seven Sins in themselves almost dominate medieval literature, a sort of shadowy evil pantheon. Moral and religious questions could scarcely be discussed without regard to them; and they maintain their commanding place even as late as in Spenser's 'Faerie Queene,' at the very end of the sixteenth century. To the Seven Sins were commonly opposed, but with much less emphasis, the Seven Cardinal Virtues, Faith, Hope, Charity (Love), Prudence, Temperance, Chastity, and Fortitude. Again, almost as prominent as the Seven Sins was the figure of Fortune with her revolving wheel, a goddess whom the violent vicissitudes and tragedies of life led the men of the Middle Ages, in spite of their Christianity, to bring over from classical literature and virtually to accept as a real divinity, with almost absolute control in human affairs. In the seventeenth century Shakespeare's plays are full of allusions to her, but so for that matter is the everyday talk of all of us in the twentieth century.

Though it is not to the purpose in a study like the present to give special attention to the literature written in England in Latin and French; we can speak only briefly of that composed in English. But in fact when the English had made its new beginning, about the year 1200, the same general forms flourished in all three languages, so that what is said in general of the English applies almost as much to the other two as well.

In fact, we can divide all the literature of the period, roughly, into (1) Religious and (2) Secular. But it must be observed that religious writings were far more important as literature during the Middle Ages than in more recent times, and the separation between religious and secular less distinct than at present.

The forms of the religious literature were largely the same as in the previous period. There were songs, many of them addressed to the Virgin, some not only beautiful in their sincere and tender devotion, speaking for the finer spirits in an age of crudeness and violence, but occasionally beautiful as poetry. There were paraphrases of many parts of the Bible, lives of saints, in both verse and prose, and various other miscellaneous work. Perhaps worthy of special mention among single productions is the 'Cursor Mundi' (Surveyor of the World), an early fourteenth century poem of twenty-four thousand lines ('Paradise Lost' has less than eleven thousand), relating universal history from the beginning, on the basis of the Biblical narrative. Most important of all for their promise of the future, there were the germs of the modern drama in the form of the Church plays; but to these we shall give special attention in a later chapter.

In secular literature the variety was greater than in religious. We may begin by transcribing one or two of the songs, which, though not as numerous then as in some later periods, show that the great tradition of English secular lyric poetry reaches back from our own time to that of the Anglo-Saxons without a break. There were also political and satirical songs and miscellaneous poems of various sorts, among them certain 'Bestiaries,' accounts of the supposed habits of animals, generally drawn originally from classical tradition, and most of them highly fantastic and allegorized in the interests of morality and religion. There was an abundance of extremely realistic coarse tales, hardly belonging to literature, in both prose and verse.

The popular ballads of the fourteenth century we must reserve for later consideration. Most numerous of all the prose works, perhaps, were the Chronicles, which were produced generally in the monasteries and chiefly in the twelfth and thirteenth centuries, the greater part in Latin, some in French, and a few in rude English verse. Many of them were mere annals like the Anglo-Saxon Chronicle, but some were the lifelong works of men with genuine historical vision. Some dealt merely with the history of England, or a part of it, others with that of the entire world as it was known to medieval Europe. The majority will never be withdrawn from the obscurity of the manuscripts on which the patient care of their authors inscribed them; others have been printed in full and serve as the main basis for our knowledge of the events of the period.

The Romances

It is pertinent to note that the chief form of secular literature during the period, beginning in the middle of the twelfth century, was the romance, especially the metrical (verse) romance. The typical romances were the literary expression of chivalry. They were composed by the professional minstrels, some of whom, as in Anglo-Saxon times, were richly supported and rewarded by kings and nobles, while others still wandered about the country, always welcome in the manor-houses. There, like Scott's Last Minstrel, they recited their sometimes almost endless works from memory, in the great halls or in the ladies' bowers, to the accompaniment of occasional strains on their harps.

For two or three centuries the romances were to the lords and ladies, and to the wealthier citizens of the towns, much what novels are to the reading public of our own day. By far the greater part of the romances current in England were written in French, whether by Normans or by French natives of the English provinces in France, and the English ones which have been preserved are mostly translations or imitations of French originals. The romances are extreme representatives of the whole class of literature of all times to which they have given the name.

Frankly abandoning in the main the world of reality, they carry into that of idealized and glamorous fancy the chief interests of the medieval lords and ladies, namely, knightly exploits in war, and lovemaking. Love in the romances, also, retains all its courtly affectations, together with that worship of woman by man which in the twelfth century was exalted into a sentimental art by the poets of wealthy and luxurious Provence in Southern France. Side by side, again, with war and love, appears in the romances medieval religion, likewise conventionalized and childishly superstitious, but in some inadequate degree a mitigator of cruelty and a restrainer of lawless passion.

Artistically, in some respects or all, the greater part of the romances are crude and immature. Their usual main or only purpose is to hold attention by successions of marvellous adventures, natural or supernatural; of structure, therefore, they are often destitute; the characters are ordinarily mere types; and motivation is little considered. There were, however, exceptional authors, genuine artists, masters of meter and narrative, possessed by a true feeling for beauty; and in some of the romances the psychological analysis of love, in particular, is subtile and powerful, the direct precursor of one of the main developments in modern fiction.

The romances may very roughly be grouped into four great classes. First in time, perhaps, come those which are derived from the earlier French epics and in which love, if it appears at all, is subordinated to the military exploits of Charlemagne and his twelve peers in their wars against the Saracens. Second are the romances which, battered salvage from a greater past, retell in strangely altered romantic fashion the great stories of classical antiquity, mainly the achievements of Alexander the Great and the tragic fortunes of Troy. Third come the Arthurian romances, and fourth those scattering miscellaneous ones which do not belong to the other classes, dealing, most of them, with native English heroes.

Of these, two, 'King Horn' and 'Havelok,' spring direct from the common people and in both substance and expression reflect the hard reality of their lives, while 'Guy of Warwick' and 'Bevis of Hampton,' which are among the best known but most tedious of all the list, belong, in their original form, to the upper classes. Of all the romances the Arthurian are by far the most important. They belong peculiarly to English literature, because they are based on traditions of British history, but they have assumed a very prominent place in the literature of the whole western world. Rich in varied characters and incidents to which a universal significance could be attached, in their own time they were the most popular works of their class; and living on vigorously after the others were forgotten, they have continued to form one of the chief quarries of literary material and one of the chief sources of inspiration for modern poets and romancers.

It seems well worth while, therefore, to outline briefly their literary history. The period in which their scene is nominally laid is that of the Anglo-Saxon conquest of Great Britain. Of the actual historical events of this period extremely little is known, and even the capital question whether such a person as Arthur ever really existed can never receive a definite answer.

The only contemporary writer of the least importance is the Briton (priest or monk), Gildas, who in a violent Latin pamphlet of about the year 550 ('The Destruction and Conquest of Britain') denounces his countrymen for their sins and urges them to unite against the Saxons; and Gildas gives only the slightest sketch of what had actually happened. He tells how a British king (to whom later tradition assigns the name Vortigern) invited in the Anglo-Saxons as allies against the troublesome northern Scots and Picts, and how the Anglo-Saxons, victorious against these tribes, soon turned in furious conquest against the Britons themselves, until, under a certain Ambrosius Aurelianus, a man 'of Roman race,' the Britons successfully defended themselves and at last in the battle of Mount Badon checked the Saxon advance.

Next in order after Gildas, but not until about the year 800, appears a strangely jumbled document, last edited by a certain Nennius, and entitled 'Historia Britonum' (The History of the Britons), which adds to Gildas' outline traditions, natural and supernatural, which had meanwhile been growing up among the Britons (Welsh). It supplies the names of the earliest Saxon leaders, Hengist and Horsa (who also figure in the 'Anglo-Saxon Chronicle'), and narrates at length their treacherous dealings with Vortigern. Among other stories we find that of Vortigern's tower, where Gildas' Ambrosius appears as a boy of supernatural nature, destined to develop in the romances into the great magician Merlin. In Nennius' book occurs also the earliest mention of Arthur, who, in a comparatively sober passage, is said, some time after the days of Vortigern, to have 'fought against the Saxons, together with the kings of the Britons, but he himself was leader in the battles.' A list, also, is given of his twelve victories, ending with Mount Badon.

It is impossible to decide whether there is really any truth in this account of Nennius, or whether it springs wholly from the imagination of the Britons, attempting to solace themselves for their national overthrow; but it allows us to believe if we choose that sometime in the early sixth century there was a British leader of the name of Arthur, who by military genius rose to high command and for a while beat back the Saxon hordes. At most, however, it should be clearly realized.

Arthur was probably only a local leader in some limited region, and, far from filling the splendid place which he occupies in the later romances, was but the hard-pressed captain of a few thousand barbarous and half-armed warriors. For three hundred years longer the traditions about Arthur continued to develop among the Welsh people.

The most important change which took place was Arthur's elevation to the position of chief hero of the British (Welsh) race and the subordination to him, as his followers, of all the other native heroes, most of whom had originally been gods. To Arthur himself certain divine attributes were added, such as his possession of magic weapons, among them the sword Excalibur. It also came to be passionately believed among the Welsh that he was not really dead but would some day return from the mysterious Other World to which he had withdrawn and reconquer the island for his people.

It was not until the twelfth century that these Arthurian traditions, the cherished heritage of the Welsh and their cousins, the Bretons across the English Channel in France, were suddenly adopted as the property of all Western

Europe, so that Arthur became a universal Christian hero. This remarkable transformation, no doubt in some degree inevitable, was actually brought about chiefly through the instrumentality of a single man, a certain English archdeacon of Welsh descent, Geoffrey of Monmouth. Geoffrey, a literary and ecclesiastical adventurer looking about for a means of making himself famous, put forth about the year 1136, in Latin, a 'History of the Britons' from the earliest times to the seventh century, in which, imitating the form of the serious chronicles, he combined in cleverly impudent fashion all the adaptable miscellaneous material, fictitious, legendary, or traditional, which he found at hand. In dealing with Arthur, Geoffrey greatly enlarges on Gildas and Nennius; in part, no doubt, from his own invention, in part, perhaps, from Welsh tradition.

He provides Arthur with a father, King Uther, makes of Arthur's wars against the Saxons only his youthful exploits, relates at length how Arthur conquered almost all of Western Europe, and adds to the earlier story the figures of Merlin, Guenevere, Modred, Gawain, Kay, and Bedivere. What is not least important, he gives to Arthur's reign much of the atmosphere of feudal chivalry which was that of the ruling class of his own age. Geoffrey may or may not have intended his astonishing story to be seriously accepted, but in fact it was received with almost universal credence. For centuries it was incorporated in outline or in excerpts into almost all the sober chronicles, and what is of much more importance for literature, it was taken up and rehandled in various fashions by very numerous romancers.

About twenty years after Geoffrey wrote, the French poet Wace, an English subject, paraphrased his entire 'History' in vivid, fluent, and diffuse verse. Wace imparts to the whole, in a thorough-going way, the manners of chivalry, and adds, among other things, a mention of the Round Table, which Geoffrey, somewhat chary of the supernatural, had chosen to omit, though it was one of the early elements of the Welsh tradition. Other poets followed, chief among them the delightful Chretien of Troyes, all writing mostly of the exploits of single knights at Arthur's court, which they made over, probably, from scattering tales of Welsh and Breton mythology.

To declare that most romantic heroes had been knights of Arthur's circle now became almost a matter of course. Prose romances also appeared, vast formless compilations, which gathered up into themselves story after story, according to the fancy of each successive editor. Greatest of the additions to the substance of the cycle was the story of the Holy Grail, originally an altogether independent legend. Important changes necessarily developed. Arthur himself, in many of the romances, was degraded from his position of the bravest knight to be the inactive figurehead of a brilliant court; and the only really historical element in the story, his struggle against the Saxons, was thrust far into the background, while all the emphasis was laid on the romantic achievements of the single knights. Thus it had come about that Arthur, originally the national hero of the Welsh, and the deadly foe of the English, was adopted, as a Christian champion, not only for one of the medieval Nine Worthies of all history, but for the special glory of the English race itself. In that light he figures in the first important work in which native English reemerges after the Norman Conquest, the 'Brut' (Chronicle) wherein, about the year 1200, Laghamon paraphrased Wace's paraphrase of Geoffrey.

Notably, Laghamon was a humble parish priest in Worcestershire, and his thirty-two thousand half-lines, in which he imperfectly follows the Anglo-Saxon alliterative meter, are rather crude; though they are by no means dull, rather are often strong with the old-time Anglo-Saxon fighting spirit. In language also the poem is almost purely Saxon; occasionally it admits the French device of rime, but it is said to exhibit, all told, fewer than a hundred words of French origin.

Expanding throughout on Wace's version, Laghamon adds some minor features; but English was not yet ready to take a place beside French and Latin with the reading class, and the poem exercised no influence on the development of the Arthurian story or on English literature.

Here, we can make special mention of only one other romance, which all students should read in modern translation, namely, 'Sir Gawain (pronounced Gaw'-wain) and the Green Knight.' This is the brief and carefully constructed work of an unknown but very real poetic artist, who lived a century and more later than Laghamon and probably a little earlier than Chaucer. The story consists of two old folk-tales, here finely united in the form of an Arthurian romance and so treated as to bring out all the better side of knightly feeling, with which the author is in charming sympathy. Like many other medieval writings, this one is preserved by mere chance in a single manuscript, which contains also three slightly shorter religious poems (of a thousand or two lines apiece), all possibly by the same author as the romance. One of them in particular, *'The Pearl,'* is a narrative of much fine feeling, which may well have come from so true a gentleman as he.

The dialect is that of the Northwest Midland, scarcely more intelligible to modern readers than Anglo-Saxon, but it indicates that the author belonged to the same border region between England and Wales from which came also

Geoffrey of Monmouth and Laghamon, a region where Saxon and Norman elements were mingled with Celtic fancy and delicacy of temperament. The meter, also, is interesting—the Anglo-Saxon unrimed alliterative verse, but divided into long stanzas of irregular length, each ending in a 'bob' of five short riming lines. *'Sir Gawain and the Green Knight'* may very fittingly bring to a close our hasty survey of the entire Norman-French period, a period mainly of formation, which has left no literary work of great and permanent fame, but in which, after all, there were some sincere and talented writers, who have fallen into forgetfulness rather through the untoward accidents of time.

After having a through discussion of the evolution of English language and literature, we will narrate this journey is succeeding chapters.

2

Early English Literature

In this chapter we will give an account of English literature during 1350 to 1500. As we know literature is the mirror of contemporary society during which it is created. So for a reader of literature it is must to know the contemporary history of the concerned society.

First we will put light an contemporary political and social conditions.

It is significant to mention that of the century and a half, from 1350 to 1500, which forms our third period, the most important part for literature was the first fifty years, which constitutes the age of Chaucer. The middle of the fourteenth century was also the middle of the externally brilliant fifty years' reign of Edward III. In 1337 Edward had begun the terrible though often-interrupted series of campaigns in France which historians group together as the Hundred Tears' War, and having won the battle of Crecy against amazing odds, he had inaugurated at his court a period of splendor and luxury.

The country as a whole was really increasing in prosperity; Edward was fostering trade, and the towns and some of the town-merchants were becoming wealthy; but the oppressiveness of the feudal system, now becoming outgrown, was apparent, abuses in society and state and church were almost intolerable, and the spirit which was to create our modern age, beginning already in Italy to move toward the Renaissance, was felt in faint stirrings even so far to the North as England. The towns, indeed, were achieving their freedom. Thanks to compact organization, they were loosening the bonds of their dependence on the lords or bishops to whom most of them paid taxes; and the alliance of their representatives with the knights of the shire (country gentlemen) in the House of Commons, now a separate division of Parliament, was laying the foundation of the political power of the whole middle class. But the feudal system continued to rest cruelly on the peasants.

Still bound, most of them, to the soil, as serfs of the land or tenants with definite and heavy obligations of service, living in dark and filthy hovels under indescribably unhealthy conditions, earning a wretched subsistence by ceaseless labor, and almost altogether at the mercy of masters who regarded them as scarcely better than beasts, their lot was indeed pitiable.

Nevertheless their spirit was not broken nor their state so hopeless as it seemed. It was by the archers of the class of yeomen (small free-holders), men akin in origin and interests to the peasants, that the victories in the French wars were won, and the knowledge that this was so created in the peasants an increased self-respect and an increased dissatisfaction.

Their groping efforts to better their condition received strong stimulus also from the ravages of the terrible Black Death, a pestilence which, sweeping off at its first visitation, in 1348, at least half the population, and on two later recurrences only smaller proportions, led to a scarcity of laborers and added strength to their demand for commutation of personal services by money-payments and for higher wages.

This demand was met by the ruling classes with sternly repressive measures, and the socialistic Peasants' Revolt of John Ball and Wat Tyler in 1381 was violently crushed out in blood, but it expressed a great human cry for justice which could not permanently be denied.

In fact, one of the earliest literary works of the period, however, was uninfluenced by these social and moral problems, being rather a very complete expression of the naive medieval delight in romantic marvels. This is the highly entertaining 'Voyage and Travels of Sir John Mandeville.' This clever book was actually written at Liege, in what is now Belgium, sometime before the year 1370, and in the French language; from which, attaining enormous popularity, it was several times translated into Latin and English, and later into various other languages. Five centuries had to pass before scholars succeeded in demonstrating that the asserted author, 'Sir John Mandeville,' never existed, that the real author is undiscoverable, and that this pretended account of his journeyings over all the known and imagined world is a compilation from a large number of previous works.

Yet the book (the English version along with the others) really deserved its long-continued reputation. Its tales of the Ethiopian Prester John, of diamonds that by proper care can be made to grow, of trees whose fruit is an odd sort of lambs, and a hundred other equally remarkable phenomena, are narrated with skilful verisimilitude and still strongly hold the reader's interest, even if they no longer command belief.

Geoffrey Chaucher, 1338-1400

Remarkably, Chaucer came into the world probably in 1338, the first important author who was born and lived in London, which with him becomes the center of English literature. About his life, as about those of many of our earlier writers, there remains only very fragmentary information, which in his case is largely pieced together from scattering entries of various kinds in such documents as court account books and public records of state matters and of lawsuits.

His father, a wine merchant, may have helped supply the cellars of the king (Edward III) and so have been able to bring his son to royal notice; at any rate, while still in his teens Geoffrey became a page in the service of one of the king's daughters-in-law. In this position his duty would be partly to perform various humble work in the household, partly also to help amuse the leisure of the inmates, and it is easy to suppose that he soon won favor as a fluent story-teller.

He early became acquainted with the seamy as well as the brilliant side of courtly life; for in 1359 he was in the campaign in France and was taken prisoner. Chaucer's poetry falls into three rather clearly marked periods. First is that of French influence, when, though writing in English, he drew inspiration from the rich French poetry of the period, which was produced partly in France, partly in England. Chaucer experimented with the numerous lyric forms which the French poets had brought to perfection; he also translated, in whole or in part, the most important of medieval French narrative poems, the thirteenth century 'Romance of the Rose' of Guillaume de Lorris and Jean de Meung, a very clever satirical allegory, in many thousand lines, of medieval love and medieval religion.

This poem, with its Gallic brilliancy and audacity, long exercised over Chaucer's mind the same dominant influence which it possessed over most secular poets of the age. Chaucer's second period, that of Italian influence, dates from his first visit to Italy in 1372-3, where at Padua he may perhaps have met the fluent Italian poet Petrarch, and where at any rate the revelation of Italian life and literature must have aroused his intense enthusiasm. From this time, and especially after his other visit to Italy, five years later, he made much direct use of the works of Petrarch and Boccaccio and to a less degree of those of their greater predecessor, Dante, whose severe spirit was too unlike Chaucer's for his thorough appreciation.

The longest and finest of Chaucer's poems of this period, 'Troilus and Criseyde' is based on a work of Boccaccio; here Chaucer details with compelling power the sentiment and tragedy of love, and the psychology of the heroine who had become for the Middle Ages a central figure in the tale of Troy. Chaucer's third period, covering his last fifteen years, is called his English period, because now at last his genius, mature and self-sufficient, worked in essential independence. First in time among his poems of these years stands 'The Legend of Good Women,' a series of romantic biographies of famous ladies of classical legend and history, whom it pleases Chaucer to designate as martyrs of love; but more important than the stories themselves is the Prolog, where he chats with delightful frankness about his own ideas and tastes. The great work of the period, however, and the crowning achievement of Chaucer's life, is *'The Canterbury Tales.'* Every one is familiar with the plan of the story (which may well have had some basis in fact): how Chaucer finds himself one April evening with thirty other men and women, all gathered at the Tabard Inn in Southwark (a suburb of London and just across the Thames from the city proper), ready to start next morning, as thousands of Englishmen did every year, on a pilgrimage to the shrine of St. Thomas a Becket at Canterbury. The travelers readily accept the proposal of Harry Bailey, their jovial and domineering host, that he go with them as leader and that they enliven the journey with a story-telling contest (two stories from each pilgrim during each half of the journey) for the prize of a dinner at his inn on their return.

Next morning, therefore, the Knight begins the series of tales and the others follow in order. This literary form—a collection of disconnected stories bound together in a fictitious framework—goes back almost to the beginning of literature itself; but Chaucer may well have been directly influenced by Boccaccio's famous book of prose tales, 'The Decameron' (Ten Days of Story-Telling). Between the two works, however, there is a striking contrast, which has often been pointed out. While the Italian author represents his gentlemen and ladies as selfishly fleeing from the misery of a frightful plague in Florence to a charming villa and a holiday of unreflecting pleasure, the gaiety of Chaucer's pilgrims rests on a basis of serious purpose, however conventional it may be.

The main principles for the pronunciation of Chaucer's language, so far as it differs from ours, are these: Every letter should be sounded, especially the final *e* (except when it is to be suppressed before another vowel). A large proportion of the rimes are therefore feminine.

John Gower

The three other chief writers contemporary with Chaucer contrast strikingly both with him and with each other. Least important is John Gower (pronounced either Go-er or Gow-er), a wealthy landowner whose tomb, with his effigy, may still be seen in St. Savior's, Southwark, the church of a priory to whose rebuilding he contributed and where he spent his latter days. Gower was a confirmed conservative, and time has left him stranded far in the rear of the forces that move and live. Unlike Chaucer's, the bulk of his voluminous poems reflect the past and scarcely hint of the future.

The earlier and larger part of them are written in French and Latin, and in 'Vox Clamantis' (The Voice of One Crying in the Wilderness) he exhausts the vocabulary of exaggerated bitterness in denouncing the common people for the insurrection in which they threatened the privileges and authority of his own class. Later on, perhaps through Chaucer's example, he turned to English, and in 'Confessio Amantis' (A Lover's Confession) produced a series of renderings of traditional stories parallel in general nature to 'The Canterbury Tales.' He is generally a smooth and fluent versifier, but his fluency is his undoing; he wraps up his material in too great a mass of verbiage. The active moral impulse which Chaucer and Gower lacked, and a consequent direct confronting of the evils of the age, appear vigorously in the group of poems written during the last forty years of the century and known from the title in some of the manuscripts as 'The Vision of William Concerning Piers the Plowman.'

From the sixteenth century, at least, until very lately this work, the various versions of which differ greatly, has been supposed to be the single poem of a single author, repeatedly enlarged and revised by him; and ingenious inference has constructed for this supposed author a brief but picturesque biography under the name of William Langland. Recent investigation, however, has made it seem at least probable that the work grew, to its final form through additions by several successive writers who have not left their names and whose points of view were not altogether identical.

In its own age the influence of 'Piers the Plowman' was very great. Despite its intended impartiality, it was inevitably adopted as a partisan document by the poor and oppressed, and together with the revolutionary songs of John Ball it became a powerful incentive to the Peasant's Insurrection. Piers himself became and continued an ideal for men who longed for a less selfish and brutal world, and a century and a half later the poem was still cherished by the Protestants for its exposure of the vices of the Church. Its medieval form and setting remove it hopelessly beyond the horizon of general readers of the present time, yet it furnishes the most detailed remaining picture of the actual social and economic conditions of its age.

The Wiclifite Bible

It is significant to mention that product of the same general forces which inspired 'Piers the Plowman' is the earliest in the great succession of the modern English versions of the Bible, the one connected with the name of John Wiclif, himself the first important English precursor of the Reformation. Wiclif was born about 1320, a Yorkshireman of very vigorous intellect as well as will, but in all his nature and instincts a direct representative of the common people. During the greater part of his life he was connected with Oxford University, as student, teacher (and therefore priest), and college head. Early known as one of the ablest English thinkers and philosophers, he was already opposing certain doctrines and practices of the Church when he was led to become a chief spokesman for King Edward and the nation in their refusal to pay the tribute which King John, a century and a half before, had promised to the Papacy and which was now actually demanded. As the controversies proceeded, Wiclif was brought at last to formulate the principle, later to be basal in the whole Protestant movement, that the final source of religious authority is not the Church, but the Bible. One by one he was led to attack also other fundamental doctrines and institutions of the Church—transubstantiation, the temporal possessions of the Church, the Papacy, and at last, for their corruption, the four orders of friars.

In the outcome the Church proved too strong for even Wiclif, and Oxford, against its will, was compelled to abandon him; yet he could be driven no farther than to his parish of Lutterworth, where he died undisturbed in 1384. Wiclif and the men associated with him, however, were always reformers first and writers only to that end. Their religious tracts are formless and crude in style, and even their final version of the Bible aims chiefly at fidelity of rendering.

In general it is not elegant, the more so because the authors usually follow the Latin idioms and sentence divisions instead of reshaping them into the native English style. Their text, again, is often interrupted by the insertion of brief phrases explanatory of unusual words. The vocabulary, adapted to the unlearned readers, is more largely Saxon than in our later versions, and the older inflected forms appear oftener than in Chaucer; so that it is only through our knowledge of the later versions that we to-day can read the work without frequent stumbling. Nevertheless this version has served as the starting point for almost all those that have come after it in English, as even a hasty reader of this one must be conscious; and no reader can fail to admire in it the sturdy Saxon vigor which has helped to make our own version one of the great masterpieces of English literature.

The Fifteenth Century

But with Chaucer's death in 1400 the half century of original creative literature in which he is the main figure comes to an end, and for a hundred and fifty years thereafter there is only a single author of the highest rank. For this decline political confusion is the chief cause; first, in the renewal of the Hundred Years' War, with its sordid effort to deprive another nation of its liberty, and then in the brutal and meaningless War of the Roses, a mere cut-throat civil butchery of rival factions with no real principle at stake.

Throughout the fifteenth century the leading poets (of prose we will speak later) were avowed imitators of Chaucer, and therefore at best only second-rate writers. Most of them were Scots, and best known is the Scottish king, James I. For tradition seems correct in naming this monarch as the author of a pretty poem, 'The King's Quair' ('The King's Quire,' that is Book), which relates in a medieval dream allegory of fourteen hundred lines how the captive author sees and falls in love with a lady whom in the end Fortune promises to bestow upon him.

This may well be the poetic record of King James' eighteen-year captivity in England and his actual marriage to a noble English wife. In compliment to him Chaucer's stanza of seven lines (riming *ababbcc)*, which King James employs, has received the name of 'rime royal.' It is remarkable to note that largely to the fifteenth century, however, belong those of the English and Scottish 'popular' ballads which the accidents of time have not succeeded in destroying. We have already considered the theory of the communal origin of this kind of poetry in the remote pre-historic past, and have seen that the ballads continue to flourish vigorously down to the later periods of civilization. The still existing

English and Scottish ballads are mostly, no doubt, the work of individual authors of the fifteenth and sixteenth centuries, but none the less they express the little-changing mind and emotions of the great body of the common people who had been singing and repeating ballads for so many thousand years. Really essentially 'popular,' too, in spirit are the more pretentious poems of the wandering professional minstrels, which have been handed down along with the others, just as the minstrels were accustomed to recite both sorts indiscriminately.

Such minstrel ballads are the famous ones on the battle of Chevy Chase, or Otterburn. The production of genuine popular ballads began to wane in the fifteenth century when the printing press gave circulation to the output of cheap London writers and substituted reading for the verbal memory by which the ballads had been transmitted, portions, as it were, of a half mysterious and almost sacred tradition.

Remarkable, some of the elements which go to make this peculiar 'popular' quality can be stated as follows:

1. The 'popular' ballads are the simple and spontaneous expression of the elemental emotion of the people, emotion often crude but absolutely genuine and unaffected. Phrases are often repeated in the ballads, just as in the talk of the common man, for the sake of emphasis, but there is neither complexity of plot or characterization nor attempt at decorative literary adornment—the story and the emotion which it calls forth are all in all. It is this simple, direct fervor of feeling, the straightforward outpouring of the authors' hearts, that gives the ballads their power and entitles them to consideration among the far more finished works of conscious literature.

Both the emotion and the morals of the ballads, also, are pagan, or at least pre-Christian; vengeance on one's enemies is as much a virtue as loyalty to one's friends; the most shameful sins are cowardice and treachery in war or love; and the love is often lawless.

2. The verbal style of the ballads, like their spirit, is vigorous and simple, generally unpolished and sometimes rough, but often powerful with its terse dramatic suggestiveness. The usual, though not the only, poetic form is the four-lined stanza in lines alternately of four and three stresses and riming only in the second and fourth lines. Besides the refrains which are perhaps a relic of communal composition and the conventional epithets which the ballads share with epic poetry there are numerous traditional ballad expressions—rather meaningless formulas and line-tags used only to complete the rime or meter, the common useful scrap-bag reserve of these unpretentious poets. The license of Anglo-Saxon poetry in the number of the unstressed syllables still remains. But it is evident that the existing versions of the ballads are generally more imperfect than the original forms; they have suffered from the corruptions of generations of oral repetition, which the scholars who have recovered them have preserved with necessary accuracy, but which for appreciative reading editors should so far as possible revise away.

3. From first to last the treatment of the themes is objective, dramatic, and picturesque. Everything is action, simple feeling, or vivid scenes, with no merely abstract moralizing (except in a few unusual cases); and often much of the story or sentiment is implied

rather than directly stated. This too, of course, is the natural manner of the common man, a manner perfectly effective either in animated conversation or in the chant of a minstrel, where expression and gesture can do so much of the work which the restraints of civilized society have transferred to words.

4. To this spirit and treatment correspond the subjects of the ballads. They are such as make appeal to the underlying human instincts—brave exploits in individual fighting or in organized war, and the romance and pathos and tragedy of love and of the other moving situations of simple life. From the 'popular' nature of the ballads it has resulted that many of them are confined within no boundaries of race or nation, but, originating one here, one there, are spread in very varying versions throughout the whole, almost, of the world. Purely English, however, are those which deal with Robin Hood and his 'merry men,' idealized imaginary heroes of the Saxon common people in the dogged struggle which they maintained for centuries against their oppressive feudal lords.

5. The characters and 'properties' of the ballads of all classes are generally typical or traditional. There are the brave champion, whether noble or common man, who conquers or falls against overwhelming odds; the faithful lover of either sex; the woman whose constancy, proving stronger than man's fickleness, wins back her lover to her side at last; the traitorous old woman (victim of the blind and cruel prejudice which after a century or two was often to send her to the stake as a witch); the loyal little child; and some few others.

Sir Thomas Malory

It is pertinent to note that the one fifteenth century author of the first rank, above referred to, is Sir Thomas Malory. He is probably to be identified with the Sir Thomas Malory who during the wars in France and the civil strife of the Roses that followed was an adherent of the Earls of Warwick and who died in 1471 under sentence of outlawry by the victorious Edward IV. And some passing observations, at least, in his book seem to indicate that if he knew and had shared all the splendor and inspiration of the last years of medieval chivalry, he had experienced also the disappointment and bitterness of defeat and prolonged captivity.

Further than this we know of him only that he wrote 'Le Morte Darthur' and had finished it by 1467. Malory's purpose was to collect in a single work the great body of important Arthurian romance and to arrange it in the form of a continuous history of King Arthur and his knights. He called his book 'Le Morte Darthur,' The Death of Arthur, from the title of several popular Arthurian romances to which, since they dealt only with Arthur's later years and death, it was properly enough applied, and from which it seems to have passed into general currency as a name for the entire story of Arthur's life. Actually to get together all the Arthurian romances was not possible for any man in Malory's day, or in any other, but he gathered up a goodly number, most of them, at least, written in French, and combined them, on the whole with unusual skill, into a work of about one-tenth their original bulk, which still ranks, with all qualifications, as one of the masterpieces of English literature.

Dealing with such miscellaneous material, he could not wholly avoid inconsistencies, so that, for example, he sometimes introduces in full health in a later book a knight whom a hundred pages earlier he had killed and regularly buried; but this need not cause the reader anything worse than mild amusement. Not Malory but his age, also, is to blame for his sometimes hazy and puzzled treatment of the supernatural element in his material. In the remote earliest form of the stories, as Celtic myths, this supernatural element was no doubt frank and very large, but Malory's authorities, the more skeptical French romancers, adapting it to their own age, had often more or less fully rationalized it; transforming, for instance, the black river of Death which the original heroes often had to cross on journeys to the Celtic Other World into a rude and forbidding moat about the hostile castle into which the romancers degraded the Other World itself.

Countless magic details, however, still remained recalcitrant to such treatment; and they evidently troubled Malory, whose devotion to his story was earnest and sincere. Some of them he omits, doubtless as incredible, but others he retains, often in a form where the impossible is merely garbled into the unintelligible. For a single instance, in his seventh book he does not satisfactorily explain why the valiant Gareth on his arrival at Arthur's court asks at first only for a year's food and drink. In the original story, we can see to-day, Gareth must have been under a witch's spell which compelled him to a season of distasteful servitude; but this motivating bit of superstition Malory discards, or rather, in this case, it had been lost from the story at a much earlier stage.

It results, therefore, that Malory's supernatural incidents are often far from clear and satisfactory; yet the reader is little troubled by this difficulty either in so thoroughly romantic a work. Other technical faults may easily be pointed out in Malory's book. Thorough unity, either in the whole or in the separate stories so loosely woven together, could not be expected; in continual reading the long succession of similar combat after combat and the constant repetition of stereotyped phrases become monotonous for a present-day reader; and it must be confessed that Malory has little of the modern literary craftsman's power of close-knit style or proportion and emphasis in details.

But these faults also may be overlooked, and the work is truly great, partly because it is an idealist's dream of chivalry, as chivalry might have been, a chivalry of faithful knights who went about redressing human wrongs and were loyal lovers and zealous servants of Holy Church; great also because Malory's heart is in his stories, so that he tells them in the main well, and invests them with a delightful atmosphere of romance which can never lose its fascination. The style, also, in the narrower sense, is strong and good, and does its part to make the book, except for the Wiclif Bible, unquestionably the greatest monument of English prose of the entire period before the sixteenth century.

There is no affectation of elegance, but rather knightly straightforwardness which has power without lack of ease. The sentences are often long, but always 'loose' and clear; and short ones are often used with the instinctive skill of sincerity. Everything is picturesque and dramatic and everywhere there is chivalrous feeling and genuine human sympathy.

William Caxton

No exaggeratopm. Malory's book is the first great English classic which was given to the world in print instead of written manuscript; for it was shortly after Malory's death that the printing press was brought to England by William Caxton. The invention of printing, perhaps the most important event of modern times, took place in Germany not long after the middle of the fifteenth century, and the development of the art was rapid. Caxton, a shrewd and enterprising Kentishman, was by first profession a cloth merchant, and having taken up his residence across the Channel, was appointed by the king to the important post of Governor of the English Merchants in Flanders. Employed later in the service of the Duchess of Burgundy (sister of Edward IV), his ardent delight in romances led him to translate into English a French 'Recueil des Histoires de Troye' (Collection of the Troy Stories).

To supply the large demand for copies he investigated and mastered the new art by which they might be so wonderfully multiplied and about 1475, at fifty years of age, set up a press at Bruges in the modern Belgium, where he issued his 'Recueil,' which was thus the first English book ever put into print. During the next year, 1476, just a century before the first theater was to be built in London, Caxton returned to England and established his shop in Westminster, then a London suburb. During the fifteen remaining years of his life he labored diligently, printing an aggregate of more than a hundred books, which together comprised over fourteen thousand pages. Aside from Malory's romance, which he put out in 1485, the most important of his publications was an edition of Chaucer's 'Canterbury Tales.'

While laboring as a publisher Caxton himself continued to make translations, and in spite of many difficulties he, together with his assistants, turned into English from French no fewer than twenty-one distinct works. From every point of view Caxton's services were great. As translator and editor his style is careless and uncertain, but like Malory's it is sincere and manly, and vital with energy and enthusiasm. As printer, in a time of rapid changes in the language, when through the wars in France and her growing influence the second great infusion of Latin-French words was coming into the English language, he did what could be done for consistency in forms and spelling. Partly medieval and partly modern in spirit, he may fittingly stand at the close, or nearly at the close, of our study of the medieval era.

Now we will turn to medieval era of English literature.

3

Major Trends in Medieval Literature

Literature was gradually moving upwards during medieval period.

Herein this chapter we shall put light an major trends in Medieval English literature.

Folk-Plays, Jugglers, Pagents

First it is pertinent to note that at the fall of the Roman Empire, which marks the beginning of the Middle Ages, the corrupt Roman drama, proscribed by the Church, had come to an unhonored end, and the actors had been merged into the great body of disreputable jugglers and inferior minstrels who wandered over all Christendom. The performances of these social outcasts, crude and immoral as they were, continued for centuries unsuppressed, because they responded to the demand for dramatic spectacle which is one of the deepest though not least troublesome instincts in human nature. The same demand was partly satisfied also by the rude country folk-plays, survivals of primitive heathen ceremonials, performed at such festival occasions as the harvest season, which in all lands continue to flourish among the country people long after their original meaning has been forgotten. In England the folk-plays, throughout the Middle Ages and in remote spots down almost to the present time, sometimes took the form of energetic dances (Morris dances, they came to be called, through confusion with Moorish performances of the same general nature). Others of them, however, exhibited in the midst of much rough-and-tumble fighting and buffoonery, a slight thread of dramatic action. Their characters gradually came to be a conventional set, partly famous figures of popular tradition, such as St. George, Robin Hood, Maid Marian, and the Green Dragon. Other offshoots of the folk-play were the 'mummings' and 'disguisings,' collective names for many forms of processions, shows, and other entertainments, such as, among the upper classes, that precursor of the Elizabethan Mask in which a group of persons in disguise, invited or uninvited, attended a formal dancing party. In the later part of the Middle Ages, also, there were the secular pageants, spectacular displays (rather different from those of the twentieth century) given on such occasions as when a king or other person of high rank made formal entry into a town.

They consisted of an elaborate scenic background set up near the city gate or on the street, with figures from allegorical or traditional history who engaged in some pantomime or declamation, but with very little dramatic dialog, or none.

Mystery Plays and Liturgical Plays

But all these forms, though they were not altogether without later influence, were very minor affairs, and the real drama of the Middle Ages grew up, without design and by the mere nature of things, from the regular services of the Church. We must try in the first place to realize clearly the conditions under which the church service, the mass, was conducted during all the medieval centuries. We should picture to ourselves congregations of persons for the most part grossly ignorant, of unquestioning though very superficial faith, and of emotions easily aroused to fever heat.

Of the Latin words of the service they understood nothing; and of the Bible story they had only a very general impression. It was necessary, therefore, that the service should be given a strongly spectacular and emotional character, and to this end no effort was spared. The great cathedrals and churches were much the finest buildings of the time, spacious with lofty pillars and shadowy recesses, rich in sculptured stone and in painted windows that cast on the walls and pavements soft and glowing patterns of many colors and shifting forms.

The service itself was in great part musical, the confident notes of the full choir joining with the resonant organ-tones; and after all the rest the richly robed priests and ministrants passed along the aisles in stately processions enveloped in fragrant clouds of incense. That the eye if not the ear of the spectator, also, might catch some definite knowledge, the priests as they read the Bible stories sometimes displayed painted rolls which vividly pictured the principal events of the day's lesson. Still, however, a lack was strongly felt, and at last, accidentally and slowly, began the process of dramatizing the services.

First, inevitably, to be so treated was the central incident of Christian faith, the story of Christ's resurrection. The earliest steps were very simple. First, during the ceremonies on Good Friday, the day when Christ was crucified, the cross which stood all the year above the altar, bearing the Savior's figure, was taken down and laid beneath the altar, a dramatic symbol of the Death and Burial; and two days later, on 'the third day' of the Bible phraseology, that is on Easter Sunday, as the story of the Resurrection was chanted by the choir, the cross was uncovered and replaced, amid the rejoicings of the congregation. Gradually, probably, as time passed, this Easter scene was further enlarged, in part by additions from the closing incidents of the Savior's life.

A similar treatment, too, was being given to the Christmas scene, still more humanly beautiful, of his birth in the manger, and occasionally the two scenes might be taken from their regular places in the service, combined, and presented at any season of the year. Other Biblical scenes, as well, came to be enacted, and, further, there were added stories from Christian tradition, such as that of Antichrist, and, on their particular days, the lives of Christian saints.

Thus far these compositions are called Liturgical Plays, because they formed, in general, a part of the church service (liturgy). But as some of them were united into extended groups and as the interest of the congregation deepened, the churches began to seem too small and inconvenient, the excited audiences forgot the proper reverence, and the performances were transferred to the churchyard, and then, when the gravestones proved troublesome, to the market place, the village-green, or any convenient field. By this time the people had ceased to be patient with the unintelligible Latin, and it was replaced at first, perhaps, and in part, by French, but finally by English; though probably verse was always retained as more appropriate than prose to the sacred subjects. Then, the religious spirit yielding inevitably in part to that of merrymaking, minstrels and mountebanks began to flock to the celebrations; and regular fairs, even, grew up about them.

Gradually, too, the priests lost their hold even on the plays themselves; skilful actors from among the laymen began to take many of the parts; and at last in some towns the trade-guilds, or unions of the various handicrafts, which had secured control of the town governments, assumed entire charge. These changes, very slowly creeping in, one by one, had come about in most places by the beginning of the fourteenth century. In 1311 a new impetus was given to the whole ceremony by the establishment of the late spring festival of Corpus Christi, a celebration of the doctrine of transubstantiation. On this occasion, or sometimes on some other festival, it became customary for the guilds to present an extended series of the plays, a series which together contained the essential substance of the Christian story, and therefore of the Christian faith. The Church generally still encouraged attendance, and not only did all the townspeople join wholeheartedly, but from all the country round the peasants flocked in.

On one occasion the Pope promised the remission of a thousand days of purgatory to all persons who should be present at the Chester plays, and to this exemption the bishop of Chester added sixty days more. The list of plays thus presented commonly included: The Fall of Lucifer; the Creation of the World and the Fall of Adam; Noah and the Flood; Abraham and Isaac and the promise of Christ's coming; a Procession of the Prophets, also foretelling Christ; the main events of the Gospel story, with some additions from Christian tradition; and the Day of Judgment. The longest cycle now known, that at York, contained, when fully developed, fifty plays, or perhaps even more. Generally each play was presented by a single guild (though sometimes two or three guilds or two or three plays might be combined), and sometimes, though not always, there was a special fitness in the assignment, as when the watermen gave the play of Noah's Ark or the bakers that of the Last Supper. In this connected form the plays are called the Mystery or Miracle Cycles.

In many places, however, detached plays, or groups of plays smaller than the full cycles, continued to be presented at one season or another. As we have said that the plays were always composed in verse. The stanza forms employed differ widely even within the same cycle, since the single plays were very diverse in both authorship and dates.

The quality of the verse, generally mediocre at the outset, has often suffered much in transmission from generation to generation. In other respects also there are great contrasts; sometimes the feeling and power of a scene are admirable, revealing an author of real ability, sometimes there is only crude and wooden amateurishness. The medieval lack of historic sense gives to all the plays the setting of the authors' own times; Roman officers appear as feudal knights; and all the heathens (including the Jews) are Saracens, worshippers of 'Mahound' and 'Termagaunt'; while the good characters, however long they may really have lived before the Christian era, swear stoutly by St. John and St. Paul and the other medieval Christian divinities. The frank coarseness of the plays is often merely disgusting, and suggests how superficial, in most cases, was the medieval religious sense.

With no thought of incongruity, too, these writers brought God the Father onto the stage in bodily form, and then, attempting in all sincerity to show him reverence, gilded his face and put into his mouth long speeches of exceedingly tedious declamation. The whole emphasis, as generally in the religion of the times, was on the fear of hell rather than on the love of righteousness. Yet in spite of everything grotesque and inconsistent, the plays no doubt largely fulfilled their religious purpose and exercised on the whole an elevating influence. The humble submission of the boy Isaac to the will of God and of his earthly father, the yearning devotion of Mary the mother of Jesus, and the infinite love and pity of the tortured Christ himself, must have struck into even callous hearts for at least a little time some genuine consciousness of the beauty and power of the finer and higher life. A literary form which supplied much of the religious and artistic nourishment of half a continent for half a thousand years cannot be lightly regarded or dismissed.

The Morality Plays

Whereas the Mystery Plays seem to have reached their greatest popularity in the fourteenth and fifteenth centuries. In the dawning light of the Renaissance and the modern spirit they gradually waned, though in exceptional places and in special revivals they did not altogether cease to be given until the seventeenth century. On the Continent of Europe, indeed, they still survive, after a fashion, in a single somewhat modernized form, the celebrated Passion Play of Oberammergau. In England by the end of the fifteenth century they had been for the most part replaced by a kindred species which had long been growing up beside them, namely the Morality Plays.

The Morality Play probably arose in part from the desire of religious writers to teach the principles of Christian living in a more direct and compact fashion than was possible through the Bible stories of the Mysteries. In its strict form the Morality Play was a dramatized moral allegory. It was in part an offshoot from the Mysteries, in some of which there had appeared among the actors abstract allegorical figures, either good or bad, such as The Seven Deadly Sins, Contemplation, and Raise-Slander.

In the Moralities the majority of the characters are of this sort—though not to the exclusion of supernatural persons such as God and the Devil—and the hero is generally a type-figure standing for all Mankind. For the control of the hero the two definitely opposing groups of Virtues and Vices contend; the commonest type of Morality presents in brief glimpses the entire story of the hero's life, that is of the life of every man.

Obviously, it shows how he yields to temptation and lives for the most part in reckless sin, but at last in spite of all his flippancy and folly is saved by Perseverance and Repentance, pardoned through God's mercy, and assured of salvation. As compared with the usual type of Mystery plays the Moralities had for the writers this advantage, that they allowed some independence in the invention of the story; and how powerful they might be made in the hands of a really gifted author has been finely demonstrated in our own time by the stage-revival of the best of them, 'Everyman' (which is probably a translation from a Dutch original).

In most cases, however, the spirit of medieval allegory proved fatal, the genuinely abstract characters are mostly shadowy and unreal, and the speeches of the Virtues are extreme examples of intolerable sanctimonious declamation. Against this tendency, on the other hand, the persistent instinct for realism provided a partial antidote; the Vices are often very lifelike rascals, abstract only in name. In these cases the whole plays become vivid studies in contemporary low life, largely human and interesting except for their prolixity and the coarseness which they inherited from the Mysteries and multiplied on their own account. During the Reformation period, in the early sixteenth century, the character of the Moralities, more strictly so called, underwent something of a change, and they were— sometimes made the vehicle for religious argument, especially by Protestants.

The Interludes

It worth mentioning that, early in the sixteenth century, the Morality in its turn was largely superseded by another sort of play called the Interlude. But just as in the case of the Mystery and the Morality, the Interlude developed out of the Morality, and the two cannot always be distinguished, some single plays being distinctly described by the authors as 'Moral Interludes.' In the Interludes the realism of the Moralities became still more pronounced, so that the typical Interlude is nothing more than a coarse farce, with no pretense at religious or ethical meaning. The name Interlude denotes literally 'a play between,' but the meaning intended between whom or what) is uncertain. The plays were given sometimes in the halls of nobles and gentlemen, either when banquets were in progress or on other festival occasions; sometimes before less select audiences in the town halls or on village greens. The actors were sometimes strolling companies of players, who might be minstrels 'or rustics, and were sometimes also retainers of the great nobles, allowed to practice their dramatic ability on tours about the country when they were not needed for their masters' entertainment. In the Interlude-Moralities and Interludes first appears *The* Vice, a rogue who sums up in himself all the Vices of the older Moralities and serves as the buffoon.

One of his most popular exploits was to belabor the Devil about the stage with a wooden dagger, a habit which took a great hold on the popular imagination, as numerous references in later literature testify. Transformed by time, the Vice appears in the Elizabethan drama, and thereafter, as the clown. The various dramatic forms from the tenth century to the middle of the sixteenth at which we have thus hastily glanced—folk-plays, mummings and disguisings, secular pageants, Mystery plays, Moralities, and Interludes—have little but a historical importance.

But besides demonstrating the persistence of the popular demand for drama, they exerted a permanent influence in that they formed certain stage traditions which were to modify or largely control the great drama of the Elizabethan period and to some extent of later times. Among these traditions were the disregard for unity, partly of action, but especially of time and place; the mingling of comedy with even the intensest scenes of tragedy; the nearly complete lack of stage scenery, with a resultant willingness in the audience to make the largest possible imaginative assumptions; the presence of certain stock figures, such as the clown; and the presentation of women's parts by men and boys. The plays, therefore, must be reckoned with in dramatic history.

4

Seventeenth Century Literature: A Survey

In the present chapter we shall present a survey of seventeenth century English literature and major writers of the period.

Prose and Poetry

It is pertinent to note that the first half of the seventeenth century as a whole, compared with the Elizabethan age, was a period of relaxing vigor. The Renaissance enthusiasm had spent itself, and in place of the danger and glory which had long united the nation there followed increasing dissension in religion and politics and uncertainty as to the future of England and, indeed, as to the whole purpose of life. Through increased experience men were certainly wiser and more sophisticated than before, but they were also more self-conscious and sadder or more pensive.

The output of literature did not diminish, but it spread itself over wider fields, in general fields of somewhat recondite scholarship rather than of creation. Nevertheless this period includes in prose one writer greater than any prose writer of the previous century, namely Francis Bacon, and, further, the book which unquestionably occupies the highest place in English literature, that is the King James version of the Bible; and in poetry it includes one of the very greatest figures, John Milton, together with a varied and highly interesting assemblage of lesser lyrists of the period.

Francis Bacon

Francis Bacon, intellectually one of the most eminent Englishmen of all times, and chief formulator of the methods of modern science, was born in 1561 (three years before Shakespeare), the son of Sir Nicholas Bacon, Lord Keeper of the Great Seal under Queen Elizabeth and one of her most trusted earlier advisers. The boy's precocity led the queen to call him her 'little Lord Keeper.' At the age of twelve he, like Wyatt, was sent to Cambridge, where his chief impression was of disgust at the unfruitful scholastic application of Aristotle's ideas, still supreme in spite of a century of Renaissance enlightenment. A very much more satisfactory three years' residence in France in the household of the English ambassador was terminated in 1579 (the year of Spenser's 'Shepherd's Calendar') by the death of Sir Nicholas. Bacon was now ready to enter on the great career for which his talents fitted him, but his uncle by marriage, Lord Burghley, though all-powerful with the queen, systematically thwarted his progress, from jealous consciousness of his superiority to his own son.

Bacon's splendid mind and unique intellectual vision produced, perhaps inevitably, considering his public activity, only fragmentary concrete achievements. The only one of his books still commonly read is the series of 'Essays,' which consist of brief and comparatively informal jottings on various subjects.

In their earliest form, in 1597, the essays were ten in number, but by additions from time to time they had increased at last in 1625 to fifty-eight. They deal with a great variety of topics, whatever Bacon happened to be interested in, from friendship to the arrangement of a house, and in their condensation they are more like bare synopses than complete discussions. But their comprehensiveness of view, sureness of ideas and phrasing, suggestiveness, and apt illustrations reveal the pregnancy and practical force of Bacon's thought (though, on the other hand, he is not altogether free from the superstitions of his time and after the lapse of three hundred years sometimes seems commonplace). The whole general tone of the essays, also, shows the man, keen and worldly, not at all a poet or idealist. How to succeed and make the most of prosperity might be called the pervading theme of the essays, and subjects which in themselves suggest spiritual treatment are actually considered in accordance with a coldly intellectual calculation of worldly advantage. The essays are scarcely less notable for style than for ideas. With characteristic intellectual independence Bacon strikes out for himself an extremely terse and clear manner of expression, doubtless influenced by such Latin authors as Tacitus, which stands in marked contrast to the formless diffuseness or artificial elaborateness of most Elizabethan and Jacobean prose. His unit of structure is always a short clause.

The sentences are sometimes short, sometimes consist of a number of connected clauses; but they are always essentially loose rather than periodic; so that the thought is perfectly simple and its movement clear and systematic. The very numerous allusions to classical history and life are not the result of affectation, but merely indicate the natural furnishing of the mind of the educated Renaissance gentleman. The essays, it should be added, were evidently suggested and more or less influenced by those of the great

French thinker, Montaigne, an earlier contemporary of Bacon. The hold of medieval scholarly tradition, it is further interesting to note, was still so strong that in order to insure their permanent preservation Bacon translated them into Latin—he took for granted that the English in which he first composed them and in which they will always be known was only a temporary vulgar tongue. But Bacon's most important work, as we have already implied, was not in the field of pure literature but in the general advancement of knowledge, particularly knowledge of natural science; and of this great service we must speak briefly. His avowal to Burghley, made as early as 1592, is famous: 'I have taken all knowledge to be my province.'

Briefly stated, his purposes, constituting an absorbing and noble ambition, were to survey all the learning of his time, in all lines of thought, natural science, morals, politics, and the rest, to overthrow the current method of *a priori* deduction, deduction resting, moreover, on very insufficient and long-antiquated bases of observation, and to substitute for it as the method of the future, unlimited fresh observation and experiment and inductive reasoning. This enormous task was to be mapped out and its results summarized in a Latin work called 'Magna Instauratio Scientiarum'; but parts of this survey were necessarily to be left for posterity to formulate, and of the rest Bacon actually composed only a fraction. What may be called the first part appeared originally in English in 1605 and is known by the abbreviated title, *'The Advancement of Learning'*; the expanded Latin form has the title, 'De Augmentis Scientiarum.' Its exhaustive enumeration of the branches of thought and knowledge, what has been accomplished in each and what may be hoped for it in the future, is thoroughly fascinating, though even here Bacon was not capable of passionate enthusiasm.

However, the second part of the work, 'Novum Organum' (The New Method), written in Latin and published in 1620, is the most important. Most interesting here, perhaps, is the classification (contrasting with Plato's doctrine of divinely perfect controlling ideas) of the 'idols' (phantoms) which mislead the human mind. Of these Bacon finds four sorts: idols of the tribe, which are inherent in human nature; idols of the cave, the errors of the individual; idols of the market-place, due to mistaken reliance on words; and idols of the theater (that is, of the schools), resulting from false reasoning. In the details of all his scholarly work Bacon's knowledge and point of view were inevitably imperfect.

Even in natural science he was not altogether abreast of his time—he refused to accept Harvey's discovery of the manner of the circulation of the blood and the Copernican system of astronomy. Neither was he, as is sometimes supposed, the *inventor* of the inductive method of observation and reasoning, which in some degree is fundamental in all study. But he did, much more fully and clearly than any one before him, demonstrate the importance and possibilities of that method; modern experimental science and thought have proceeded directly in the path which he pointed out; and he is fully entitled to the great honor of being called their father, which certainly places him high among the great figures in the history of human thought.

Among the prose authors of the period who hold an assured secondary position in the history of English literature three or four may be mentioned: Robert Burton, Oxford scholar, minister, and recluse, whose 'Anatomy of Melancholy' (1621), a vast and quaint compendium of information both scientific and literary, has largely influenced numerous later writers; Jeremy Taylor, royalist clergyman and bishop, one of the most eloquent and spiritual of English preachers, author of 'Holy Living' (1650) and 'Holy Dying' (1651); Izaak Walton, London tradesman and student, best known for his 'Compleat Angler' (1653), but author also of charming brief lives of Donne, George Herbert, and others of his contemporaries; and Sir Thomas Browne, a scholarly physician of Norwich, who elaborated a fastidiously poetic Latinized prose style for his pensively delightful 'Religio Medici' (A Physician's Religion—1643) and other works.

Lyric Poetry

Apart from the drama and the *King James Bible,* the most enduring literary achievement of the period was in poetry. Milton—distinctly, after Shakespeare, the greatest writer of the century—must receive separate consideration; the more purely lyric poets may be grouped together. The absence of any sharp line of separation between the literature of the reign of Elizabeth and of those of James I and Charles I is no less marked in the case of the lyric poetry than of the drama. Some of the poets whom we have already discussed in Chapter V continued writing until the second decade of the seventeenth century, or later, and some of those whom we shall here name had commenced their career well before 1600. Just as in the drama, therefore, something of the Elizabethan spirit remains in the lyric poetry; yet here also before many years there is a perceptible change; the Elizabethan spontaneous joyousness largely vanishes and is replaced by more self-conscious artistry or thought. The Elizabethan note is perhaps most unmodified in certain anonymous songs and other poems of the early years of James I, such as the exquisite 'Weep you no more, sad fountains.' It is clear also in the charming songs of Thomas Campion, a physician who composed both words and music for several song-books, and in Michael Drayton, a voluminous poet and dramatist who is known to most readers only for his finely rugged patriotic ballad on the battle of Agincourt. Sir Henry Wotton, statesman and Provost (head) of Eton School, displays the Elizabethan idealism in 'The Character of a Happy Life' and in his stanzas in praise of Elizabeth, daughter of King James, wife of the ill-starred Elector-Palatine and King of Bohemia, and ancestress of the present English royal family.

The Elizabethan spirit is present but mingled with seventeenth century melancholy in the sonnets and other poems of the Scotch gentleman William Drummond of Hawthornden (the name of his estate near Edinburgh), who in quiet life-long retirement lamented the untimely death of the lady to whom he had been betrothed or meditated on heavenly things. Herrick belongs in part to a group of poets who, being attached to the Court, and devoting some, at least, of their verses to conventional love-making, are called the Cavalier Poets. Among the others Thomas Carew follows the classical principles of Jonson in lyrics which are facile, smooth, and sometimes a little frigid. Sir John Suckling, a handsome and capricious representative of all the extravagances of the Court set, with whom he was enormously popular, tossed off with affected carelessness a mass of slovenly lyrics of which a few audaciously impudent ones are worthy to survive. From the equally chaotic product of Colonel Richard Lovelace stand out the two well-known bits of noble idealism, 'To Lucasta, Going to the Wars,' and 'To Althea, from Prison.' George Wither (1588-1667), a much older man than Suckling and Lovelace, may be mentioned with them as the writer in his youth of light-hearted love-poems. But in the Civil War he took the side of Parliament and under Cromwell he rose to the rank of major-general. In his later life he wrote a great quantity of Puritan religious verse, largely prosy in spite of his fluency. The last important group among these lyrists is that of the more distinctly religious poets. The chief of these, George Herbert (1593-1633), the subject of one of the most delightful of the short biographies of Izaak Walton, belonged to a distinguished family of the Welsh Border, one branch of which held the earldom of Pembroke, so that the poet was related to the young noble who may have been Shakespeare's patron. He was also younger brother of Lord Edward Herbert of Cherbury, an inveterate duellist and the father of English Deism.

Destined by his mother to peaceful pursuits, he wavered from the outset between two forces, religious devotion and a passion for worldly comfort and distinction. For a long period the latter had the upper hand, and his life has been described by his best editor, Professor George Herbert Palmer, as twenty-seven years of vacillation and three of consecrated service. Appointed Public Orator, or showman, of his university, Cambridge, he spent some years in enjoying the somewhat trifling elegancies of life and in truckling to the great. Then, on the death of his patrons, he passed through a period of intense crisis from which he emerged wholly spiritualized.

The three remaining years of his life he spent in the little country parish of Bemerton, just outside of Salisbury, as a fervent High Church minister, or as he preferred to name himself, priest, in the strictest devotion to his professional duties and to the practices of an ascetic piety which to the usual American mind must seem about equally admirable and conventional. His religious poems, published after his death in a volume called 'The Temple,' show mainly two things, first his intense and beautiful consecration to his personal God and Saviour, which, in its earnest sincerity, renders him distinctly the most representative poet of the Church of England, and second the influence of Donne, who was a close friend of his mother. The titles of most of the poems, often consisting of a single word, are commonly fantastic and symbolical—for example, 'The Collar,' meaning the yoke of submission to God; and his use of conceits, though not so pervasive as with Donne, is equally contorted.

To a present-day reader the apparent affectations may seem at first to throw doubt on Herbert's genuineness; but in reality he was aiming to dedicate to religious purposes what appeared to him the highest style of poetry. Without question he is, in a true if special sense, a really great poet. The second of these religious poets, Richard Crashaw, whose life (1612-1649) was not quite so short as Herbert's, combined an ascetic devotion with a glowingly sensuous esthetic nature that seems rather Spanish than English. Born into an extreme Protestant family, but outraged by the wanton iconoclasm of the triumphant Puritans, and deprived by them of his fellowship, at Cambridge, he became a Catholic and died a canon in the church of the miracle-working Lady (Virgin Mary) of Loretto in Italy.

His most characteristic poetry is marked by extravagant conceits and by ecstatic outbursts of emotion that have been called more ardent than anything else in English; though he sometimes writes also in a vein of calm and limpid beauty. He was a poetic disciple of Herbert, as he avowed by humbly entitling his volume 'Steps to the Temple.' The life of Henry Vaughan (1621-1695) stands in contrast to those of Herbert and Crashaw both by its length and by its quietness. Vaughan himself emphasized his Welsh race by designating himself 'The Silurist' (native of South Wales).

After an incomplete university course at Jesus College (the Welsh college), Oxford, and some apparently idle years in London among Jonson's disciples, perhaps also after serving the king in the war, he settled down in his native mountains to the self-denying life of a country physician. His important poems were mostly published at this time, in 1650 and 1655, in the collection which he named 'Silex Scintillans' (The Flaming Flint), a title explained by the frontispiece, which represents a flinty heart glowing under the lightning stroke of God's call. Vaughan's chief traits are a very fine and calm philosophic-religious spirit and a carefully observant love of external Nature, in which he sees mystic revelations of God. In both respects he is closely akin to the later and greater Wordsworth, and his 'Retreat' has the same theme as Wordsworth's famous 'Ode on Intimations of Immortality,' the idea namely that children have a greater spiritual sensitiveness than older persons, because they have come to earth directly from a former life in Heaven.

The contrast between the chief Anglican and Catholic religious poets of this period has been thus expressed by a discerning critic: 'Herrick's religious emotions are only as ripples on a shallow lake when compared to the crested waves of Crashaw, the storm-tides of Herbert, and the deep-sea stirrings of Vaughan.' We may give a further word of mention to the voluminous Francis Quarles, who in his own day and long after enjoyed enormous popularity, especially among members of the Church of England and especially for his 'Emblems,' a book of a sort common in Europe for a century before his time, in which fantastic woodcuts, like Vaughan's 'Silex Scintillans,' were illustrated with short poems of religious emotion, chiefly dominated by fear.

But Quarles survives only as an interesting curiosity. Three other poets whose lives belong to the middle of the century may be said to complete this entire lyric group. Andrew Marvell, a very moderate Puritan, joined with Milton in his office of Latin Secretary under Cromwell, wrote much poetry of various sorts, some of it in the Elizabethan octosyllabic couplet. He voices a genuine love of Nature, like Wither often in the pastoral form; but his best-known poem is the 'Horatian Ode upon Cromwell's Return from Ireland,' containing the famous eulogy of King Charles' bearing at his execution. Abraham Cowley, a youthful prodigy and always conspicuous for intellectual power, was secretary to Queen Henrietta Maria after her flight to France and later was a royalist spy in England. His most conspicuous poems are his so-called 'Pindaric Odes,' in which he supposed that he was imitating the structure of the Greek Pindar but really originated the pseudo-Pindaric Ode, a poem in irregular, non-correspondent stanzas. He is the last important representative of the 'Metaphysical' style. In his own day he was acclaimed as the greatest poet of all time, but as is usual in such cases his reputation very rapidly waned.

Edmund Waller (1606-1687), a very wealthy gentleman in public life who played a flatly discreditable part in the Civil War, is most important for his share in shaping the riming pentameter couplet into the smooth pseudo-classical form rendered famous by Dryden and Pope; but his only notable single poems are two Cavalier love-lyrics in stanzas, 'On a Girdle' and 'Go, Lovely Rose.'

John Milton (1608-1674)

John Milton's life falls naturally into three periods: first, Youth and preparation, 1608-1639, when he wrote his shorter poems. Second, Public life, 1639-1660, when he wrote, or at least published, in poetry, only a few sonnets. Finally, later years, 1660-1674, of outer defeat, but of chief poetic achievement, the period of *'Paradise Lost,' 'Paradise Regained,'* and *'Samson Agonistes.'*

Noted poet, John Milton was born in London in December, 1608. His father was a prosperous scrivener, or lawyer of the humbler sort, and a Puritan, but broad-minded, and his children were brought up in the love of music, beauty, and learning. At the age of twelve the future poet was sent to St. Paul's School, and he tells us that from this time on his devotion to study seldom allowed him to leave his books earlier than midnight. At sixteen, in 1625, he entered Cambridge, where he remained during the seven years required for the M.A. degree, and where he was known as 'the lady of Christ's' [College], perhaps for his beauty, of which all his life he continued proud, perhaps for his moral scrupulousness.

Milton was never, however, a conventional prig, and a quarrel with a self-important tutor led at one time to his informal suspension from the University. His nature, indeed, had many elements quite inconsistent with the usual vague popular conception of him. He was always not only inflexible in his devotion to principle, but—partly, no doubt, from consciousness of his intellectual superiority—haughty as well as reserved, self-confident, and little respectful of opinions and feelings that clashed with his own. Nevertheless in his youth he had plenty of animal spirits and always for his friends warm human sympathies.

To his college years belong two important poems. His Christmas hymn, the 'Ode on the Morning of Christ's Nativity,' shows the influence of his early poetical master, Spenser, and of contemporary pastoral poets, though it also contains some conceits—truly poetic conceits, however, not exercises in intellectual cleverness like many of those of Donne and his followers. With whatever qualifications, it is certainly one of the great English lyrics, and its union of Renaissance sensuousness with grandeur of conception and sureness of expression foretell clearly enough at twenty the poet of 'Paradise Lost.' The sonnet on his twenty-third birthday, further, is known to almost every reader of poetry as the best short expression in literature of the dedication of one's life and powers to God. Milton had planned to enter the ministry, but the growing predominance of the High-Church party made this impossible for him, and on leaving the University in 1632 he retired to the country estate which his parents now occupied at Horton, twenty miles west of London.

Here, for nearly six years, amid surroundings which nourished his poet's love for Nature, he devoted his time chiefly to further mastery of the whole range of approved literature, Greek, Latin, French, Italian, and English. His poems of these years also are few, but they too are of the very highest quality. 'L'Allegro' and 'Il Penseroso' are idealized visions, in the tripping Elizabethan octosyllabic couplet, of the pleasures of suburban life viewed in moods respectively of light-hearted happiness and of reflection.

'Comus,' the last of the Elizabethan and Jacobean masks, combines an exquisite poetic beauty and a real dramatic action more substantial than that of any other mask with a serious moral theme (the security of Virtue) in a fashion that renders it unique. 'Lycidas' is one of the supreme English elegies; though the grief which helps to create its power sprang more from the recent death of the poet's mother than from that of the nominal subject, his college acquaintance, Edward King, and though in the hands of a lesser artist the solemn denunciation of the false leaders of the English Church might not have been wrought into so fine a harmony with the pastoral form. Milton's first period ends with an experience designed to complete his preparation for his career, a fifteen months' tour in France and Italy, where the highest literary circles received him cordially.

From this trip he returned in 1639, sooner than he had planned, because, he said, the public troubles at home, foreshadowing the approaching war, seemed to him a call to service; though in fact some time intervened before his entrance on public life. Now at last Milton was drawn into active public life. The execution of the King by the extreme Puritan minority excited an outburst of indignation not only in England but throughout Europe. Milton, rising to the occasion, defended the act in a pamphlet, thereby beginning a paper controversy, chiefly with the Dutch scholar Salmasius, which lasted for several years.

By 1652 it had resulted in the loss of Milton's eyesight, previously over-strained by his studies—a sacrifice in which he gloried but which lovers of poetry must always regret, especially since the controversy largely consisted, according to the custom of the time, in a disgusting exchange of personal scurrilities. Milton's championship of the existing government, however, together with his scholarship, had at once secured for him the position of Latin secretary, or conductor of the diplomatic correspondence of the State with foreign countries.

He held this office, after the loss of his eyesight, with Marvell as a colleague, under both Parliament and Cromwell, but it is an error to suppose that he exerted any influence in the management of affairs or that he was on familiar terms with the Protector.

Remarkably, at the Restoration he necessarily lost both the position and a considerable part of his property, and for a while he went into hiding; but through the efforts of Marvell and others he was finally included in the general amnesty. In the remaining fourteen years which make the third period of his life Milton stands out for subsequent ages as a noble figure. His very obstinacy and egoism now enabled him, blind, comparatively poor, and the representative of a lost cause, to maintain his proud and patient dignity in the midst of the triumph of all that was most hateful to him, and, as he believed, to God. His isolation, indeed, was in many respects extreme, though now as always he found the few sympathetic friends on whom his nature was quite dependent.

His religious beliefs had become what would at present be called Unitarian, and he did not associate with any of the existing denominations; in private theory he had even come to believe in polygamy. At home he is said to have suffered from the coldness or more active antipathy of his three daughters, which is no great cause for wonder if we must credit the report that he compelled them to read aloud to him in foreign languages of which he had taught them the pronunciation but not the meaning.

Their mother had died some years before, and he had soon lost the second wife who is the subject of one of his finest sonnets. In 1663, at the age of fifty-four, he was united in a third marriage to Elizabeth Minshull, a woman of twenty-four, who was to survive him for more than fifty years. The important fact of this last period, however, is that Milton now had the leisure to write, or to complete, 'Paradise Lost.' For a quarter of a century he had avowedly cherished the ambition to produce 'such a work as the world would not willingly let die' and had had in mind, among others, the story of Man's Fall.

Outlines for a treatment of it not in epic but in dramatic

form are preserved in a list of a hundred possible subjects for a great work which he drew up as early as 1640, and during the Commonwealth period he seems not only to have been slowly maturing the plan but to have composed parts of the existing poem; nevertheless the actual work of composition belongs chiefly to the years following 1660. The story as told in Genesis had received much elaboration in Christian tradition from a very early period and Milton drew largely from this general tradition and no doubt to some extent from various previous treatments of the Bible narrative in several languages which he might naturally have read and kept in mind. But beyond the simple outline the poem, like every great work, is essentially the product of his own genius.

He aimed, specifically, to produce a Christian epic which should rank with the great epics of antiquity and with those of the Italian Renaissance. In this purpose he was entirely successful. As a whole, by the consent of all competent judges, 'Paradise Lost' is worthy of its theme, perhaps the greatest that the mind of man can conceive, namely 'to justify the ways of God.' Of course there are defects.

The seventeenth century theology, like every successive theological, philosophical, and scientific system, has lost its hold on later generations, and it becomes dull indeed in the long expository passages of the poem. The attempt to express spiritual ideas through the medium of the secular epic, with its battles and councils and all the forms of physical life, is of course rationally paradoxical. It was early pointed out that in spite of himself Milton has in some sense made Satan the hero of the poem—a reader can scarcely fail to sympathize with the fallen archangel in his unconquerable Puritan-like resistance to the arbitrary decrees of Milton's despotic Deity. Further, Milton's personal, English, and

Puritan prejudices sometimes intrude in various ways. But all these things are on the surface. In sustained imaginative grandeur of conception, expression, and imagery 'Paradise Lost' yields to no human work, and the majestic and varied movement of the blank verse, here first employed in a really great non-dramatic English poem, is as magnificent as anything else in literature.

It cannot be said that the later books always sustain the greatness of the first two; but the profusely scattered passages of sensuous description, at least, such as those of the Garden of Eden and of the beauty of Eve, are in their own way equally fine. Stately and more familiar passages alike show that however much his experience had done to harden Milton's Puritanism, his youthful Renaissance love of beauty for beauty's sake had lost none of its strength, though of course it could no longer be expressed with youthful lightness of fancy and melody.

The poem is a magnificent example of classical art, in the best Greek spirit, united with glowing romantic feeling. Lastly, the value of Milton's scholarship should by no means be overlooked. All his poetry, from the 'Nativity Ode' onward, is like a rich mosaic of gems borrowed from a great range of classical and modern authors, and in 'Paradise Lost' the allusions to literature and history give half of the romantic charm and very much of the dignity. The poem could have been written only by one who combined in a very high degree intellectual power, poetic feeling, religious idealism, profound scholarship and knowledge of literature, and also experienced knowledge of the actual world of men. *'Paradise Lost'* was published in 1677. It was followed in 1671 by 'Paradise Regained,' only one-third as long and much less important; and by 'Samson Agonistes' (Samson in his Death Struggle).

In the latter Milton puts the story of the fallen hero's last days into the majestic form of a Greek drama, imparting to it the passionate but lofty feeling evoked by the close similarity of Samson's situation to his own. This was his last work, and he died in 1674. Whatever his faults, the moral, intellectual and poetic greatness of his nature sets him apart as in a sense the grandest figure in English literature.

John Bunyan

John Bunyan was born in 1628 at the village of Elstow, just outside of Bedford, in central England. After very slight schooling and some practice at his father's trade of tinker, he was in 1644 drafted for two years and a half into garrison service in the Parliamentary army. Released from this occupation, he married a poor but excellent wife and worked at his trade; but the important experiences of his life were the religious ones. Endowed by nature with great moral sensitiveness, he was nevertheless a person of violent impulses and had early fallen into profanity and laxity of conduct, which he later described with great exaggeration as a condition of abandoned wickedness. But from childhood his abnormally active dramatic imagination had tormented him with dreams and fears of devils and hell-fire, and now he entered on a long and agonizing struggle between his religious instinct and his obstinate self-will.

He has told the whole story in his spiritual autobiography, 'Grace Abounding to the Chief of Sinners,' which is one of the notable religious books of the world. A reader of it must be filled about equally with admiration for the force of will and perseverance that enabled Bunyan at last to win his battle, and pity for the fantastic morbidness that created out of next to nothing most of his well-nigh intolerable tortures. One Sunday, for example, fresh from a sermon on

Sabbath observance, he was engaged in a game of 'cat,' when he suddenly heard within himself the question, 'Wilt thou leave thy sins and go to heaven, or have thy sins and go to hell?' Stupefied, he looked up to the sky and seemed there to see the Lord Jesus gazing at him 'hotly displeased' and threatening punishment. Again, one of his favorite diversions was to watch bellmen ringing the chimes in the church steeples, and though his Puritan conscience insisted that the pleasure was 'vain,' still he would not forego it.

Suddenly one day as he was indulging in it the thought occurred to him that God might cause one of the bells to fall and kill him, and he hastened to shield himself by standing under a beam. But, he reflected, the bell might easily rebound from the wall and strike him; so he shifted his position to the steeple-door. Then 'it came into his head, "How if the steeple itself should fall?"' and with that he fled alike from the controversy and the danger. Relief came when at the age of twenty-four he joined a non-sectarian church in Bedford (his own point of view being Baptist). A man of so energetic spirit could not long remain inactive, and within two years he was preaching in the surrounding villages. A dispute with the Friends had already led to the beginning of his controversial writing when in 1660 the Restoration rendered preaching by persons outside the communion of the Church of England illegal, and he was arrested and imprisoned in Bedford jail.

Consistently refusing to give the promise of submission and abstention from preaching which at any time would have secured his release, he continued in prison for twelve years, not suffering particular discomfort and working for the support of his family by fastening the ends onto shoestrings. During this time he wrote and published several of the most important of his sixty books and pamphlets. At last, in 1672, the authorities abandoned the ineffective requirement of conformity, and he was released and became pastor of his church. Three years later he was again imprisoned for six months, and it was at that time that he composed the first part of 'The Pilgrim's Progress,' which was published in 1678. During the remaining ten years of his life his reputation and authority among the Dissenters almost equalled his earnest devotion and kindness, and won for him from his opponents the good-naturedly jocose title of 'the Baptist bishop.' He died in 1688.

Criticism, no doubt, easily discovers in 'Pilgrim's Progress' technical faults. The story often lacks the full development and balance of incidents and narration which a trained literary artist would have given it; the allegory is inconsistent in a hundred ways and places; the characters are only types; and Bunyan, always more preacher than artist, is distinctly unfair to the bad ones among them. But these things are unimportant. Every allegory is inconsistent, and Bunyan repeatedly takes pains to emphasize that this is a dream; while the simplicity of character-treatment increases the directness of the main effect. When all is said, the book remains the greatest example in literature of what absolute earnestness may make possible for a plain and untrained man.

Nothing, of course, can alter the fundamental distinctions. 'Paradise Lost' is certainly greater than 'Pilgrim's Progress,' because it is the work of a poet and a scholar as well as a religious enthusiast. But 'Pilgrim's Progress,' let it be said frankly, will always find a dozen readers where Milton has one by choice, and no man can afford to think otherwise than respectfully of achievements which speak powerfully and nobly to the underlying instincts and needs of all mankind.

THE RESTORATION (1660-1700)

It is remarkable that the revolt of the nation was directed partly against the irresponsible injustice of the Puritan military government but largely also against the excessive moral severity of the whole Puritan regime. Accordingly a large part of the nation, but particularly the Court, now plunged into an orgy of self-indulgence in which moral restraints almost ceased to be regarded. The new king and his nobles had not only been led by years of proscription and exile to hate on principle everything that bore the name of Puritan, but had spent their exile at the French Court, where utterly cynical and selfish pursuit of pleasure and licentiousness of conduct were merely masked by conventionally polished manners.

The upshot was that the quarter century of the renewed Stuart rule was in almost all respects the most disgraceful period of English history and life. In everything, so far as possible, the restored Cavaliers turned their backs on their immediate predecessors. The Puritans, in particular, had inherited the enthusiasm which had largely made the greatness of the Elizabethan period but had in great measure shifted it into the channel of their religion. Hence to the Restoration courtiers enthusiasm and outspoken emotion seemed marks of hypocrisy and barbarism. In opposition to such tendencies they aimed to realize the ideal of the man of the world, sophisticated, skeptical, subjecting everything to the scrutiny of the reason, and above all, well-bred.

Well-bred, that is, according to the artificial social standards of a selfish aristocratic class; for the actual manners of the courtiers, as of such persons at all times, were in many respects disgustingly crude. In religion most of them professed adherence to the English Church (some to the

Catholic), but it was a conventional adherence to an institution of the State and a badge of party allegiance, not a matter of spiritual conviction or of any really deep feeling. The Puritans, since they refused to return to the English (Established) Church, now became known as Dissenters. The men of the Restoration, then, deliberately repudiated some of the chief forces which seem to a romantic age to make life significant.

As a natural corollary they concentrated their interest on the sphere of the practical and the actual. In science, particularly, they continued with marked success the work of Bacon and his followers. Very shortly after the Restoration the Royal Society was founded for the promotion of research and scientific knowledge, and it was during this period that Sir Isaac Newton (a man in every respect admirable) made his vastly important discoveries in physics, mathematics, and astronomy. In literature, both prose and verse, the rationalistic and practical spirit showed itself in the enthroning above everything else of the principles of utility and common sense in substance and straightforward directness in style. The imaginative treatment of the spiritual life, as in 'Paradise Lost' or 'The Faerie Queene,' or the impassioned exaltation of imaginative beauty, as in much Elizabethan poetry, seemed to the typical men of the Restoration unsubstantial and meaningless, and they had no ambition to attempt flights in those realms. In anything beyond the tangible affairs of visible life, indeed, they had little real belief, and they preferred that literature should restrain itself within the safe limits of the known and the demonstrable.

Hence the characteristic Restoration verse is satire of a prosaic sort which scarcely belongs to poetry at all. More fortunate results of the prevailing spirit were the gradual abandonment of the conceits and irregularities of the 'metaphysical' poets, and, most important, the perfecting of the highly regular rimed pentameter couplet, the one great formal achievement of the time in verse.

Notably, in prose style the same tendencies resulted in a distinct advance. Thitherto English prose had seldom attained to thorough conciseness and order; it had generally been more or less formless or involved in sentence structure or pretentious in general manner; but the Restoration writers substantially formed the more logical and clear-cut manner which, generally speaking, has prevailed ever since. Quite consistent with this commonsense spirit, as the facts were then interpreted, was the allegiance which Restoration writers rendered to the literature of classical antiquity, an allegiance which has gained for this period and the following half-century, where the same attitude was still more strongly emphasized, the name 'pseudo-classical.'

We have before noted that the enthusiasm for Greek and Latin literature which so largely underlay the Renaissance took in Ben Jonson and his followers, in part, the form of a careful imitation of the external technique of the classical writers. In France and Italy at the same time this tendency was still stronger and much more general.

The seventeenth century was the great period of French tragedy (Corneille and Racine), which attempted to base itself altogether on classical tragedy. One particular social institution of the period should be mentioned for its connection with literature, namely the coffee houses, which, introduced about the middle of the century, soon became very popular and influential. They were, in our own idiom, cafes, where men met to sip coffee or chocolate and discuss current topics. Later, in the next century, they often developed into clubs.

Minor Writers

The contempt which fell upon the Puritans as a deposed and unpopular party found stinging literary expression in one of the most famous of English satires, Samuel Butler's 'Hudibras.' Butler, a reserved and saturnine man, spent much of his uneventful life in the employ (sometimes as steward) of gentlemen and nobles, one of whom, a Puritan officer, Sir Samuel Luke, was to serve as the central lay-figure for his lampoon. 'Hudibras,' which appeared in three parts during a period of fifteen years, is written, like previous English satires, in rough-and-ready doggerel verse, in this case verse of octosyllabic couplets and in the form of a mock-epic. It ridicules the intolerance and sanctimonious hypocrisy of the Puritans as the Cavaliers insisted on seeing them in the person of the absurd Sir Hudibras and his squire Ralph (partly suggested by Cervantes' Don Quixote and Sancho). These sorry figures are made to pass very unheroically through a series of burlesque adventures. The chief power of the production lies in its fire of witty epigrams, many of which have become familiar quotations.

Though the king and Court took unlimited delight in 'Hudibras' they displayed toward Butler their usual ingratitude and allowed him to pass his latter years in obscure poverty. Some of the other central characteristics of the age appear in a unique book, the voluminous 'Diary' which Samuel Pepys, a typical representative of the thrifty and unimaginative citizen class, kept in shorthand for ten years beginning in 1660. Pepys, who ultimately became Secretary to the Admiralty, and was a hard-working and very able naval official, was also astonishingly naif and vain.

In his 'Diary' he records in the greatest detail, without the least reserve (and with no idea of publication) all his daily doings, public and private, and a large part of his thoughts. The absurdities and weaknesses, together with the better traits, of a man spiritually shallow and yet very human are here revealed with a frankness unparalleled and almost incredible. Fascinating as a psychological study, the book also affords the fullest possible information about all the life of the period, especially the familiar life, not on dress-parade.

In rather sharp contrast stands the 'Diary' of John Evelyn, which in much shorter space and virtually only in a series of glimpses covers seventy years of time. Evelyn was a real gentleman and scholar who occupied an honorable position in national life; his 'Diary,' also, furnishes a record, but a dignified record, of his public and private experience.

Restoration Drama

The moral anarchy of the period is most strikingly exhibited in its drama, particularly in its comedy and 'comedy of manners.' These plays, dealing mostly with love-actions in the setting of the Court or of fashionable London life, and carrying still further the general spirit of those of Fletcher and Shirley a generation or two earlier, deliberately ridicule moral principles and institutions, especially marriage, and are always in one degree or another grossly indecent.

John Dryden (1631-1700)

It is pertinent to note that no other English literary period is so thoroughly represented and summed up in the works of a single man as is the Restoration period in John Dryden, a writer in some respects akin to Ben Jonson, of prolific and vigorous talent without the crowning quality of genius. Dryden, the son of a family of Northamptonshire country gentry, was born in 1631. From Westminster School and Cambridge he went, at about the age of twenty-six and possessed by inheritance of a minimum living income, to London, where he perhaps hoped to get political preferment through his relatives in the Puritan party. His serious entrance into literature was made comparatively late, in 1659, with a eulogizing poem on Cromwell on the occasion of the latter's death.

When, the next year, Charles II was restored, Dryden shifted to the Royalist side and wrote some poems in honor of the king. Dryden's character should not be judged from this incident and similar ones in his later life too hastily nor without regard to the spirit of the times. Aside from the fact that Dryden had never professed, probably, to be a radical Puritan, he certainly was not, like Milton and Bunyan, a heroic person, nor endowed with deep and dynamic convictions; on the other hand, he was very far from being base or dishonorable—no one can read his works attentively without being impressed by their spirit of straightforward manliness.

As such controlled, like his age, by cool common sense and practical judgment, he kept his mind constantly open to new impressions, and was more concerned to avoid the appearance of bigotry and unreason than to maintain that of consistency. In regard to politics and even religion he evidently shared the opinion, bred in many of his contemporaries by the wasteful strife of the previous generations, that beyond a few fundamental matters the good citizen should make no close scrutiny of details but rather render loyal support to the established institutions of the State, by which peace is preserved and anarchy restrained. Since the nation had recalled Charles II, overthrown Puritanism, and reestablished the Anglican Church, it probably appeared to Dryden an act of patriotism as well as of expediency to accept its decision. Dryden's marriage with the daughter of an earl, two or three years after the Restoration, secured his social position, and for more than fifteen years thereafter his life was outwardly successful.

He first turned to the drama. In spite of the prohibitory Puritan law, a facile writer, Sir William Davenant, had begun, cautiously, a few years before the Restoration, to produce operas and other works of dramatic nature; and the returning Court had brought from Paris a passion for the stage, which therefore offered the best and indeed the only field for remunerative literary effort. Accordingly, although Dryden himself frankly admitted that his talents were not especially adapted to writing plays, he proceeded to do so energetically, and continued at it, with diminishing productivity, nearly down to the end of his life, thirty-five years later.

But his activity always found varied outlets. He secured a lucrative share in the profits of the King's Playhouse, one of the two theaters of the time which alone were allowed to present regular plays, and he held the mainly honorary positions of poet laureate and historiographer-royal. Later, like Chaucer, he was for a time collector of the customs of the port of London. He was not much disturbed by 'The Rehearsal,' a burlesque play brought out by the Duke of Buckingham and other wits to ridicule current dramas and dramatists, in which he figured as chief butt under the name 'Bayes' (poet laureate); and he took more than full revenge ten years later when in 'Absalom and Achitophel' he drew the portrait of Buckingham as Zimri.

But in 1680 an outrage of which he was the victim, a brutal and unprovoked beating inflicted by ruffians in the employ of the Earl of Rochester, seems to mark a permanent change for the worse in his fortunes, a change not indeed to disaster but to a permanent condition of doubtful prosperity.

The next year he became engaged in political controversy, which resulted in the production of his most famous work. Charles II was without a legitimate child, and the heir to the throne was his brother, the Duke of York, who a few years later actually became king as James II. But while Charles was outwardly, for political reasons, a member of the Church of England (at heart he was a Catholic), the Duke of York was a professed and devoted Catholic, and the powerful Whig party, strongly Protestant, was violently opposed to him. The monstrous fiction of a 'Popish Plot,' brought forward by Titus Oates, and the murderous frenzy which it produced, were demonstrations of the strength of the Protestant feeling, and the leader of the Whigs, the Earl of Shaftesbury, proposed that the Duke of York should be excluded by law from the succession to the throne in favor of the Duke of Monmouth, one of the king's illegitimate sons.

At last, in 1681, the nation became afraid of another civil war, and the king was enabled to have Shaftesbury arrested on the charge of treason. Hereupon Dryden, at the suggestion, it is said, of the king, and with the purpose of securing Shaftesbury's conviction, put forth the First Part of 'Absalom and Achitophel,' a masterly satire of Shaftesbury, Monmouth, and their associates in the allegorical disguise of the (somewhat altered) Biblical story of David and Absalom.

Variety, fluency, and not ungraceful strength are perhaps the chief qualities of Dryden's work, displayed alike in his verse and in his prose. Since he was primarily a poet it is natural to speak first of his verse; and we must begin with a glance at the history of the rimed pentameter couplet, which he carried to the highest point of effectiveness thus far attained. This form had been introduced into English, probably from French, by Chaucer, who used it in many thousand lines of the 'Canterbury Tales.' It was employed to some extent by the Elizabethans, especially in scattered passages of their dramas, and in some poems of the early seventeenth century.

Up to that time it generally had a free form, with frequent 'running-on' of the sense from one line to the next and marked irregularity of pauses. The process of developing it into the representative pseudo-classical measure of Dryden and Pope consisted in making the lines, or at least the couplets, generally end-stopt, and in securing a general regular movement, mainly by eliminating pronounced pauses within the line, except for the frequent organic cesura in the middle. This process, like other pseudo-classical tendencies, was furthered by Ben Jonson, who used the couplet in more than half of his non-dramatic verse; but it was especially carried on by the wealthy politician and minor poet Edmund Waller, who for sixty years, from 1623 on, wrote most of his verse (no very great quantity) in the couplet. Dryden and all his contemporaries gave to Waller, rather too unreservedly, the credit of having first perfected the form, that is of first making it (to their taste) pleasingly smooth and regular.

The great danger of the couplet thus treated is that of over-great conventionality, as was partly illustrated by Dryden's successor, Pope, who carried Waller's method to the farthest possible limit. Dryden's vigorous instincts largely saved him from this fault; by skilful variations in accents and pauses and by terse forcefulness of expression he gave the couplet firmness as well as smoothness. He employed, also, two other more questionable means of variety, namely, the insertion (not original with him) of occasional Alexandrine lines and of frequent triplets, three lines instead of two riming together.

In fact, a present-day reader may like the pentameter couplet or may find it frigid and tedious; at any rate Dryden employed it in the larger part of his verse and stamped it unmistakably with the strength of his strong personality. In satiric and didactic verse Dryden is accepted as the chief English master, and here 'Absalom and Achitophel' is his greatest achievement. It is formally a narrative poem, but in fact almost nothing happens in it; it is really expository and descriptive—a very clever partisan analysis of a situation, enlivened by a series of the most skilful character sketches with very decided partisan coloring.

The sketches, therefore, offer an interesting contrast with the sympathetic and humorous portraits of Chaucer's 'Prolog.' Among the secrets of Dryden's success in this particular field are his intellectual coolness, his vigorous masculine power of seizing on the salient points of character, and his command of terse, biting phraseology, set off by effective contrast. Of Dryden's numerous comedies and 'tragi-comedies' (serious plays with a sub-action of comedy) it may be said summarily that some of them were among the best of their time but that they were as licentious as all the others. Dryden was also the chief author of another kind of play, peculiar to this period in England, namely the 'Heroic' (Epic) Play. The material and spirit of these works came largely from the enormously long contemporary French romances, which were widely read in England, and of which a prominent representative was 'The Great Cyrus' of Mlle. de Scudery, in ten volumes of a thousand pages or more apiece.

These romances, carrying further the tendency which

appears in Sidney's 'Arcadia,' are among the most extravagant of all products of the romantic imagination—strange melanges of ancient history, medieval chivalry, pastoralism, seventeenth century artificial manners, and allegory of current events. The English 'heroic' plays, partly following along these lines, with influence also from Fletcher, lay their scenes in distant countries; their central interest is extravagant romantic love; the action is more that of epic adventure than of tragedy; and incidents, situations, characters, sentiments, and style, though not without power, are exaggerated or overstrained to an absurd degree. Breaking so violently through the commonplaceness and formality of the age, however, they offer eloquent testimony to the irrepressibility of the romantic instinct in human nature. Dryden's most representative play of this class is 'Almanzor and Almahide, or the Conquest of Granada,' in two long five-act parts. Dryden's work in other forms of verse, also, is of high quality. In his dramas he inserted songs whose lyric sweetness is reminiscent of the similar songs of Fletcher.

Early in his career he composed (in pentameter quatrains of alternate rime, like Gray's 'Elegy') 'Annus Mirabilis' (The Wonderful Year—namely 1666), a long and vigorous though far from faultless narrative of the war with the Dutch and of the Great Fire of London. More important are the three odes in the 'irregular Pindaric' form introduced by Cowley. The first, that to Mrs. (i. e., Miss) Anne Killigrew, one of the Queen's maids of honor, is full, thanks to Cowley's example, of 'metaphysical' conceits and science. The two later ones, 'Alexander's Feast' and the 'Song for St. Cecilia's Day,' both written for a musical society's annual festival in honor of the patron saint of their art, are finely spirited and among the most striking, though not most delicate, examples of onomatopoeia in all poetry. Dryden's prose, only less important than his verse, is mostly in the form of long critical essays, virtually the first in English, which are prefixed to many of his plays and poems.

In them, following French example, he discusses fundamental questions of poetic art or of general esthetics. His opinions are judicious; independent, so far as the despotic authority of the French critics permitted, at least honest; and interesting. Most important, perhaps, is his attitude toward the French pseudo-classical formulas. He accepted French theory even in details which we now know to be absurd—agreed, for instance, that even Homer wrote to enforce an abstract moral (namely that discord destroys a state).

In fact, the field of his main interest, further, his reason was persuaded by the pseudo-classical arguments that English (Elizabethan) tragedy, with its violent contrasts and irregularity, was theoretically wrong. Nevertheless his greatness consists throughout partly in the common sense which he shares with the best English critics and thinkers of all periods; and as regards tragedy he concludes, in spite of rules and theory, that he 'loves Shakespeare.'

In expression, still again, Dryden did perhaps more than any other man to form modern prose style, a style clear, straightforward, terse, forceful, easy and simple and yet dignified, fluent in vocabulary, varied, and of pleasing rhythm. Dryden's general quality and a large part of his achievement are happily summarized in Lowell's epigram that he 'was the greatest poet who ever was or ever could be made wholly out of prose.' He can never again be a favorite with the general reading-public; but he will always remain one of the conspicuous figures in the annals of English literature.

Other Playwrights

In fact, the other dramatists of the Restoration period may be dismissed with a few words. In tragedy the overdrawn but powerful plays of Thomas Otway, a man of short and pathetic life, and of Nathaniel Lee, are alone of any importance. In comedy, during the first part of the period, stand Sir George Etherege and William Wycherley. The latter's 'Country Wife' has been called the most heartless play ever written. To the next generation and the end of the period (or rather of the Restoration literature, which actually lasted somewhat beyond 1700), belong William Congreve, a master of sparkling wit, Sir John Vanbrugh, and George Farquhar. So corrupt a form of writing as the Restoration comedy could not continue to flaunt itself indefinitely.

The growing indignation was voiced from time to time in published protests, of which the last, in 1698, was the over-zealous but powerful 'Short View of the Immorality and Profaneness of the English Stage' by Jeremy Collier, which carried the more weight because the author was not a Puritan but a High-Church bishop and partisan of the Stuarts. Partly as a result of such attacks and partly by the natural course of events the pendulum, by the end of the period, was swinging back, and not long thereafter Restoration comedy died and the stage was left free for more decent, though, as it proved, not for greater, productions of the time.

In the next chapter we will discuss Elizabethan period and Ben Jonson.

5

Elizabethan Literature and Ben Jonson

> "When a virtuous man is raised, it brings gladness to his friends, grief to enemies, and glory to his posterity."
>
> —*Ben Jonson*

Elizabethan period in English literature is an important epoch when many great literatures like Marlow, William Shakespeare and many notable personalities created the literature of all times. Ben Jonson is a luminary of the period.

In this chapter we will make an assessment of contribution and influence of Ben Jonson.

A contemporary of William Shakespeare, Ben Jonson is best known for his satirical plays, particularly *Volpone*, *The Alchemist*, and *Bartholomew Fair*, which are considered his best, and his lyric poems. A man of vast reading and a seemingly insatiable appetite for controversy, Jonson had an unparalleled breadth of influence on Jacobean and Caroline playwrights and poets.

Born in Westminster, London, on 11 June 1572 Jonson claimed his family was of Scottish Border country descent, and this claim may have been supported by the fact that his coat of arms bears three spindles or rhombi, a device shared by a Borders family, the Johnstones of Annandale. His father died a month before Ben's birth, and his mother remarried two years later, to a master bricklayer. Jonson attended school in St. Martin's Lane, and was later sent to Westminster School, where one of his teachers was William Camden. Jonson remained friendly with Camden, whose broad scholarship evidently influenced his own style, until the latter's death in 1623. On leaving, Jonson was once thought to have gone on to the University of Cambridge; Jonson himself said that he did not go to university, but was put to a trade immediately: a legend recorded by Fuller indicates that he worked on a garden wall in Lincoln's Inn.

He soon had enough of the trade, probably bricklaying, and spent some time in the Low Countries as a volunteer with the regiments of Francis Vere.

In conversations with the poet William Drummond, subsequently published as the *Hawthornden Manuscripts*, Jonson reports that while in the Netherlands he killed an opponent in single combat and stripped him of his weapons. Ben Jonson married, some time before 1594, a woman he described to Drummond as "a shrew, yet honest." His wife has not been definitively identified, but she is sometimes identified as the Ann Lewis who married a Benjamin Jonson at St Magnus-the-Martyr, near London Bridge. The registers of St. Martin's Church state that his eldest daughter Mary died in November, 1593, when she was only six months old.

His eldest son Benjamin died of the plague ten years later (Jonson's epitaph to him *On My First Sonne* was written shortly after), and a second Benjamin died in 1635. For five years somewhere in this period, Jonson lived separately from his wife, enjoying instead the hospitality of Lord Aubigny. By the summer of 1597, Jonson had a fixed engagement in the Admiral's Men, then performing under Philip Henslowe's management at The Rose. John Aubrey reports, on uncertain authority, that Jonson was not successful as an actor; whatever his skills as an actor, he was evidently more valuable to the company as a writer. By this time, Jonson had begun to write original plays for the Lord Admiral's Men; in 1598, he was mentioned by Francis Meres in his *Palladis Tamia* as one of "the best for tragedy." None of his early tragedies survive, however. An undated comedy, *The Case is Altered*, may be his earliest surviving play.

Remarkably in 1597, a play co-written with Thomas Nashe entitled *The Isle of Dogs* was suppressed after causing great offence. Arrest warrants for Jonson and Nashe were subsequently issued by Elizabeth's so-called interrogator, Richard Topcliffe. Jonson was jailed in Marshalsea Prison and famously charged with "Leude and mutynous behavior", while Nashe managed to escape to Great Yarmouth. A year later, Jonson was again briefly imprisoned, this time in Newgate Prison, for killing another man, an actor Gabriel Spenser, in a duel on 22 September 1598 in Hogsden Fields, (today part of Hoxton).

Tried on a charge of manslaughter, Jonson pleaded guilty but was subsequently released by benefit of clergy, a legal ploy through which he gained leniency by reciting a brief bible verse in Latin, forfeiting his 'goods and chattels' and being branded on his left thumb. In 1598, Jonson produced his first great success, *Every Man in his Humour*, capitalising on the vogue for humour plays that had been begun by George Chapman with *An Humorous Day's Mirth*. William Shakespeare was among the first cast. This play was followed the next year by *Every Man Out of His*

Humour, a pedantic attempt to imitate Aristophanes. It is not known whether this was a success on stage, but when published, it proved popular and went through several editions. Jonson's other work for the theater in the last years of Elizabeth I's reign was unsurprisingly marked by fighting and controversy. *Cynthia's Revels* was produced by the Children of the Chapel Royal at Blackfriars Theatre in 1600. It satirized both John Marston, who Jonson believed had accused him of lustfulness, probably in *Histrio-Mastix*, and Thomas Dekker, against whom Jonson's animus is not known.

Jonson attacked the same two poets again in 1601's *Poetaster*. Dekker responded with *Satiromastix*, subtitled "the untrussing of the humorous poet". The final scene of this play, whilst certainly not to be taken at face value as a portrait of Jonson, offers a caricature that is recognisable from Drummond's report - boasting about himself and condemning other poets, criticising performances of his plays, and calling attention to himself in any available way. This "War of the Theatres" appears to have been concluded with reconciliation on all sides. Jonson collaborated with Dekker on a pageant welcoming James I to England in 1603 although Drummond reports that Jonson called Dekker a rogue. Marston dedicated *The Malcontent* to Jonson and the two collaborated with Chapman on *Eastward Ho*, a 1605 play whose anti-Scottish sentiment landed both authors in jail for a brief time. At the beginning of the reign of James I of England in 1603 Jonson joined other poets and playwrights in welcoming the reign of the new king. Jonson flourished as a dramatist during the first decade or so of James's reign; by 1616, he had produced all the plays on which his reputation as a dramatist depends. These include the tragedy of *Catiline* (acted and printed 1611), which achieved only limited success, and the comedies

Volpone, (acted 1605 and printed in 1607), *Epicoene, or the Silent Woman* (1609), *The Alchemist* (1610), *Bartholomew Fair* (1614) and *The Devil is an Ass* (1616). *The Alchemist* and *Volpone* appear to have been successful at once. Of *Epicoene*, Jonson told Drummond of a satirical verse which reported that the play's subtitle was appropriate, since its audience had refused to applaud the play (i.e., remained silent). Yet *Epicoene*, along with *Bartholomew Fair* and (to a lesser extent) *The Devil is an Ass* have in modern times achieved a certain degree of recognition. While his life during this period was apparently more settled than it had been in the 1590s, his financial security was still not assured.

In 1603, Overbury reported that Jonson was living on Aurelian Townsend and "scorning the world." His trouble with English authorities continued. In 1603, he was questioned by the Privy Council about *Sejanus*, a politically-themed play about corruption in the Roman Empire. He was again in trouble for topical allusions in a play, now lost, in which he took part. After the discovery of the Gunpowder Plot, he appears to have been asked by the Privy Council to attempt to prevail on a certain priest to cooperate with the government; the priest he found was Father Thomas Wright, who heard Fawkes's confession (Teague, 249). At the same time, Jonson pursued a more prestigious career as a writer of masques for James' court.

The Satyr (1603) and *The Masque of Blackness* (1605) are but two of the some two dozen masques Jonson wrote for James or for Queen Anne; the latter was praised by Swinburne as the consummate example of this now-extinct genre, which mingled speech, dancing, and spectacle. On many of these projects he collaborated, not always peacefully, with designer Inigo Jones. Perhaps partly as a result of this new career, Jonson gave up writing plays for the public theaters for a decade. Jonson later told Drummond that he had made less than two hundred pounds on all his plays together. 1616 saw a pension of 100 marks a year conferred upon him, leading some to identify him as England's first Poet Laureate.

This sign of royal favour may have encouraged him to publish the first volume of the folio collected edition of his works that year. Other volumes followed in 1640–41 and 1692. In 1618, Ben Jonson set out for his ancestral Scotland on foot. He spent over a year there, and the best-remembered hospitality which he enjoyed was that of the Scottish poet, Drummond of Hawthornden. Drummond undertook to record as much of Jonson's conversation as he could in his diary, and thus recorded aspects of Jonson's personality that would otherwise have been less clearly seen.

Jonson delivers his opinions, in Drummond's terse reporting, in an expansive and even magisterial mood. In the postscript added by Drummond, he is described as "a great lover and praiser of himself, a contemner and scorner of others". While in Scotland, he was made an honorary citizen of Edinburgh. On returning to England, he was awarded an honorary Master of Arts degree from Oxford University. The period between 1605 and 1620 may be viewed as Jonson's heyday. In addition to his popularity on the public stage and in the royal hall, he enjoyed the patronage of aristocrats such as Elizabeth Sidney (daughter of Sir Philip Sidney) and Lady Mary Wroth.

This connection with the Sidney family provided the impetus for one of Jonson's most famous lyrics, the country house poem *To Penshurst*. The 1620s began a lengthy and slow decline for Jonson. He was still well-known; from this time dates the prominence of the Sons of Ben or the "Tribe of Ben", those younger poets such as Robert Herrick, Richard Lovelace, and Sir John Suckling who took their bearing in verse from Jonson. However, a series of setbacks drained his strength and damaged his reputation. Jonson returned to writing regular plays in the 1620s, but these are not considered among his best. They are of significant interest for the study of the culture of Charles I's England. *The Staple of News*, for example, offers a remarkable look at the earliest stage of English journalism.

The lukewarm reception given that play was, however, nothing compared to the dismal failure of *The New Inn*; the cold reception given this play prompted Jonson to write a poem condemning his audience (the *Ode to Myself*), which in turn prompted Thomas Carew, one of the "Tribe of Ben," to respond in a poem that asks Jonson to recognize his own decline. The principal factor in Jonson's partial eclipse was, however, the death of James and the accession of King Charles I in 1625. Justly or not, Jonson felt neglected by the new court. A decisive quarrel with Jones harmed his career as a writer of court masques, although he continued to entertain the court on an irregular basis. For his part, Charles displayed a certain degree of care for the great poet of his father's day: he increased Jonson's annual pension to £100 and included a tierce of wine. Despite the strokes that he suffered in the 1620s, Jonson continued to write. At his death in 1637 he seems to have been working on another play, *The Sad Shepherd*. Though only two acts are extant, this represents a remarkable new direction for Jonson: a move into pastoral drama.

During the early 1630s he also conducted a correspondence with James Howell, who warned him about disfavour at court in the wake of his dispute with Jones. Jonson is buried in Westminster Abbey, with the inscription

"O Rare Ben Johnson" *(sic)* set in the slab over his grave. It has been suggested that this could be read "Orare Ben Jonson" (pray for Ben Jonson), which would indicate a deathbed return to Catholicism, but the carving shows a distinct space between "O" and "rare".Researchers suggest that the tribute came from William D'Avenant, Jonson's successor as Poet Laureate, as the same phrase appears on his gravestone nearby. The fact that he was buried in an upright grave could be an indication of his reduced circumstances at the time of his death, although it has also been written that Jonson asked for a grave exactly 18 inches square from the monarch and received an upright grave to fit in the requested space. The same source claims that the epitaph came from the remark of a passerby to the grave.

Drama

Besides two tragedies, *Sejanus* and *Catiline*, that largely failed to impress Renaissance audiences, Jonson's work for the public theatres was in comedy. These plays vary in some respects. The minor early plays, particularly those written for the boy players, present somewhat looser plots and less-developed characters than those written later, for adult companies. Already in the plays which were his salvos in the Poet's War, he displays the keen eye for absurdity and hypocrisy that marks his best-known plays; in these early efforts, however, plot mostly takes second place to variety of incident and comic set-pieces. They are, also, notably ill-tempered. Thomas Davies called *Poetaster* "a contemptible mixture of the serio-comic, where the names of Augustus Caesar, Maecenas, Virgil, Horace, Ovid, and Tibullus, are all sacrificed upon the altar of private resentment." Another early comedy in a different vein, *The Case is Altered*, is markedly similar to Shakespeare's romantic comedies in its foreign setting, emphasis on genial wit, and love-plot. Henslowe's diary indicates that Jonson had a hand in numerous other plays, including many in genres such as English history with which he is not otherwise associated. The comedies of his middle career, from *Eastward Ho* to *The Devil is an Ass* are for the most part city comedy, with a London setting, themes of trickery and money, and a distinct moral ambiguity, despite Jonson's professed aim in the Prologue to *Volpone* to "mix profit with your pleasure".

His late plays or "dotages," particularly *The Magnetic Lady* and *The Sad Shepherd*, exhibit some signs of an accommodation with the romantic tendencies of Elizabethan comedy. Within this general progression, however, Jonson's comic style remained constant and easily recognizable.

He announces his programme in the prologue to the folio version of *Every Man in His Humour*; he promises to represent "deeds, and language, such as men do use." He planned to write comedies that revived the classical premises of Elizabethan dramatic theory—or rather, since all but the loosest English comedies could claim some descent from Plautus and Terence, he intended to apply those premises with rigour.

This commitment entailed negations: after *The Case is Altered*, Jonson eschewed distant locations, noble characters, romantic plots, and other staples of Elizabethan comedy. Jonson focused instead on the satiric and realistic inheritance of new comedy. He sets his plays in contemporary settings, peoples them with recognizable types, and sets them to actions that, if not strictly realistic, involve everyday motives such as greed and jealousy. In accordance with the temper of his age, he was often so broad in his characterisation that many of his most famous scenes border on the farcical (as Congreve, for example, judged *Epicoene*.)

He was, moreover, more diligent in adhering to the classical unities than many of his peers—although as Margaret Cavendish noted, the unity of action in the major comedies was rather compromised by Jonson's abundance of incident. To this classical model Jonson applies the two features of his style which save his classical imitations from mere pedantry: the vividness with which he depicts the lives of his characters, and the intricacy of his plots. Coleridge, for instance, claimed that *The Alchemist* had one of the three most perfect plots in literature.

Poetry

Jonson's poetry, like his drama, is informed by his classical learning. Some of his better-known poems are close translations of Greek or Roman models; all display the careful attention to form and style that often came naturally to those trained in classics in the humanist manner. Jonson, however, largely avoided the debates about rhyme and meter that had consumed Elizabethan classicists such as Campion and Harvey. Accepting both rhyme and stress, Jonson uses them to mimic the classical qualities of simplicity, restraint, and precision. "Epigrams" (published in the 1616 folio) is an entry in a genre that was popular among late-Elizabethan and Jacobean audiences, although Jonson was perhaps the only poet of his time to work in its full classical range. The epigrams explore various attitudes, most but not all of them from the satiric stock of the day: complaints against women, courtiers, and spies abound. The condemnatory poems are short and anonymous; Jonson's epigrams of praise, including a famous poem to Camden and lines to Lucy Harington, are somewhat longer and mostly addressed to specific individuals.

Although it is an epigram in the classical sense of the genre, "On My First Son" is neither satirical nor long; the poem, and others like it, resemble what a later age sometimes called "lyric poetry." The poems of "The Forest" also appeared in the first folio. Most of the fifteen poems are addressed to Jonson's aristocratic supporters, but the most famous are his country-house poem "To Penshurst" and the poem "To Celia" ("Come, my Celia, let us prove") that appears also in "Volpone." "Underwoods," published in the expanded folio of 1640, is a larger and more heterogeneous group of poems. It contains "A Celebration of Charis," Jonson's most extended effort at love poetry; various religious pieces; encomiastic poems including the poem to Shakespeare and a sonnet on Mary Wroth; the "Execration against Vulcan" and others. The 1640 volume also contains three elegies which have often been ascribed to Donne.

It is pertinent to note that are many legends about Jonson's rivalry with Shakespeare, some of which may be true. Drummond reports that during their conversation, Jonson scoffed at two apparent absurdities in Shakespeare's plays: a nonsensical line in Julius Caesar, and the setting of *The Winter's Tale* on the non-existent seacoast of Bohemia. Drummond also reports Jonson saying that Shakespeare "wanted art." Whether Drummond is viewed as accurate or not, the comments fit well with Jonson's well-known théories about literature.

In *Timber,* which was published posthumously and reflects his lifetime of practical experience, Jonson offers a fuller and more conciliatory comment. He recalls being told by certain actors that Shakespeare never blotted (i.e., crossed out) a line when he wrote. His own response, "Would he had blotted a thousand," was taken as malicious. However, Jonson explains, "He was, indeed, honest, and of an open and free nature, had an excellent phantasy, brave notions, and gentle expressions, wherein he flowed with that facility that sometimes it was necessary he should be stopped". Jonson concludes that "there was ever more in him to be praised than to be pardoned."

Also when Shakespeare died he said "He was not of an age, but for all time." Thomas Fuller relates stories of Jonson and Shakespeare engaging in debates in the Mermaid Tavern; Fuller imagines conversations in which Shakespeare would run rings around the more learned but more ponderous Jonson. That the two men knew each other personally is beyond doubt, not only because of the tone of Jonson's references to him but because Shakespeare's company produced a number of Jonson's plays, at least one of which (*Every Man in his Humour*) Shakespeare certainly acted in. However, it is now impossible to tell how much personal communication they had, and tales of their friendship cannot be substantiated in the present state of knowledge.

Jonson's most influential and revealing commentary on Shakespeare is the second of the two poems that he contributed to the prefatory verse that opens Shakespeare's First Folio. This poem, "To the memory of my beloved, The AUTHOR, Mr. William Shakespeare: And what he hath left us," did a good deal to create the traditional view of Shakespeare as a poet who, despite "small Latine, and lesse Greeke", had a natural genius. The poem has traditionally been thought to exemplify the contrast Jonson perceived between himself, the disciplined and erudite classicist, scornful of ignorance and skeptical of the masses, and Shakespeare, represented in the poem as a kind of natural wonder whose genius was not subject to any rules except those of the audiences for which he wrote.

Some view this elegy as a conventional exercise, but a rising number of critics see it as a heartfelt tribute to the

"Sweet Swan Of Avon," the "Soul of the Age!" It has been compellingly argued that Jonson helped to edit the First Folio, and he may have been inspired to write this poem, surely one of his greatest, by reading his fellow playwright's works, a number of which had been previously either unpublished or available in less satisfactory versions, in a relatively complete shape.

Critical Analysis

During most of the seventeenth century Jonson was a towering literary figure, and his influence was enormous. Before the civil war The Tribe of Ben touted his importance, and during the Restoration Jonson's satirical comedies and his theory and practice of "humour characters" was extremely influential, providing the blueprint for many Restoration comedies. In the eighteenth century Jonson's status began to decline.

In the Romantic era, Jonson suffered the fate of being unfairly compared and contrasted to Shakespeare, as the taste for Jonson's type of satirical comedy decreased. Jonson was at times greatly appreciated by the Romantics, but overall he was denigrated for not writing in a Shakespearean vein. In the twentieth century, Jonson's status rose significantly. As G.E. Bentley notes in *Shakespeare and Jonson: Their Reputations in the Seventeenth Century Compared*, Jonson's reputation was in some respects equal to Shakespeare's in the seventeenth century.

After the English theatres were reopened on the Restoration of Charles II, Jonson's work, along with Shakespeare's and Fletcher's work, formed the initial core of the Restoration repertory. It was not until after 1710 that Shakespeare's plays (ordinarily in heavily revised forms) were more frequently performed than those of his Renaissance contemporaries. Many critics since the eighteenth century have ranked Jonson below only Shakespeare among English Renaissance dramatists. Critical judgment has tended to emphasize the very qualities that Jonson himself lauds in his prefaces, in Timber, and in his scattered prefaces and dedications: the realism and propriety of his language, the bite of his satire, and the care with which he plotted his comedies.

For some critics, the temptation to contrast Jonson (representing art or craft) with Shakespeare (representing nature, or untutored genius) has seemed natural; Jonson himself may be said to initiate this interpretation in his poem on Shakespeare. Leonard Digges echoed this line of thought in his verses affixed to the second folio, and Samuel Butler drew the same comparison in his commonplace book later in the century. At the Restoration, this sensed difference became a kind of critical dogma. Saint-Évremond, indeed, placed Jonson's comedies above all else in English drama, and Charles Gildon called Jonson the father of English comedy.

John Dryden offered a more common assessment in the Essay of Dramatic Poesie, in which his avatar Neander compares Shakespeare to Homer and Jonson to Virgil: the former represented profound creativity, the latter polished artifice. But "artifice" was in the seventeenth century almost synonymous with "art"; Jonson, for instance, used "artificer" as a synonym for "artist" (*Discoveries,* 33). For Lewis Theobald, too, Jonson "ow[ed] all his Excellence to his Art," in contrast to Shakespeare, the natural genius. Rowe, to whom may be traced the legend that Jonson owed the production of *Every Man in his Humour* to Shakespeare's intercession, likewise attributed Jonson's excellence to learning, which did not raise him quite to the level of genius.

A consensus formed: Jonson was the first English poet to understand classical precepts with any accuracy, and he was the first to apply those precepts successfully to contemporary life. But there were also more negative spins on Jonson's learned art; for instance, in the 1750s, Edward Young casually remarked on the way in which Jonson's learning worked, like Samson's strength, to his own detriment. Earlier, Aphra Behn, writing in defence of female playwrights, had pointed to Jonson as a writer whose learning did not make him popular; unsurprisingly, she compares him unfavorably to Shakespeare. Particularly in the tragedies, with their lengthy speeches abstracted from Sallust and Cicero, Augustan critics saw a writer whose learning had swamped his aesthetic judgment.

In this period, Alexander Pope is exceptional in that he noted the tendency to exaggeration in these competing critical portraits: "It is ever the nature of Parties to be in extremes; and nothing is so probable, as that because Ben Johnson had much the most learning, it was said on the one hand that Shakespear had none at all; and because Shakespear had much the most wit and fancy, it was retorted on the other, that Johnson wanted both."

For the most part, the eighteenth century consensus remained committed to the division that Pope doubted; as late as the 1750s, Sarah Fielding could put a brief recapitulation of this analysis in the mouth of a "man of sense" encountered by David Simple.

Though his stature declined during the eighteenth century, Jonson was still read and commented on throughout the century, generally in the kind of comparative and dismissive terms just described. Heinrich Wilhelm von Gerstenberg translated parts of Peter Whalley's edition into German in 1765. Shortly before the Romantic revolution, Edward Capell offered an almost unqualified rejection of Jonson as a dramatic poet, who (he writes) "has very poor pretensions to the high place he holds among the English Bards, as there is no original manner to distinguish him, and the tedious sameness visible in his plots indicates a defect of Genius."

In fact, the disastrous failures of productions of *Volpone* and *Epicoene* in the early 1770s no doubt bolstered a widespread sense that Jonson had at last grown too antiquated for the contemporary public; if Jonson still attracted enthusiasts such as Earl Camden and William Gifford, he all but disappeared from the stage in the last quarter of the century. The romantic revolution in criticism brought about an overall decline in the critical estimation of Jonson. Hazlitt refers dismissively to Jonson's "laborious caution."

Coleridge, while more respectful, describes Jonson as psychologically superficial: "He was a very accurately observing man; but he cared only to observe what was open to, and likely to impress, the senses." Coleridge placed Jonson second only to Shakespeare; other romantic critics were less approving. The early nineteenth century was the great age for recovering Renaissance drama. Jonson, whose reputation had survived, appears to have been less interesting to some readers than writers such as Thomas Middleton or John Heywood, who were in some senses "discoveries" of the nineteenth century. Moreover, the emphasis the romantic writers placed on imagination, and their concomitant tendency to distrust studied art, lowered Jonson's status, if it also sharpened their awareness of the difference traditionally noted between Jonson and Shakespeare. This trend was by no means universal, however; William Gifford, Jonson's first editor of the nineteenth century, did a great deal to defend Jonson's reputation during this period of general decline. In the next era, Swinburne, who was more interested in Jonson than most Victorians, wrote, "The flowers of his growing have every quality but one which belongs to the rarest and finest among flowers: they have colour, form, variety, fertility, vigour: the one thing they want is fragrance" — by "fragrance," Swinburne means spontaneity. In the twentieth century, Jonson's body of work has been subject to a more varied set of analyses, broadly consistent with the interests and programmes of modern literary criticism.

In an essay printed in *The Sacred Wood* T.S. Eliot attempts to repudiate the charge that Jonson was an arid classicist by analysing the role of imagination in his dialogue. Eliot was appreciative of Jonson's overall conception and his "surface," a view consonant with the modernist reaction against Romantic criticism, which tended to denigrate playwrights who did not concentrate on representations of psychological depth. Around mid-century, a number of critics and scholars followed Eliot's lead, producing detailed studies of Jonson's verbal style. At the same time, study of Elizabethan themes and conventions, such as those by E. E. Stoll and M. C. Bradbrook, provided a more vivid sense of how Jonson's work was shaped by the expectations of his time. The proliferation of new critical perspectives after mid-century touched on Jonson inconsistently.

Jonas Barish was the leading figure in a group of critics that was appreciative of Jonson's artistry. On the other hand, Jonson received less attention from the new critics than did some other playwrights and his work was not of programmatic interest to psychoanalytic critics. But Jonson's career eventually made him a focal point for the revived sociopolitical criticism. Jonson's work, particularly his masques and pageants, offers significant information regarding the relations of literary production and political power, as do his contacts with and poems for aristocratic patrons; moreover, his career at the centre of London's emerging literary world has been seen as exemplifying the development of a fully commodified literary culture.

It is pertinent to note that Jonson's reputation as a playwright has traditionally been linked to Shakespeare, his reputation as a poet has, since the early twentieth century, been linked to that of John Donne. In this comparison, Jonson represents the cavalier strain of poetry, which emphasized grace and clarity of expression; Donne, by contrast, epitomized the metaphysical school of poetry, with its reliance on strained, baroque metaphors and often vague phrasing.

Since the critics who made this comparison (Herbert Grierson for example), were to varying extents rediscovering Donne, this comparison often worked to the detriment of Jonson's reputation. In his time, though, Jonson was at least as influential as Donne. In 1623, historian Edmund Bolton named him the best and most polished English poet.

That this judgment was widely shared is indicated by the admitted influence he had on younger poets. The grounds for describing Jonson as the "father" of cavalier poets are clear: many of the cavalier poets described themselves as his "sons" or his "tribe." For some of this tribe, the connection was as much social as poetic; Herrick describes meetings at "the Sun, the Dog, the Triple Tunne." All of them, including those like Herrick whose accomplishments in verse are generally regarded as superior to Jonson's, took inspiration from Jonson's revival of classical forms and themes, his subtle melodies, and his disciplined use of wit. In all of these respects, Jonson may be regarded as among the most important figures in the prehistory of English neoclassicism.

His total literary output is furnished below in chronological order.

Plays

1. *A Tale of a Tub,* comedy (ca. 1596? revised? performed 1633; printed 1640)
2. *The Case is Altered,* comedy (ca. 1597–98; printed 1609), with Henry Porter and Anthony Munday?
3. *Every Man in His Humour,* comedy (performed 1598; printed 1601)
4. *Every Man out of His Humour,* comedy (performed 1599; printed 1600)
5. *Cynthia's Revels* (performed 1600; printed 1601)
6. *The Poetaster,* comedy (performed 1601; printed 1602)
7. *Sejanus His Fall,* tragedy (performed 1603; printed 1605)
8. *Eastward Ho,* comedy (performed and printed 1605)
9. *Volpone,* comedy (ca. 1605–06; printed 1607)
10. *Epicoene, or the Silent Woman,* comedy (performed 1609; printed 1616)
11. *The Alchemist,* comedy (performed 1610; printed 1612)
12. *Catiline His Conspiracy,* tragedy (performed and printed 1611)
13. *Bartholomew Fair,* comedy (performed 31 October 1614; printed 1631)

14. *The Devil is an Ass,* comedy (performed 1616; printed 1631)
15. *The Staple of News,* comedy (performed Feb. 1626; printed 1631)
16. *The New Inn, or The Light Heart,* comedy (licensed 19 January 1629; printed 1631)
17. *The Magnetic Lady, or Humors Reconciled,* comedy (licensed 12 October 1632; printed 1641)
18. *The Sad Shepherd,* pastoral (ca. 1637, printed 1641), unfinished
19. *Mortimer his Fall,* history (printed 1641).

Masques

20. *The Coronation Triumph,* or *The King's Entertainment* (performed 15 March 1604; printed 1604); with Thomas Dekker
21. *A Private Entertainment of the King and Queen on May-Day (The Penates)* (1 May 1604; printed 1616)
22. *The Entertainment of the Queen and Prince Henry at Althorp (The Satyr)* (25 June 1603; printed 1604)
23. *The Masque of Blackness* (6 January 1605; printed 1608)
24. *Hymenaei* (5 January 1606; printed 1606)
25. *The Entertainment of the Kings of Great Britain and Denmark (The Hours)* (24 July 1606; printed 1616)
26. *The Masque of Beauty* (10 January 1608; printed 1608)
27. *The Masque of Queens* (2 February 1609; printed 1609)

28. *The Hue and Cry after Cupid,* or *The Masque at Lord Haddington's Marriage* (9 February 1608; printed ca. 1608)
29. *The Speeches at Prince Henry's Barriers,* or *The Lady of the Lake* (6 January 1610; printed 1616)
30. *Oberon, the Faery Prince* (1 January 1611; printed 1616)
31. *Love Freed from Ignorance and Folly* (3 February 1611; printed 1616)
32. *Love Restored* (6 January 1612; printed 1616)
33. *A Challenge at Tilt, at a Marriage* (27 December 1613/1 January 1614; printed 1616)
34. *The Irish Masque at Court* (29 December 1613; printed 1616)
35. *Mercury Vindicated from the Alchemists* (6 January 1615; printed 1616)
36. *The Golden Age Restored* (1 January 1616; printed 1616)
37. *Christmas, His Masque* (Christmas 1616; printed 1641)
38. *The Vision of Delight* (6 January 1617; printed 1641)
39. *Lovers Made Men,* or *The Masque of Lethe,* or *The Masque at Lord Hay's* (22 February 1617; printed 1617)
40. *Pleasure Reconciled to Virtue* (6 January 1618; printed 1641)
41. *For the Honour of Wales* (17 February 1618; printed 1641)

42. *News from the New World Discovered in the Moon* (7 January 1620: printed 1641)
43. *The Entertainment at Blackfriars, or The Newcastle Entertainment* (May 1620?; MS)
44. *Pan's Anniversary, or The Shepherd's Holy-Day* (19 June 1620?; printed 1641)
45. *The Gypsies Metamorphosed* (3 and 5 August 1621; printed 1640)
46. *The Masque of Augurs* (6 January 1622; printed 1622)
47. *Time Vindicated to Himself and to His Honours* (19 January 1623; printed 1623)
48. *Neptune's Triumph for the Return of Albion* (26 January 1624; printed 1624)
49. *The Masque of Owls at Kenilworth* (19 August 1624; printed 1641)
50. *The Fortunate Isles and Their Union* (9 January 1625; printed 1625)
51. *Love's Triumph Through Callipolis* (9 January 1631; printed 1631)
52. *Chloridia: Rites to Chloris and Her Nymphs* (22 February 1631; printed 1631)
53. *The King's Entertainment at Welbeck in Nottinghamshire* (21 May 1633; printed 1641)
54. *Love's Welcome at Bolsover* (30 July 1634; printed 1641).

Other Works

55. *Epigrams* (1612)
56. *The Forest* (1616), including *To Penshurst*

57. *A Discourse of Love* (1618)
58. Barclay's *Argenis,* translated by Jonson (1623)
59. *The Execration against Vulcan* (1640)
60. *Horace's Art of Poetry*, translated by Jonson (1640), with a commendatory verse by Edward Herbert
61. *Underwoods* (1640).

Now we will try to make an assessment of seventeenth century literature.

6

A Survey of Augustan Literature

First it is pertinent to note that, Augustan era in English is a literary epoch that featured the rapid development of the novel, an explosion in satire, the mutation of drama from political satire into melodrama, and an evolution toward poetry of personal exploration. In philosophy, it was an age increasingly dominated by empiricism, while in the writings of political-economy it marked the evolution of mercantilism as a formal philosophy, the development of capitalism, and the triumph of trade.

The chronological anchors of the era are generally vague, largely since the label's origin in contemporary 18th century criticism has made it a shorthand designation for a somewhat nebulous age of satire. This new Augustan period exhibited exceptionally bold political writings in all genres, with the satires of the age marked by an arch, ironic pose, full of nuance, and a superficial air of dignified calm that hid sharp criticisms beneath. With the growth and development of literacy, literature began to appear from all over the United Kingdom.

Authors gradually began to accept literature that went in unique directions rather than the formerly monolithic conventions and, through this, slowly began to honor and recreate various folk compositions. Beneath the appearance of a placid and highly regulated series of writing modes, many developments of the later Romantic era were beginning to take place—while politically, philosophically, and literarily, modern consciousness was being hewn out of hitherto feudal and courtly notions of past ages.

Before proceeding to Augustan literature we must acquaint with enlightenment.

In fact, "Augustan" derives from George I wishing to be seen as Augustus Caesar. Alexander Pope, who had been imitating Horace, wrote an *Epistle to Augustus* that was to George II and seemingly endorsed the notion of his age being like that of Augustus, when poetry became more mannered, political and satirical than in the era of Julius Caesar (Thornton 275). Later, Voltaire and Oliver Goldsmith (in his *History of Literature* in 1764) used the term "Augustan" to refer to the literature of the 1720s and '30s (Newman and Brown 32).

Outside of poetry, however, the Augustan era is generally known by other names. Partially because of the rise of empiricism and partially due to the self-conscious naming of the age in terms of Ancient Rome, two imprecise labels have been affixed to the age. One is that it is the age of neoclassicism. The other is that it is the Age of Reason. Both terms have some usefulness, but both also obscure much. While neoclassical criticism from France was imported to English letters, the English had abandoned their strictures in all but name by the 1720s. As for whether the era was "the Enlightenment" or not, the critic Donald Greene wrote vigorously against it, arguing persuasively that the age should be known as "The Age of Exuberance," while T.H. White made a case for "The Age of Scandal". Most recently, Roy Porter attempted again to argue for the developments of science dominating all other areas of endeavor in the age unmistakably making it the Enlightenment (Porter).

One of the most critical elements of the 18th century was the increasing availability of printed material, both for readers and authors. Books fell in price dramatically, and used books were sold at Bartholomew Fair and other fairs. Additionally, a brisk trade in chapbooks and broadsheets carried London trends and information out to the farthest reaches of the kingdom. This was only furthered with the establishment of periodicals, including *The Gentleman's Magazine* and the *London Magazine.* Not only, therefore, were people in York aware of the happenings of Parliament and the court, but people in London were more aware than before of the happenings of York. Furthermore, in this age before copyright, pirate editions were commonplace, especially in areas without frequent contact with London. Pirate editions thereby encouraged booksellers to increase their shipments to outlying centers like Dublin, which increased, again, awareness across the whole realm.

This was compounded by the end of the Press Restriction Act in 1693, which allowed for provincial printing presses to be established, creating a printing structure that was no longer under government control. (Clair 158-176) Mostly, all types of literature were spread quickly in all directions. Newspapers not only began, but they multiplied. Furthermore, the newspapers were immediately compromised, as the political factions created their own newspapers, planted stories, and bribed journalists.

Leading clerics had their sermon collections printed, and these were top selling books. Since dissenting, Establishment, and Independent divines were in print, the constant movement of these works helped defuse any one region's religious homogeneity and fostered emergent latitudinarianism. Periodicals were exceedingly popular, and the art of essay writing was at nearly its apex. Furthermore, the happenings of the Royal Society were published regularly, and these events were digested and explained or celebrated in more popular presses. The latest books of scholarship had "keys" and "indexes" and "digests" made of them that could popularize, summarize, and explain them to a wide audience.

The cross-index, now commonplace, was a novelty in the 18th century, and several persons created indexes for older books of learning, allowing anyone to find what an author had to say about a given topic at a moment's notice.

Books of etiquette, of correspondence, and of moral instruction and hygiene multiplied Economics began as a serious discipline, but it did so in the form of numerous "projects" for solving England's (and Ireland's, and Scotland's) ills. Sermon collections, dissertations on religious controversy, and prophecies, both new and old and explained, cropped up in endless variety. In short, readers in the 18th century were overwhelmed by competing voices.

True and false sat side by side on the shelves, and anyone could be a published author, just as anyone could quickly pretend to be a scholar by using indexes and digests (Clair 45, 158-187). The positive side of the explosion in information was that the 18th century was markedly more generally educated than the centuries before.

Education was less confined to the upper classes than it had been in prior centuries, and consequently contributions to science, philosophy, economics, and literature came from all parts of the newly United Kingdom. It was the first time when literacy and a library were all that stood between a person and education. It was an age of "enlightenment" in the sense that the insistence and drive for reasonable explanations of nature and mankind was a rage.

It was an "age of reason" in that it was an age that accepted clear, rational methods as superior to tradition. However, there was a dark side to such literacy as well, a dark side which authors of the 18th century felt at every turn, and that was that nonsense and insanity were also getting more adherents than ever before. Charlatans and mountebanks were fooling more, just as sages were educating more, and alluring and lurid apocalypses vied with sober philosophy on the shelves. As with the world-wide web in the 21st century, the democratization of publishing meant that older systems for determining value and uniformity of view were both in shambles. Thus, it was increasingly difficult to trust books in the 18th century, because books were increasingly easy to make and buy. Remarkably, the Restoration period ended with the exclusion crisis and the Glorious Revolution, where Parliament set up a new rule for succession to the British throne that would always favor Protestantism over sanguinity.

This had brought William and Mary to the throne instead of James II, and was codified in the Act of Settlement 1701. James had fled to France from where his son James Francis Edward Stuart launched an attempt to retake the throne in 1715. Another attempt was launched by the latter's son Charles Edward Stuart in 1745. The attempted invasions are often referred to as "the 15" and "the 45". When William died, Anne Stuart came to the throne. Anne was reportedly immoderately stupid: Thomas Babington Macaulay would say of Anne that "when in good humour, [she] was meekly stupid and, when in bad humour, was sulkily stupid." Anne's reign saw two wars and great triumphs by John Churchill, the Duke of Marlborough. Marlborough's wife, Sarah Churchill, was Anne's best friend, and many supposed that she secretly controlled the Queen in every respect.

With a weak ruler and the belief that true power rested in the hands of the leading ministers, the two factions of politics stepped up their opposition to each other, and Whig and Tory were at each others' throats. This weakness at the throne would lead quickly to the expansion of the powers of the party leader in Parliament and the establishment in all but name of the Prime Minister office in the form of Robert Walpole. When Anne died without issue, George I, Elector of Hanover, came to the throne. George I never bothered to learn the English language, and his isolation from the English people was instrumental in keeping his power relatively irrelevant. His son, George II, on the other hand, spoke some English and some more French, and his was the first full Hanoverian rule in England.

By that time, the powers of Parliament had silently expanded, and George II's power was perhaps equal only to that of Parliament. London's population exploded spectacularly. During the Restoration, it grew from around 350,000 to 600,000 in 1700 (*Old Bailey*) (*Millwall history*). By 1800, it had reached 950,000. Not all of these residents were prosperous. The enclosure act had destroyed lower-class farming in the countryside, and rural areas experienced painful poverty. When the Black Act was expanded to cover all protestors to enclosure, the communities of the country poor were forced to migrate or suffer.

Therefore, young people from the country often moved to London with hopes of achieving success, and this swelled the ranks of the urban poor and cheap labor for city employers. It also meant an increase in numbers of criminals, prostitutes and beggars. The fears of property crime, rape, and starvation found in Augustan literature should be kept in the context of London's growth, as well as the depopulation of the countryside. Partially because of these population pressures, property crime became a business both for the criminals and for those who fed off of the criminals.

Major crime lords like Jonathan Wild invented new schemes for stealing, and the newspapers were eager to report crime. Biographies of the daring criminals became popular, and these spawned fictional biographies of fictional criminals. Cautionary tales of country women abused by sophisticated rakes (such as Anne Bond) and libertines in the city were popular fare, and these prompted fictional accounts of exemplary women abused (or narrowly escaping abuse). The population pressure also meant that urban discontent was never particularly difficult to find for political opportunists, and London suffered a number of riots, most of them against supposed Roman Catholic agent provocateurs. When highly potent, inexpensive distilled spirits were introduced, matters worsened, and authors and artists protested the innovation of gin.

From 1710, the government encouraged distilling as a source of revenue and trade goods, and there were no licenses required for the manufacturing or selling of gin. There were documented instances of women drowning their infants to sell the child's clothes for gin, and so these facilities created both the fodder for riots and the conditions against which riots would occur (Loughrey and Treadwell, 14). Dissenters (those radical Protestants who would not join with the Church of England) recruited and preached to the poor of the city, and various offshoots of the Puritan and "Independent" (Baptist) movements increased their numbers substantially. One theme of these ministers was the danger of the Roman Catholic Church, which they frequently saw as the Whore of Babylon. While Anne was high church, George I came from a far more Protestant nation than England, and George II was almost low church, as the events of the Bangorian Controversy would show.

The convocation was effectively disbanded by George I (who was struggling with the House of Lords), and George II was pleased to keep it in abeyance. Additionally, both of the first two Hanoverians were concerned with James Francis Edward Stuart and Charles Edward Stuart who had considerable support in Scotland and Ireland, and anyone too high church was suspected of being a closet Jacobite, thanks in no small part to Walpole's inflating fears of Stuart sympathizers among any group that did not support him.

The literature of the 18th century—particularly the early 18th century, which is what "Augustan" most commonly indicates—is explicitly political in ways that few others are. Because the professional author was still not distinguishable from the hack-writer, those who wrote poetry, novels, and plays were frequently either politically active or politically funded. At the same time, an aesthetic of artistic detachment from the everyday world had yet to develop, and the aristocratic ideal of an author so noble as to be above political concerns was largely archaic and irrelevant.

The period may be an "Age of Scandal," for it is an age when authors dealt specifically with the crimes and vices. In fact, satire, both in prose, drama, and poetry, was the genre that attracted the most energetic and voluminous writing. The satires produced during the Augustan period were occasionally gentle and non-specific—commentaries on the comically flawed human condition—but they were at least as frequently specific critiques of specific policies, actions, and persons.

Even those works studiously non-topical were, in fact, transparently political statements in the 18th century. Consequently, readers of 18th-century literature today need to understand the history of the period more than most readers of other literature do. The authors were writing for an informed audience and only secondarily for posterity. Even the authors who criticized writing that lived for only a day (e.g. Jonathan Swift and Alexander Pope, in *The Dedication to Prince Posterity* of *A Tale of a Tub* and *Dunciad*, among other pieces) were criticizing specific authors who are unknown without historical knowledge of the period. 18th-century poetry of all forms was in constant dialog: each author was responding and commenting upon the others. 18th-century novels were written against other 18th-century novels.

Similarly, plays were written to make fun of plays, or to counter the success of plays (e.g. the reaction against and for *Cato* and, later, Fielding's *The Authors Farce*). Therefore, history and literature are linked in a way rarely seen at other times. On the one hand, this metropolitan and political writing can seem like coterie or salon work, but, on the other, it was the literature of people deeply committed to sorting out a new type of government, new technologies, and newly vexatious challenges to philosophical and religious certainty.

Prose

The essay, satire, and dialogue (in philosophy and religion) thrived in the age, and the English novel was truly begun as a serious art form. Literacy in the early 18th century passed into the working classes, as well as the middle and upper classes (Thompson, Class). Furthermore, literacy was not confined to men, though rates of female literacy are very difficult to establish. For those who were literate, circulating libraries in England began in the Augustan period. Libraries were open to all, but they were mainly associated with female patronage and novel reading.

Mostly, English essayists were aware of Continental models, but they developed their form independently from that tradition, and periodical literature grew between 1692 and 1712. Periodicals were inexpensive to produce, quick to read, and a viable way of influencing public opinion, and consequently there were many broadsheet periodicals headed by a single author and staffed by hirelings (so-called "Grub Street" authors). One periodical outsold and dominated all others, however, and that was *The Spectator*, written by Joseph Addison and Richard Steele (with occasional contributions from their friends). *The Spectator* developed a number of pseudonymous characters, including "Mr. Spectator," Roger de Coverley, and "Isaac Bickerstaff", and both Addison and Steele created fictions to surround their narrators. The dispassionate view of the world (the pose of a spectator, rather than participant) was essential for the development of the English essay, as it set out a ground wherein Addison and Steele could comment and meditate upon manners and events. Rather than being philosophers like Montesquieu, the English essayist could be an honest observer and his reader's peer.

After the success of *The Spectator,* more political periodicals of comment appeared. However, the political factions and coalitions of politicians very quickly realized the power of this type of press, and they began funding newspapers to spread rumors. The Tory ministry of Robert Harley (1710–1714) reportedly spent over 50,000 pounds sterling on creating and bribing the press (Butt); we know this figure because their successors publicized it, but they (the Walpole government) were suspected of spending even more. Politicians wrote papers, wrote into papers, and supported papers, and it was well known that some of the periodicals, like *Mist's Journal,* were party mouthpieces.

Religious Writing and Philosophy

It is significant to note that Augustan period showed less literature of controversy than the Restoration. There were Puritan authors, however, and one of the names usually associated with the novel is perhaps the most prominent in Puritan writing: Daniel Defoe. After the coronation of Anne, dissenter hopes of reversing the Restoration were at an ebb, and dissenter literature moved from the offensive to the defensive, from revolutionary to conservative. Defoe's infamous volley in the struggle between high and low church came in the form of *The Shortest Way with the Dissenters; Or, Proposals for the Establishment of the Church.* The work is satirical, attacking all of the worries of Establishment figures over the challenges of dissenters. It is, in other words, defensive.

Later still, the most majestic work of the era, and the one most quoted and read, was William Law's *A Serious Call to a Devout and Holy Life* (1728). The *Meditations* of Robert Boyle remained popular as well. Both Law and Boyle called for revivalism, and they set the stage for the later development of Methodism and George Whitefield's sermon style. However, their works aimed at the individual, rather than the community. The age of revolutionary divines and militant evangelists in literature was over for a considerable time. Also in contrast to the Restoration, when philosophy in England was fully dominated by John Locke, the 18th century had a vigorous competition among followers of Locke.

Bishop Berkeley extended Locke's emphasis on perception to argue that perception entirely solves the Cartesian problem of subjective and objective knowledge by saying "to be is to be perceived." Only, Berkeley argued, those things that are perceived by a consciousness are real. For Berkeley, the persistence of matter rests in the fact that God perceives those things that humans are not, that a living and continually aware, attentive, and involved God is the only rational explanation for the existence of objective matter. In essence, then, Berkeley's skepticism leads to faith.

David Hume, on the other hand, took empiricist skepticism to its extremes, and he was the most radically empiricist philosopher of the period. He attacked surmise and unexamined premises wherever he found them, and his skepticism pointed out metaphysics in areas that other empiricists had assumed were material. Hume doggedly refused to enter into questions of his personal faith in the divine, but his assault on the logic and assumptions of theodicy and cosmogeny was devastating, and he concentrated on the provable and empirical in a way that would lead to utilitarianism and naturalism later. In social and political philosophy, economics underlies much of the debate.

Bernard de Mandeville's *The Fable of the Bees* (1714) became a center point of controversy regarding trade, morality, and social ethics. Mandeville argued that wastefulness, lust, pride, and all the other "private" vices were good for the society at large, for each led the individual to employ others, to spend freely, and to free capital to flow through the economy. Mandeville's work is full of paradox and is meant, at least partially, to problematize what he saw as the naive philosophy of human progress and inherent virtue. However, Mandeville's arguments, initially an attack on graft of the War of the Spanish Succession, would be quoted often by economists who wished to strip morality away from questions of trade. Adam Smith is remembered by lay persons as the father of capitalism, but his *Theory of Moral Sentiments* of 1759 also attempted to strike out a new ground for moral action.

His emphasis on "sentiment" was in keeping with the era, as he emphasized the need for "sympathy" between individuals as the basis of fit action. These ideas, and the psychology of David Hartley, were influential on the sentimental novel and even the nascent Methodist movement. If sympathetic sentiment communicated morality, would it not be possible to induce morality by providing sympathetic circumstances? Smith's greatest work was *An Inquiry into the Nature and Causes of the Wealth of Nations* in 1776. What it held in common with de Mandeville, Hume, and Locke was that it began by analytically examining the history of material exchange, without reflection on morality. Instead of deducing from the ideal or moral to the real, it examined the real and tried to formulate inductive rules.

Novel

In fact, the ground for the novel had been laid by journalism, drama and satire. Long prose satires like Swift's *Gulliver's Travels* (1726) had a central character who goes through adventures and may (or may not) learn lessons. However, the most important single satirical source for the writing of novels came from Cervantes's *Don Quixote* (1605, 1615). In general, one can see these three axes, drama, journalism, and satire, as blending in and giving rise to three different types of novel. Daniel Defoe's *Robinson*

Crusoe (1719) was the first major novel of the new century and was published in more editions than any other works besides *Gulliver's Travels* (Mullan 252). Defoe worked as a journalist during and after its composition, and therefore he encountered the memoirs of Alexander Selkirk, who had been stranded in South America on an island for some years.

Defoe took aspects of the actual life and, from that, generated a fictional life, satisfying an essentially journalistic market with his fictio (Hunter 331-338). In the 1720s, Defoe interviewed famed criminals and produced accounts of their lives. In particular, he investigated Jack Sheppard and Jonathan Wild and wrote *True Accounts* of the former's escapes (and fate) and the latter's life. From his reportage on the prostitutes and criminals, Defoe may have become familiar with the real-life Mary Mollineaux, who may have been the model for Moll in *Moll Flanders* (1722).

Remarkably, in the same year, Defoe produced *A Journal of the Plague Year* (1722), which summoned up the horrors and tribulations of 1665 for a journalistic market for memoirs, and an attempted tale of a working-class male rise in *Colonel Jack* (1722). His last novel returned to the theme of fallen women in *Roxana* (1724). Thematically, Defoe's works are consistently Puritan. They all involve a fall, a degradation of the spirit, a conversion, and an ecstatic elevation. This religious structure necessarily involved a *bildungsroman*, for each character had to learn a lesson about him or herself and emerge the wiser. Though there were novels in the interim, Samuel Richardson's *Pamela, or, Virtue Rewarded* (1740) is the next landmark development in the English novel. Richardson's generic models were quite distinct from those of Defoe. Instead of working from the journalistic biography, Richardson had in mind the books of improvement that were popular at the time.

Pamela Andrews enters the employ of a "Mr. B." As a dutiful girl, she writes to her mother constantly, and as a Christian girl, she is always on guard for her "virtue" (i.e. her virginity), for Mr. B lusts after her. The novel ends with her marriage to her employer and her rising to the position of lady. *Pamela*, like its author, presents a dissenter's and a Whig's view of the rise of the classes.

The work drew a nearly instantaneous set of satires, of which Henry Fielding's *Shamela, or an Apology for the Life of Miss Shamela Andrews* (1742) is the most memorable. Fielding continued to bait Richardson with *Joseph Andrews* (1742), the tale of Shamela's brother, Joseph, who goes through his life trying to protect his own virginity, thus reversing the sexual predation of Richardson and satirizing the idea of sleeping one's way to rank. However, *Joseph Andrews* is not a parody of Richardson, for Fielding proposed his belief in "good nature," which is a quality of inherent virtue that is independent of class and which can always prevail. Joseph's friend Parson Adams, although not a fool, is a naïf and possessing good nature. His own basic good nature blinds him to the wickedness of the world, and the incidents on the road (for most of the novel is a travel story) allow Fielding to satirize conditions for the clergy, rural poverty (and squires), and the viciousness of businessmen.

In 1747 through 1748, Samuel Richardson published *Clarissa* in serial form. Unlike *Pamela,* it is not a tale of virtue rewarded. Instead, it is a highly tragic and affecting account of a young girl whose parents try to force her into an uncongenial marriage, thus pushing her into the arms of a scheming rake named Lovelace. In the end, Clarissa dies by her own will. The novel is a masterpiece of psychological realism and emotional effect, and when Richardson was drawing to a close in the serial publication, even Henry Fielding wrote to him, begging him not to kill Clarissa. As with *Pamela,* Richardson emphasized the individual over the social and the personal over the class. Even as Fielding was reading and enjoying *Clarissa,* he was also writing a counter to its messages. His *Tom Jones* of 1749 offers up the other side of the argument from *Clarissa. Tom Jones* agrees substantially in the power of the individual to be more or less than his or her birth would indicate, but it again emphasizes the place of the individual in society and the social ramifications of individual choices.

Fielding answers Richardson by featuring a similar plot device (whether a girl can choose her own mate) but showing how family and village can complicate and expedite matches and felicity. Two other novelists should be mentioned, for they, like Fielding and Richardson, were in dialog through their works.

It is pertinent to note that Laurence Sterne's and Tobias Smollett's works offered up oppositional views of the self in society and the method of the novel. The clergyman Laurence Sterne consciously set out to imitate Jonathan Swift with his *Tristram Shandy* (1759–1767). Tristram seeks to write his autobiography, but like Swift's narrator in *A Tale of a Tub,* he worries that nothing in his life can be understood without understanding its context. For example, he tells the reader that at the very moment he was conceived, his mother was saying, "Did you wind the clock?" To explain how he knows this, he explains that his father took care of winding the clock and "other family business" on one day a month. To explain why the clock had to be wound then, he has to explain his father. In other words, the biography moves backward rather than forward in time, only to then jump forward years, hit another knot, and move backward again. It is a novel of exceptional energy, of multi-layered digressions, of multiple satires, and of frequent parodies. Journalist, translator, and historian Tobias Smollett, on the other hand, wrote more seemingly traditional novels.

He concentrated on the picaresque novel, where a low-born character would go through a practically endless series of adventures. Sterne thought that Smollett's novels always paid undue attention to the basest and most common elements of life, that they emphasized the dirt. Although this is a superficial complaint, it points to an important difference between the two as authors. Sterne came to the novel from a satirical background, while Smollett approached it from journalism. In the 19th century, novelists would have plots much nearer to Smollett's than either Fielding's or Sterne's or Richardson's, and his sprawling, linear development of action would prove most successful. In the midst of this development of the novel, other trends were taking place. The novel of sentiment was beginning in the 1760s and would experience a brief period of dominance.

This type of novel emphasized sympathy. In keeping with the theories of Adam Smith and David Hartley (see above), the sentimental novel concentrated on emotionally labile characters capable of extraordinary empathy. Sarah Fielding's *David Simple* outsold her brother Henry Fielding's *Joseph Andrews* and took the theory of "good nature" to be a sentimental nature. Other women were also writing novels and moving away from the old romance plots that had dominated before the Restoration. There were utopian novels, like Sarah Scott's *Millennium Hall* (1762), autobiographical women's novels like Frances Burney's works, female adaptations of older, male motifs, such as Charlotte Lennox's *The Female Quixote* (1752) and many others. These novels do not generally follow a strict line of development or influence. However, they were popular works that were celebrated by both male and female readers and critics.

Ian Watt's *The Rise of the Novel* (1957) still dominates attempts at writing a history of the novel. Watt's view is that the critical feature of the 18th-century novel is the creation of psychological realism. This feature, he argued, would continue on and influence the novel as it has been known in the 20th century.

Satire

A single name overshadows all others in 18th-century prose satire: Jonathan Swift. Swift wrote poetry as well as prose, and his satires range over all topics. Critically, Swift's satire marked the development of prose parody away from simple satire or burlesque. A burlesque or lampoon in prose would imitate a despised author and quickly move to *reductio ad absurdum* by having the victim say things coarse or idiotic. On the other hand, other satires would argue against a habit, practice, or policy by making fun of its reach or composition or methods. What Swift did was to combine parody, with its imitation of form and style of another, and satire in prose. Swift's works would pretend to speak in the voice of an opponent and imitate the style of the opponent and have the parodic work itself be the satire.

Swift's first major satire was *A Tale of a Tub* (1703–1705), which introduced an ancients/moderns division that would serve as a distinction between the old and new conception of value. The "moderns" sought trade, empirical science, the individual's reason above the society's, while the "ancients" believed in inherent and immanent value of birth, and the society over the individual's determinations of the good.

In Swift's satire, the moderns come out looking insane and proud of their insanity, and dismissive of the value of history. In Swift's most significant satire, *Gulliver's Travels* (1726), autobiography, allegory, and philosophy mix together in the travels. Thematically, *Gulliver's Travels* is a critique of human vanity, of pride. Book one, the journey to Liliput, begins with the world as it is. Book two shows that the idealized nation of Brobdingnag with a philosopher king is no home for a contemporary Englishman. Book four depicts the land of the Houyhnhnms, a society of horses ruled by pure reason, where humanity itself is portrayed as a group of "yahoos" covered in filth and dominated by base desires. It shows that, indeed, the very desire for reason may be undesirable, and humans must struggle to be neither Yahoos nor Houyhnhnms, for book three shows what happens when reason is unleashed without any consideration of morality or utility (i.e. madness, ruin, and starvation). There were other satirists who worked in a less virulent way, who took a bemused pose and only made lighthearted fun. Tom Brown, Ned Ward, and Tom D'Urfey were all satirists in prose and poetry whose works appeared in the early part of the Augustan age.

Tom Brown's most famous work in this vein was *Amusements Serious and Comical, Calculated for the Meridian of London* (1700). Ned Ward's most memorable work was *The London Spy* (1704–1706). *The London Spy,* before *The Spectator,* took up the position of an observer and uncomprehendingly reporting back. Tom D'Urfey's *Wit and Mirth: or Pills to Purge Melancholy* (1719) was another satire that attempted to offer entertainment, rather than a specific bit of political action, in the form of coarse and catchy songs. Particularly after Swift's success, parodic satire had an attraction for authors throughout the 18th century.

A variety of factors created a rise in political writing and political satire, and Robert Walpole's success and domination of House of Commons was a very effective proximal cause for polarized literature and thereby the rise of parodic satire. The parodic satire takes apart the cases and plans of policy without necessarily contrasting a normative or positive set of values. Therefore, it was an ideal method of attack for ironists and conservatives—those who would not be able to enunciate a set of values to change toward but could condemn present changes as ill-considered. Satire was present in all genres during the Augustan period. Perhaps primarily, satire was a part of political and religious debate. Every significant politician and political act had satires to attack it. Few of these were parodic satires, but parodic satires, too, emerged in political and religious debate. So omnipresent and powerful was satire in the Augustan age that more than one literary history has referred to it as the "Age of satire" in literature.

Poetry

It is noteworthy the Augustan era, poets wrote in direct counterpoint and direct expansion of one another, with each poet writing satire when in opposition. There was a great struggle over the nature and role of the pastoral in the early part of the century, reflecting two simultaneous movements: the invention of the subjective self as a worthy topic, with the emergence of a priority on individual psychology, against the insistence on all acts of art being performance and public gesture designed for the benefit of society at large. The development seemingly agreed upon by both sides was a gradual adaptation of all forms of poetry from their older uses.

Odes would cease to be encomium, ballads cease to be narratives, elegies cease to be sincere memorials, satires no longer be specific entertainments, parodies no longer be performance pieces without sting, song no longer be pointed, and the lyric would become a celebration of the individual rather than a lover's complaint. These developments can be seen as extensions of Protestantism, as Max Weber argued, for they represent a gradual increase in the implications of Martin Luther's doctrine of the priesthood of all believers, or they can be seen as a growth of the power and assertiveness of the bourgeoisie and an echo of the displacement of the worker from the home in growing industrialization, as Marxists such as E.P. Thompson have argued. It can be argued that the development of the subjective individual against the social individual was a natural reaction to trade over other methods of economic production.

Whatever the prime cause, a largely conservative set of voices argued for a social person and largely emergent voices argued for the individual person. The entire Augustan age's poetry was dominated by Alexander Pope. His lines were repeated often enough to lend quite a few clichés and proverbs to modern English usage. Pope had few poetic rivals, but he had many personal enemies and political, philosophical, or religious opponents, and Pope himself was quarrelsome in print. Pope and his enemies (often called "the Dunces" because of Pope's successful satirizing of them in *The Dunciad*) fought over central matters of the proper subject matter for poetry and the proper pose of the poetic voice. There was a great struggle over the nature and role of the pastoral in the early part of the century. After Pope published his Pastorals of the four seasons in 1709, an evaluation in the *Guardian* praised Ambrose Philips's pastorals above Pope's, and Pope replied with a mock praise of Philips's Pastorals that heaped scorn on them.

Pope quoted Philips's worst lines, mocked his execution, and delighted in pointing out his empty lines. Pope later explained that any depictions of shepherds and their mistresses in the pastoral must not be updated shepherds, that they must be icons of the Golden Age: "we are not to describe our shepherds as shepherds at this day really are, but as they may be conceived then to have been, when the best of men followed the employment" (Gordon). Philips's *Pastorals* were not particularly awful poems, but they did reflect his desire to "update" the pastoral. In 1724, Philips would update poetry again by writing a series of odes dedicated to "all ages and characters, from Walpole, the steerer of the realm, to Miss Pulteney in the nursery."

Henry Carey was one of the best at satirizing these poems, and his *Namby Pamby* became a hugely successful obliteration of Philips and Philips's endeavor. What is notable about Philips against Pope, however, is the fact that both poets were adapting the pastoral and the ode, both altering it. Pope's insistence upon a Golden Age pastoral no less than Philips's desire to update it meant making a political statement.

While it is easy to see in Ambrose Philips an effort at modernist triumph, it is no less the case that Pope's artificially restricted pastoral was a statement of what the ideal should be. Pope's friend John Gay also adapted the pastoral. Gay, working at Pope's suggestion, wrote a parody of the updated pastoral in *The Shepherd's Week*. He also imitated the Satires of Juvenal with his *Trivia*.

In 1728, his The Beggar's Opera was an enormous success, running for an unheard-of eighty performances. All of these works have in common a gesture of compassion. In *Trivia,* Gay writes as if commiserating with those who live in London and are menaced by falling masonry and bedpan slops, and *The Shepherd's Week* features great detail of the follies of everyday life and eccentric character. Even *The Beggar's Opera*, which is a satire of Robert Walpole, portrays its characters with compassion: the villains have pathetic songs in their own right and are acting out of exigency rather than boundless evil. Throughout the Augustan era the "updating" of Classical poets was a commonplace. These were not translations, but rather they were imitations of Classical models, and the imitation allowed poets to veil their responsibility for the comments they made.

Alexander Pope would manage to refer to the King himself in unflattering tones by "imitating" Horace in his *Epistle to Augustus.* Similarly, Samuel Johnson wrote a poem that falls into the Augustan period in his "imitation of Juvenal" entitled London. The imitation was inherently conservative, since it argued that all that was good was to be found in the old classical education, but these imitations were used for progressive purposes, as the poets who used them were often doing so to complain of the political situation. In satire, Pope achieved two of the greatest poetic satires of all time in the Augustan period. *The Rape of the Lock* (1712 and 1714) was a gentle mock-heroic. Pope applies Virgil's heroic and epic structure to the story of a young woman (Arabella Fermor) having a lock of hair snipped by an amorous baron (Lord Petre). The structure of the comparison forces Pope to invent mythological forces to overlook the struggle, and so he creates an epic battle, complete with a mythology of sylphs and metempsychosis, over a game of Ombre, leading to a fiendish appropriation of the lock of hair.

Finally, a deux ex machina appears and the lock of hair experiences an apotheosis. To some degree, Pope was adapting Jonathan Swift's habit, in *A Tale of a Tub,* of pretending that metaphors were literal truths, and he was inventing a mythos to go with the everyday. The poem was an enormous public success. A decade after the gentle, laughing satire of *The Rape of the Lock,* Pope wrote his masterpiece of invective and specific opprobrium in *The Dunciad*. The story is that of the goddess Dulness choosing a new avatar. She settles upon one of Pope's personal enemies, Lewis Theobald, and the poem describes the coronation and heroic games undertaken by all of the dunces of Great Britain in celebration of Theobald's ascension. When Pope's enemies responded to *The Dunciad* with attacks, Pope produced the Dunciad Variorum, with a "learned" commentary upon the original Dunciad. In 1743, he added a fourth book and changed the hero from Lewis Theobald to Colley Cibber.

In the fourth book of the new *Dunciad*, Pope expressed the view that, in the battle between light and dark (enlightenment and the Dark Ages), Night and Dulness were fated to win, that all things of value were soon going to be subsumed under the curtain of unknowing. John Gay and Alexander Pope belong on one side of a line separating the celebrants of the individual and the celebrants of the social. Pope wrote *The Rape of the Lock,* he said, to settle a disagreement between two great families, to laugh them into peace.

Even *The Dunciad,* which seems to be a serial killing of everyone on Pope's enemies list, sets up these figures as expressions of dangerous and antisocial forces in letters. Theobald and Cibber are marked by vanity and pride, by having no care for morality. The hireling pens Pope attacks mercilessly in the heroic games section of the *Dunciad* are all embodiments of avarice and lies. Similarly, Gay writes of political society, of social dangers, and of follies that must be addressed to protect the greater whole. Gay's individuals are microcosms of the society at large. On the other side of this line were people who agreed with the politics of Gay and Pope (and Swift), but not in approach. They include, early in the Augustan Age, James Thomson and Edward Young.

Thomson's *The Seasons* (1730) is poetry of natural description, but they are unlike Pope's notion of the Golden Age pastoral. Thomson's poet speaks in the first person from direct observation, and his own mood and sentiment color the descriptions of landscape. Unlike Pope's Windsor Forest, Thomson's seasons have no mythology, no celebration of Britain or the crown. Winter, in particular, is melancholy and meditative. Edward Yonge's *Night Thoughts* (1742–1744) was immediately popular. It was, even more than *Winter,* a poem of deep solitude, melancholy, and despair. In these two poets, there are the stirrings of the lyric as the Romantics would see it: the celebration of the private individual's idiosyncratic, yet paradigmatic, responses to the visions of the world.

These hints at the solitary poet were carried into a new realm with Thomas Gray, whose *Elegy Written in a Country Church-Yard* (1750) set off a new craze for poetry of melancholy reflection. It was written in the "country," and not in or as opposed to London, and the poem sets up the solitary observer in a privileged position. It is only by being solitary that the poet can speak of a truth that is wholly individually realized.

After Gray, a group often referred to as the Churchyard Poets began imitating his pose, if not his style. Oliver Goldsmith *(The Deserted Village),* Thomas Warton, and even Thomas Percy *(The Hermit of Warkworth),* each conservative by and large and Classicist (Gray himself was a professor of Greek), took up the new poetry of solitude and loss. It is remarkable that when the Romantics emerged at the end of the 18th century, they were not assuming a radically new invention of the subjective self themselves, but merely formalizing what had gone before. Similarly, the later 18th century saw a ballad revival, with Thomas Percy's *Reliques of Ancient English Poetry*.

Drama

No exaggeration, the "Augustan era" is difficult to define chronologically in prose and poetry, but it is very easy to date its end in drama. The Augustan era's drama ended definitively in 1737, with the Licensing Act. Prior to 1737, however the English stage was changing rapidly from the Restoration comedy and Restoration drama and their noble subjects to the quickly developing melodrama (Munns 97-100).

George Lillo and Richard Steele wrote the trend-setting plays of the early Augustan period. Lillo's plays consciously turned from heroes and kings and toward shopkeepers and apprentices. They emphasized drama on a household scale, rather than a national scale, and the hamartia and agon in his tragedies are the common flaws of yielding to temptation and the commission of Christian sin. The plots are resolved with Christian forgiveness and repentance. Steele's *The Conscious Lovers* (1722) hinges upon his young hero avoiding fighting a duel.

These plays set up a new set of values for the stage. Instead of amusing the audience or inspiring the audience, they sought to instruct the audience and ennoble it. Further, the plays were popular precisely because they seemed to reflect the audience's own lives and concerns (Legouis 782-

787, 879-383). Joseph Addison also wrote a play, entitled Cato, in 1713. Cato concerned the Roman statesman. The year of its première was important, for Queen Anne was in serious illness at the time, and both the Tory ministry of the day and the Whig opposition (already being led by Robert Walpole) were concerned about the succession. Both groups were contacting the Old Pretender about bringing the Young Pretender over. Londoners sensed this anxiety, for Anne had no heirs, and all of the natural successors in the Stuart family were Roman Catholic or unavailable.

Therefore, the figure of Cato was a transparent symbol of Roman integrity, and the Whigs saw in him a champion of Whig values, while the Tories saw in him an embodiment of Tory sentiments or, like the Tory Examiner, tried to claim that Cato was above political "faction". Both sides cheered the play, even though Addison was himself clearly Whig (Bloom and Bloom 266, 269). John Home's play *Douglas* (1756) would have a similar fate to Cato in the next generation, after the Licensing Act. As during the Restoration, economics drove the stage in the Augustan period. Under Charles II court patronage meant economic success, and therefore the Restoration stage featured plays that would suit the monarch and/or court.

The drama that celebrated kings and told the history of Britain's monarchs was fit fare for the crown and courtiers. Charles II was a philanderer, and so Restoration comedy featured a highly sexualized set of plays. However, after the reign of William and Mary, the court and crown stopped taking a great interest in the playhouse. Theaters had to get their money from the audience of city dwellers, therefore, and consequently plays that reflected city anxieties and celebrated the lives of citizens drew and were staged (Munns 96-99).

Thus, there were quite a few plays that were, in fact, not literary that were staged more often than the literary plays. John Rich and Colley Cibber duelled over special theatrical effects. They put on plays that were actually just spectacles, where the text of the play was almost an afterthought. Dragons, whirlwinds, thunder, ocean waves, and even actual elephants were on stage. Battles, explosions, and horses were put on the boards. Rich specialized in pantomime and was famous as the character "Lun" in harlequin presentations.

The plays put on in this manner are not generally preserved or studied, but their monopoly on the theaters infuriated established literary authors. Additionally, opera made its way to England during this period. Inasmuch as opera combined singing with acting, it was a mixed genre, and this violated all the strictures of neo-classicism. Further, high melodies would cover the singers' expressions of grief or joy, thus breaking "decorum." To add insult to injury, the casts and celebrated stars were foreigners, and, as with Farinelli, castrati.

The satirists saw in opera the non plus ultra of invidiousness. John Gay parodied the opera with his satirical *Beggar's Opera* (1728) and offered up a parody of Robert Walpole's actions during the South Sea Bubble. Superficially, the play is about a man named Macheath who keeps being imprisoned by a thief named Peachum and who escapes prison over and over again because the daughter of the jailor, Lucy Lockitt, is in love with him.

This is an obvious parallel with the case of Jonathan Wild (Peachum) and Jack Sheppard (Macheath). However, it was also the tale of Robert Walpole (Peachum) and the South Sea directors (Macheath). The play was a hit, and its songs were printed up and sold. However, when Gay wrote a follow up called *Polly,* Walpole had the play suppressed before performance (Winn 112-114). Playwrights were therefore in straits. On the one hand, the playhouses were doing without plays by turning out hack-written pantomimes. On the other hand, when a satirical play appeared, the Whig ministry would suppress it. This antagonism was picked up by Henry Fielding, who was not afraid to fight Walpole.

His *Tom Thumb* (1730) was a satire on all of the tragedies written before him, with quotations from all the worst plays patched together for absurdity, and the plot concerned the eponymous tiny man attempting to run things. It was, in other words, an attack on Robert Walpole and the way that he was referred to as "the Great Man." Here, the Great Man is made obviously deficient by being a midget. Walpole responded, and Fielding's revision of the play was in print only. It was written by "Scribblerus Secundus," its title page announced, and it was the *Tragedy of Tragedies,* which functioned as a clearly Swiftian parodic satire. Anti-Walpolean sentiment also showed in increasingly political plays, and the theaters began to stage them.

A particular play of unknown authorship entitled *A Vision of the Golden Rump* was cited when Parliament passed the Licensing Act of 1737. (The "rump" in question is Parliament, on the one hand, and buttocks on the other.) The Licensing Act required all plays to go to a censor before staging, and only those plays passed by the censor were allowed to be performed. The first play to be banned by the new Act was *Gustavus Vasa,* by Henry Brooke. Samuel Johnson wrote a Swiftian parodic satire of the licensers, entitled *A Complete Vindication of the Licensers of the English Stage*. The satire was, of course, not a vindication at all, but rather a *reductio ad absurdum* of the position for censorship. Had the licensers not exercised their authority in a partisan manner, the Act might not have chilled the stage so dramatically, but the public was well aware of the bannings and censorship, and consequently any play that *did* pass the licensers was regarded with suspicion by the public. Therefore, the playhouses had little choice but to present old plays and pantomime and plays that had no conceivable political content.

In the next chapter we will put light on major writers of early eighteenth century. In the subsequent chapter an overview of the entire Eighteenth Century English literature.

7

Eighteenth Century Literature: An Overview

Though we have introduced the readers in the chapter on Augustan literature with major trends of Eighteenth century literature—here we will try to present an overview of the literary movement of this important epoch.

First it is remarkable that during the first part of the eighteenth century the direct connection between politics and literature was closer than at any previous period of English life; for the practical spirit of the previous generation continued to prevail, so that the chief writers were very ready to concern themselves with the affairs of State, and in the uncertain strife of parties ministers were glad to enlist their aid. On the death of King William in 1702, Anne, sister of his wife Queen Mary and daughter of James II, became Queen. Unlike King William she was a Tory and at first filled offices with members of that party. But the English campaigns under the Duke of Marlborough against Louis XIV were supported by the Whigs, who therefore gradually regained control, and in 1708 the Queen had to submit to a Whig ministry. She succeeded in ousting them in 1710, and a Tory cabinet was formed by Henry Harley (afterwards Earl of Oxford) and Henry St. John (afterwards Viscount Bolingbroke).

On the death of Anne in 1714 Bolingbroke, with other Tories, was intriguing for a second restoration of the Stuarts in the person of the son of James II (the 'Old Pretender'). But the nation decided for a Protestant German prince, a descendant of James I through his daughter Elizabeth, and this prince was crowned as George I—an event which brought England peace at the price of a century of rule by an unenlightened and sordid foreign dynasty. The Tories were violently turned out of office; Oxford was imprisoned, and Bolingbroke, having fled to the Pretender, was declared a traitor. Ten years later he was allowed to come back and attempted to oppose Robert Walpole, the Whig statesman who for twenty years governed England in the name of the first two Georges; but in the upshot Bolingbroke was again obliged to retire to France.

Salient Feature

It is pertinent to note that the main characteristics of the period and its literature continue, with some further development, those of the Restoration, and may be summarily indicated as follows:

1. The men of this age carried still further the distrust and dislike felt by the previous generation for emotion, enthusiasm, and strong individuality both in life and in literature, and exalted Reason and Regularity as their guiding stars. The terms 'decency' and 'neatness' were forever on their lips. They sought a conventional uniformity in manners, speech, and indeed in nearly everything else, and were uneasy if they deviated far from the approved, respectable standards of the body of their fellows. Great poetic imagination, therefore, could scarcely exist among them, or indeed supreme greatness of any sort.

2. Interest was largely centered in the practical well-being either of society as a whole or of one's own social class or set. The majority of writers, furthermore, belonged by birth or association to the upper social stratum and tended to overemphasize its artificial conventions, often looking with contempt on the other classes. To them conventional good breeding, fine manners, the pleasures of the leisure class, and the standards of 'The Town' (fashionable London society) were the only part of life much worth regarding.
3. They had little appreciation for external Nature or for any beauty except that of formalized Art. A forest seemed to most of them merely wild and gloomy, and great mountains chiefly terrible, but they took delight in gardens of artificially trimmed trees and in regularly plotted and alternating beds of domestic flowers. The Elizabethans also, as we have seen, had had much more feeling for the terror than for the grandeur of the sublime in Nature, but the Elizabethans had had nothing of the elegant primness of the Augustans.
4. In speech and especially in literature, most of all in poetry, they were given to abstractness of thought and expression, intended to secure elegance, but often serving largely to substitute superficiality for definiteness and significant meaning. They abounded in personifications of abstract qualities and ideas ('Laughter, heavenly maid,' Honor, Glory, Sorrow, and so on, with prominent capital letters), a sort of a pseudo-classical substitute for emotion.
5. They were still more fully confirmed than the men of the Restoration in the conviction that the ancients

had attained the highest possible perfection in literature, and some of them made absolute submission of judgment to the ancients, especially to the Latin poets and the Greek, Latin, and also the seventeenth century classicizing French critics. Some authors seemed timidly to desire to be under authority and to glory in surrendering their independence, individuality, and originality to foreign and long-established leaders and principles.

6. There was a strong tendency to moralizing, which also was not altogether free from conventionality and superficiality.
7. Under these circumstances the effort to attain the finished beauty of classical literature naturally resulted largely in a more or less shallow formal smoothness.

No doubt, the 'Augustan Age' must be considered to end before the middle of the century, the same spirit continued dominant among many writers until near its close, so that almost the whole of the century may be called the period of pseudo-classicism.

Daniel Defoe

The two earliest notable writers of the period, however, though they display some of these characteristics, were men of strong individual traits which in any age would have directed them largely along paths of their own choosing. The first of them is Daniel Defoe, who belongs, furthermore, quite outside the main circle of high-bred and polished fashion. Defoe was born in London about 1660, the son of James Foe, a butcher, to whose name the son arbitrarily and with characteristic eye to effect prefixed the 'De' in middle life. Educated for the Dissenting ministry, Defoe, a man of inexhaustible practical energy, engaged instead in several successive lines of business, and at the age of thirty-five, after various vicissitudes, was in prosperous circumstances. He now became a pamphleteer in support of King William and the Whigs.

His first very significant work, a satire against the High-Church Tories entitled 'The Shortest Way with Dissenters,' belongs early in the reign of Queen Anne. Here, parodying extreme Tory bigotry, he argued, with apparent seriousness, that the Dissenters should all be hanged. The Tories were at first delighted, but when they discovered the hoax became correspondingly indignant and Defoe was set in the pillory, and (for a short time) imprisoned. In this confinement he began The Review a newspaper which he continued for eleven years and whose department called 'The Scandal Club' suggested 'The Tatler' to Steele. During many years following his release Defoe issued an enormous number of pamphlets and acted continuously as a secret agent and spy of the government. Though he was always at heart a thorough-going Dissenter and Whig, he served all the successive governments, Whig and Tory, alike; for his character and point of view were those of the 'practical' journalist and middle-class money-getter. This of course means that all his professed principles were superficial, or at least secondary, that he was destitute of real religious feeling and of the gentleman's sense of honor. Defoe's influence in helping to shape modern journalism and modern every-day English style was large; but the achievement which has given him world-wide fame came late in life.

In 1706 he had written a masterly short story, 'The Apparition of Mrs. Veal.' Its real purpose, characteristically enough, was the concealed one of promoting the sale of an unsuccessful religious book, but its literary importance lies first in the extraordinarily convincing mass of minute details which it casts about an incredible incident and second in the complete knowledge (sprung from Defoe's wide experience in journalism, politics, and business) which it displays of a certain range of middle-class characters and ideas. It is these same elements, together with the vigorous presentation and emphasis of basal practical virtues, that distinguished 'Robinson Crusoe,' of which the First Part appeared in 1719, when Defoe was nearly or quite sixty years of age. The book, which must have been somewhat influenced by 'Pilgrim's Progress,' was more directly suggested by a passage in William Dampier's 'Voyage Round the World,' and also, as every one knows, by the experience of Alexander Selkirk, a sailor who, set ashore on the island of Juan Fernandez, off the coast of Chile, had lived there alone from 1709 to 1713. Selkirk's story had been briefly told in the year of his return in a newspaper of Steele, 'The Englishman'; it was later to inspire the most famous poem of William Cowper. 'Robinson Crusoe,' however, turned the material to account in a much larger, more clever, and more striking fashion. Its success was immediate and enormous, both with the English middle class and with a wider circle of readers in the other European countries; it was followed by numerous imitations and it will doubtless always continue to be one of the best known of world classics.

The precise elements of its power can be briefly indicated. As a story of unprecedented adventure in a distant and unknown region it speaks thrillingly to the universal human sense of romance. Yet it makes a still stronger appeal to the instinct for practical, every-day realism which is the controlling quality in the English dissenting middle class for whom Defoe was writing.

Defoe has put himself with astonishingly complete

dramatic sympathy into the place of his hero. In spite of not a few errors and oversights (due to hasty composition) in the minor details of external fact, he has virtually lived Crusoe's life with him in imagination and he therefore makes the reader also pass with Crusoe through all his experiences, his fears, hopes and doubts. Here also, as we have implied, Defoe's vivid sense for external minutiae plays an important part. He tells precisely how many guns and cheeses and flasks of spirit Crusoe brought away from the wreck, how many days or weeks he spent in making his earthen vessels and his canoe—in a word, thoroughly actualizes the whole story. Defoe's energy had not diminished with age and a hard life, and the success of 'Robinson Crusoe' led him to pour out a series of other works of romantic-realistic fiction. The second part of 'Robinson Crusoe' is no more satisfactory than any other similar continuation, and the third part, a collection of moralizings, is today entirely and properly forgotten. On the other hand, his usual method, the remarkable imaginative re-creation and vivifying of a host of minute details, makes of the fictitious 'Journal of the Plague Year' (1666) a piece of virtual history.

Defoe's other later works are rather unworthy attempts to make profit out of his reputation and his full knowledge of the worst aspects of life; they are mostly very frank presentations of the careers of adventurers or criminals, real or fictitious. In this coarse realism they are picaresque, and in structure also they, like 'Robinson Crusoe,' are picaresque in being mere successions of adventures without artistic plot. In Defoe's last years he suffered a great reverse of fortune, paying the full penalty for his opportunism and lack of ideals. His secret and unworthy long-standing connection with the Government was disclosed, so that his reputation was sadly blemished, and he seems to have gone into hiding, perhaps as the result of half-insane delusions. He died in 1731. His place in English literature is secure, though he owes it to the lucky accident of finding not quite too late special material exactly suited to his peculiar talent.

Jonathan Swift

Another unique figure of very mixed traits, Jonathan Swift, is like Defoe in that he connects the reign of William III with that of his successors and that, in accordance with the spirit of his age, he wrote for the most part not for literary but for practical purposes; in many other respects the two are widely different. Swift is one of the best representatives in English literature of sheer intellectual power, but his character, his aims, his environment, and the circumstances of his life denied to him also literary achievement of the greatest permanent significance. Swift, though of unmixed English descent, related to both Dryden and Robert Herrick, was born in Ireland, in 1667. Brought up in poverty by his widowed mother, he spent the period between his fourteenth and twentieth years recklessly and without distinction at Trinity College, Dublin.

From the outbreak attending the Revolution of 1688 he fled to England, where for the greater part of nine years he lived in the country as a sort of secretary to the retired statesman, Sir William Temple, who was his distant relative by marriage. Here he had plenty of time for reading, but the position of dependence and the consciousness that his great though still unformed powers of intellect and of action were rusting away in obscurity undoubtedly did much to increase the natural bitterness of his disposition. In 1704 Swift published his first important works (written earlier, while he was living with Temple), which are among the masterpieces of his satirical genius. In 'The Battle of the Books' he supports Temple, who had taken the side of the Ancients in a hotly-debated and very futile quarrel then being carried on by French and English writers as to whether ancient or modern authors are the greater. 'The Tale of a Tub' is a keen, coarse, and violent satire on the actual irreligion of all Christian Churches. It takes the form of a burlesque history of three brothers, Peter (the Catholics, so called from St. Peter), Martin (the Lutherans and the Church of England, named from Martin Luther), and Jack (the Dissenters, who followed John Calvin); but a great part of the book is made up of irrelevant introductions and digressions in which Swift ridicules various absurdities, literary and otherwise, among them the very practice of digressions. The great range of the satires which make the greater part of Swift's work is supported in part by variety of satiric method. Sometimes he pours out a savage direct attack. Sometimes, in a long ironical statement, he says exactly the opposite of what he really means to suggest. Sometimes he uses apparently logical reasoning where either, as in 'A Modest Proposal,' the proposition, or, as in the 'Argument Against Abolishing Christianity,' the arguments are absurd.

He often shoots out incidental humorous or satirical shafts. But his most important and extended method is that of allegory. The pigmy size of the Lilliputians symbolizes the littleness of mankind and their interests; the superior skill in rope-dancing which with them is the ground for political advancement, the political intrigues of real men; and the question whether eggs shall be broken on the big or the little end, which has embroiled Lilliput in a bloody war, both civil and foreign, the trivial causes of European conflicts. In Brobdingnag, on the other hand, the coarseness of mankind is exhibited by the magnifying proces. Swift, like Defoe, generally increases the verisimilitude of his fictions and his ironies by careful accuracy in details, which is sometimes arithmetically genuine, sometimes only a hoax. In Lilliput all the dimensions are scientifically computed on a scale one-twelfth as large as that of man; in Brobdingnag, by an exact reversal, everything is twelve times greater than among men. But the long list of technical nautical terms which seem to make a spirited narrative at the beginning of the second of Gulliver's voyages is merely an incoherent hodge-podge. Swift, then, is the greatest of English satirists and the only one who as a satirist claims large attention in a brief general survey of English literature. He is one of the most powerfully intellectual of all English writers, and the clear force of his work is admirable; but being first a man of affairs and only secondarily a man of letters, he stands only on the outskirts of real literature.

Steele and Addison

Richard Steele was born in Dublin in 1672 of an English father and an Irish mother. The Irish strain was conspicuous throughout his life in his warm-heartedness, impulsiveness and lack of self-control and practical judgment. Having lost his father early, he was sent to the Charterhouse School in London, where he made the acquaintance of Addison, and then to Oxford. He abandoned the university to enlist in the aristocratic regiment of Life Guards, and he remained in the army, apparently, for seven or eight years, though he seems not to have been in active service and became a recognized wit at the London coffee-houses. Thackeray in 'Henry Esmond' gives interesting though freely imaginative pictures of him at this stage of his career and later.

His reckless instincts and love of pleasure were rather strangely combined with a sincere theoretical devotion to religion, and his first noticeable work (1701), a little booklet called 'The Christian Hero,' aimed, in opposition to fashionable license, to show that decency and goodness are requisites of a real gentleman. The resultant ridicule forced him into a duel (in which he seriously wounded his antagonist), and thenceforth in his writings duelling was a main object of his attacks. During the next few years he turned with the same reforming zeal to comedy, where he attempted to exalt pure love and high ideals, though the standards of his age and class leave in his own plays much that to-day seems coarse. Otherwise his plays are by no means great; they initiated the weak 'Sentimental Comedy,' which largely dominated the English stage for the rest of the century. During this period Steele was married twice in rather rapid succession to wealthy ladies whose fortunes served only very temporarily to respite him from his chronic condition of debt and bailiff's duns. Now succeeds the brief period of his main literary achievement. All his life a strong Whig, he was appointed in 1707 Gazetteer, or editor, of *'The London Gazette,'* the official government newspaper. This led him in 1709 to start *'The Tatler.'*

English periodical literature, in forms which must be called the germs both of the modern newspaper and of the modern magazine, had begun in an uncertain fashion, of which the details are too complicated for record here, nearly a hundred years before, and had continued ever since with increasing vigor. The lapsing of the licensing laws in 1695 had given a special impetus. Defoe's 'Review,' from 1704 to 1713, was devoted to many interests, including politics, the Church and commerce.

Steele's 'Tatler' at first likewise dealt in each number with several subjects, such as foreign news, literary criticism, and morals, but his controlling instinct to inculcate virtue and good sense more and more asserted itself. The various departments were dated from the respective coffee-houses where those subjects were chiefly discussed, Poetry from 'Will's,' Foreign and Domestic News from 'St. James's,' and so on. The more didactic papers were ascribed to an imaginary Isaac Bickerstaff, a nom-de-plume which Steele borrowed from some of Swift's satires. Steele himself wrote two-thirds of all the papers, but before proceeding far he accepted Addison's offer of assistance and later he occasionally called in other contributors. *'The Tatler'* appeared three times a week and ran for twenty-one months; it came to an end shortly after the return of the Tories to power had deprived Steele and Addison of some of their political offices.

Its discontinuance may have been due to weariness on Steele's part or, since it was Whig in tone, to a desire to be done with partisan writing; at any rate, two months later, in March, 1711, of Marlborough's victory at Blenheim, secured the favor of the ministers of the day, and throughout almost all the rest of his life he held important political places, some even, thanks to Swift, during the period of Tory dominance. During his last ten years he was a member of Parliament; but though he was a delightful conversationalist in a small group of friends, he was unable to speak in public. Addison's great fame as 'The Spectator' was increased when in 1713 he brought out the play 'Cato,' mostly written years before. This is a characteristic example of the pseudo-classical tragedies of which a few were produced during the first half of the eighteenth century.

They are the stiffest and most lifeless of all forms of pseudo-classical literature; Addison, for his part, attempts not only to observe the three unities, but to follow many of the minor formal rules drawn up by the French critics, and his plot, characterization, and language are alike excessively pale and frigid. Paleness and frigidity, however, were taken for beauties at the time, and the moral idea of the play, the eulogy of Cato's devotion to liberty in his opposition to Caesar, was very much in accord with the prevailing taste, or at least the prevailing affected taste.

Both political parties loudly claimed the work as an expression of their principles, the Whigs discovering in Caesar an embodiment of arbitrary government like that of the Tories, the Tories declaring him a counterpart of Marlborough, a dangerous plotter, endeavoring to establish a military despotism. 'Cato,' further, was a main cause of a famous quarrel between Addison and Pope. Addison, now recognized as the literary dictator of the age, had greatly pleased Pope, then a young aspirant for fame, by praising his 'Essay on Criticism,' and Pope rendered considerable help in the final revision of 'Cato.' When John Dennis, a rather clumsy critic, attacked the play, Pope came to its defense with a reply written in a spirit of railing bitterness which sprang from injuries of his own.

Addison, a real gentleman, disowned the defense, and this, with other slights suffered or imagined by Pope's jealous disposition, led to estrangement and soon to the composition of Pope's very clever and telling satire on Addison as 'Atticus,' which Pope did not publish, however, until he included it in his 'Epistle to Dr. Arbuthnot,' many years after Addison's death. 'The Tatler' and the more important 'Spectator' accomplished two results of main importance: they developed the modern essay as a comprehensive and fluent discussion of topics of current interest; and they performed a very great service in elevating the tone of English thought and life. The later 'Tatlers' and all the 'Spectators' dealt, by diverse methods, with a great range of themes—amusements, religion, literature, art, dress, clubs, superstitions, and in general all the fashions and follies of the time.

The writers, especially Addison, with his wide and mature scholarship, aimed to form public taste. But the chief purpose of the papers, professedly, was 'to banish Vice and Ignorance' (though here also, especially in Steele's papers, the tone sometimes seems to twentieth-century readers far from unexceptionable). When the papers began to appear, in spite of some weakening of the Restoration spirit, the idea still dominated, or was allowed to appear dominant, that immorality and lawlessness were the proper marks of a gentleman. An appeal was made, also, to women no less than to men.

During the previous period woman, in fashionable circles, had been treated as an elegant toy, of whom nothing was expected but to be frivolously attractive. Addison and Steele held up to her the ideal of self-respecting intellectual development and of reasonable preparation for her own particular sphere. The great effectiveness of 'The Spectator's' preaching was due largely to its tactfulness. The method was never violent denunciation, rather gentle admonition, suggestion by example or otherwise, and light or humorous raillery. Indeed, this almost uniform urbanity and good-nature makes the chief charm of the papers. Their success was largely furthered, also, by the audience provided in the coffee-houses, virtually eighteenth century middle-class clubs whose members and points of view they primarily addressed. The external style has been from the first an object of unqualified and well-merited praise. Both the chief authors are direct, sincere, and lifelike, and the many short sentences which they mingle with the longer, balanced, ones give point and force. Steele is on the whole somewhat more colloquial and less finished, Addison more balanced and polished, though without artificial formality. Dr. Johnson's repeatedly quoted description of the style can scarcely be improved on—'familiar but not coarse, and elegant but not ostentatious.'

Alexander Pope (1688-1744)

Pope was born in 1688 (just a hundred years before Byron), the son of a Catholic linen-merchant in London. Scarcely any other great writer has ever had to contend against such hard and cruel handicaps as he. He inherited a deformed and dwarfed body and an incurably sickly constitution, which carried with it abnormal sensitiveness of both nerves and mind. Though he never had really definite religious convictions of his own, he remained all his life formally loyal to his parents' faith, and under the laws of the time this closed to him all the usual careers of a gentleman.

But he was predestined by Nature to be a poet. Brought up chiefly at the country home near Windsor to which his father had retired, and left to himself for mental training, he never acquired any thoroughness of knowledge or power of systematic thought, but he read eagerly the poetry of many languages. He was one of the most precocious of the long list of precocious versifiers; his own words are: 'I lisped in numbers, for the numbers came.'

The influences which would no doubt have determined his style in any case were early brought to a focus in the advice given him by an amateur poet and critic, William Walsh. Walsh declared that England had had great poets, 'but never one great poet that was correct' (that is of thoroughly regular style). Pope accepted this hint as his guiding principle and proceeded to seek correctness by giving still further polish to the pentameter couplet of Dryden. For the next dozen years he occupied himself chiefly with the formidable task (suggested, no doubt, by

Dryden's 'Virgil,' but expressive also of the age) of translating 'The Iliad' and 'The Odyssey.' 'The Iliad' he completed unaided, but then, tiring of the drudgery, he turned over half of 'The Odyssey' to two minor writers. So easy, however, was his style to catch that if the facts were not on record the work of his assistants would generally be indistinguishable from his own. From an absolute point of view many criticisms must be made of Pope's version.

In fact, the publication of Pope's Homer marks an important stage in the development of authorship. Until the time of Dryden no writer had expected to earn his whole living by publishing works of real literature. The medieval minstrels and romancers of the higher class and the dramatists of the sixteenth and seventeenth centuries had indeed supported themselves largely or wholly by their works, but not by printing them.

When, in Dryden's time, with the great enlargement of the reading public, conditions were about to change, the publisher took the upper hand; authors might sometimes receive gifts from the noblemen to whom they inscribed dedications, but for their main returns they must generally sell their works outright to the publisher and accept his price. Pope's 'Iliad' and 'Odyssey' afforded the first notably successful instance of another method, that of publication by subscription—individual purchasers at a generous price being secured beforehand by solicitation and in acknowledgment having their names printed in a conspicuous list in the front of the book.

From the two Homeric poems together, thanks to this device, Pope realized a profit of nearly L9000, and thus proved that an author might be independent of the publisher. On the success of 'The Iliad' alone Pope had retired to an estate at a London suburb, Twickenham (then pronounced 'Twitnam'), where he spent the remainder of his life. Here he laid out five acres with skill, though in the formal landscape-garden taste of his time. In particular, he excavated under the road a 'grotto,' which he adorned with mirrors and glittering stones and which was considered by his friends, or at least by himself, as a marvel of artistic beauty.

During his last fifteen years Pope's original work was done chiefly in two very closely related fields, first in a group of what he called 'Moral' essays, second in the imitation of a few of the Satires and Epistles of Horace, which Pope applied to circumstances of his own time. In the 'Moral' Essays he had intended to deal comprehensively with human nature and institutions, but such a systematic plan was beyond his powers. The longest of the essays which he accomplished, the 'Essay on Man,' aims, like 'Paradise Lost,' to 'vindicate the ways of God to man,' but as regards logic chiefly demonstrates the author's inability to reason. He derived the ideas, in fragmentary fashion, from Bolingbroke, who was an amateur Deist and optimist of the shallow eighteenth century type, and so far was Pope from understanding what he was doing that he was greatly disturbed when it was pointed out to him that the theology of the poem was Deistic rather than Christian In this poem, as in all Pope's others of this period, the best things are the detached observations. Some of the other poems, especially the autobiographical 'Epistle to Dr. Arbuthnot,' are notable for their masterly and venomous satirical sketches of various contemporary characters.

Almost all of them, it will be observed, result from the habit of generalizing instead of searching for the pictorial and the particular.

1. There is a constant preference (to enlarge on what was briefly stated above) for abstract expressions instead of concrete ones, such expressions as 'immortal powers' or 'Heaven' for 'God.' These abstract expressions are especially noticeable in the descriptions of emotion, which the pseudo-classical writers often describe without really feeling it, in such colorless words as 'joys, 'delights,' and 'ecstasies,' and which they uniformly refer to the conventionalized 'heart, 'soul,' or 'bosom.' Likewise in the case of personal features, instead of picturing a face with blue eyes, rosy lips, and pretty color, these poets vaguely mention 'charms,' 'beauties,' 'glories,' 'enchantments,' and the like.
2. There is an excessive use of adjectives, often one to nearly every important noun, which creates monotony.
3. There is a constant use of generic or generalizing articles, pronouns, and adjectives, 'the,' 'a,' 'that,' 'every,' and 'each' as in some of the preceding and in the following examples: 'The wise man's passion and the vain man's boast.' 'Wind the shrill horn or spread the waving net.' 'To act a Lover's or a Roman's part.' 'That bleeding bosom.'
4. The poets imitate the Latin language to some extent; especially they often prefer long words of Latin origin to short Saxon ones, and Latin names to English—'Sol' for 'Sun, 'temple' for 'church,' 'Senate' for 'Parliament,' and so on.]
5. The vocabulary is largely conventionalized, with, certain favorite words usurping the place of a full and free variety, such words as 'conscious,' 'generous, 'soft,' and 'amorous.' The metaphors employed are

largely conventionalized ones, like 'Now burns with glory, and then melts with love.'

Samuel Johnson, 1709-1785

Johnson was born in 1709, the son of a bookseller in Lichfield. He inherited a constitution of iron, great physical strength, and fearless self-assertiveness, but also hypochondria (persistent melancholy), uncouthness of body and movement, and scrofula, which disfigured his face and greatly injured his eyesight. In his early life as well as later, spasmodic fits of abnormal mental activity when he 'gorged' books, especially the classics, as he did food, alternated with other fits of indolence. The total result, however, was a very thorough knowledge of an extremely wide range of literature; when he entered Oxford in 1728 the Master of his college assured him that he was the best qualified applicant whom he had ever known. Johnson, on his side, was not nearly so well pleased with the University; he found the teachers incompetent, and his pride suffered intensely from his poverty, so that he remained at Oxford little more than a year.

The death of his father in 1731 plunged him into a distressingly painful struggle for existence which lasted for thirty years. After failing as a subordinate teacher in a boarding-school he became a hack-writer in Birmingham, where, at the age of twenty-five, he made a marriage with a widow, Mrs. Porter, an unattractive, rather absurd, but good-hearted woman of forty-six. He set up a school of his own, where he had only three pupils, and then in 1737 tramped with one of them, David Garrick, later the famous actor, to London to try his fortune in another field. When the two reached the city their combined funds amounted to sixpence.

Sir Robert Walpole, ruling the country with unscrupulous absolutism, had now put an end to the employment of literary men in public life, and though Johnson's poem 'London,' a satire on the city written in imitation of the Roman poet Juvenal and published in 1738, attracted much attention, he could do no better for a time than to become one of that undistinguished herd of hand-to-mouth and nearly starving Grub Street writers whom Pope was so contemptuously abusing and who chiefly depended on the despotic patronage of magazine publishers. Living in a garret or even walking the streets at night for lack of a lodging, Johnson was sometimes unable to appear at a tavern because he had no respectable clothes. It was ten years after the appearance of 'London' that he began to emerge, through the publication of his 'Vanity of Human Wishes,' a poem of the same kind as 'London' but more sincere and very powerful. A little later Garrick, who had risen very much more rapidly and was now manager of Drury Lane theater, gave him substantial help by producing his early play 'Irene,' a representative pseudo-classical tragedy of which it has been said that a person with a highly developed sense of duty may be able to read it through.

Meanwhile, by an arrangement with leading booksellers, Johnson had entered on the largest, and, as it proved, the decisive, work of his life, the preparation of his 'Dictionary of the English Language.' The earliest mentionable English dictionary had appeared as far back as 1604, 'containing 3000 hard words ... gathered for the benefit and help of ladies, gentle women, or any other unskilful persons.' Others had followed; but none of them was comprehensive or satisfactory. Johnson, planning a far more thorough work, contracted to do it for L1575—scanty pay for himself and his copyists, the more so that the task occupied more than twice as much time as he had expected, over seven years.

The result, then, of very great labor, the 'Dictionary' appeared in 1755. It had distinct limitations. The knowledge of Johnson's day was not adequate for tracing the history and etymology of words, and Johnson himself on being asked the reason for one of his numerous blunders could only reply, with his characteristic blunt frankness, 'sheer ignorance.' Moreover, he allowed his strong prejudices to intrude, even though he colored them with humor; for example in defining 'oats' as 'a grain which in England is generally given to horses, but in Scotland supports the people.' Jesting at himself he defined 'lexicographer' as 'a writer of dictionaries, a harmless drudge.' Nevertheless the work, though not creative literature, was a great and necessary one, and Johnson did it, on the whole, decidedly well.

The 'Dictionary,' in successive enlargements, ultimately, though not until after Johnson's death, became the standard, and it gave him at once the definite headship of English literary life. Of course, it should be added, the English language has vastly expanded since his time, and Johnson's first edition contained only a tithe of the 400,000 words recorded in the latest edition of Webster (1910). With the 'Dictionary' is connected one of the best-known incidents in English literary history. At the outset of the undertaking Johnson exerted himself to secure the patronage and financial aid of Lord Chesterfield, an elegant leader of fashion and of fashionable literature.

At the time Chesterfield, not foreseeing the importance of the work, was coldly indifferent, but shortly before the Dictionary appeared, being better informed, he attempted to gain a share in the credit by commending it in a periodical. Johnson responded with a letter which is a perfect masterpiece of bitter but polished irony and which should be familiar to every student. In the substance of his work Johnson is most conspicuously, and of set purpose, a moralist. In all his writing, so far as the subject permitted, he aimed chiefly at the inculcation of virtue and the formation of character. His uncompromising resoluteness in this respect accounts for much of the dulness which it is useless to try to deny in his work.

'The Rambler' and 'The Idler' altogether lack Addison's lightness of touch and of humor; for Johnson, thoroughly Puritan at heart, and dealing generally with the issues of personal conduct and responsibility, can never greatly relax his seriousness, while Addison, a man of the world, is content if he can produce some effect on society as a whole.

Again, a present-day reader can only smile when he finds Johnson in his Preface to Shakespeare blaming the great dramatist for omitting opportunities of instructing and delighting, as if the best moral teachers were always explicit. But Johnson's moral and religious earnestness is essentially admirable, the more so because his deliberate view of the world was thoroughly pessimistic. His own long and unhappy experience had convinced him that life is for the most part a painful tribulation, to be endured with as much patience and courage as possible, under the consciousness of the duty of doing our best where God has put us and in the hope (though with Johnson not a confident hope) that we shall find our reward in another world.

James Boswell

It is an interesting paradox that while Johnson's reputation as the chief English man of letters of his age seems secure for all time, his works, for the most part, do not belong to the field of pure literature, and, further, have long ceased, almost altogether, to be read. His reputation is really due to the interest of his personality, and that is known chiefly by the most famous of all biographies, the life of him by James Boswell. Boswell was a Scotch gentleman, born in 1740, the son of a judge who was also laird of the estate of Auchinleck in Ayrshire, near the English border. James Boswell studied law, but was never very serious in any regular activity. Early in life he became possessed by an extreme boyish-romantic admiration for Johnson's works and through them for their author, and at last in 1763 (only twenty years before Johnson's death) secured an introduction to him. Boswell took pains that acquaintance should soon ripen into intimacy, though it was not until nine years later that he could be much in Johnson's company.

Indeed it appears from Boswell's account that they were personally together, all told, only during a total of one hundred and eighty days at intermittent intervals, plus a hundred more continuously when in 1773 they went on a tour to the Hebrides. Boswell, however, made a point of recording in minute detail, sometimes on the spot, all of Johnson's significant conversation to which he listened, and of collecting with the greatest care his letters and all possible information about him. He is the founder and still the most thorough representative of the modern method of accurate biographical writing. After Johnson's death he continued his researches, refusing to be hurried or disturbed by several hasty lives of his subject brought out by other persons, with the result that when his work appeared in 1791 it at once assumed the position among biographies which it has ever since occupied.

Boswell lived only four years longer, sinking more and more under the habit of drunkenness which had marred the greater part of his life. Boswell's character, though absolutely different from Johnson's, was perhaps as unusual a mixture. He was shallow, extremely vain, often childishly foolish, and disagreeably jealous of Johnson's other friends. Only extreme lack of personal dignity can account for the servility of his attitude toward Johnson and his acceptance of the countless rebuffs from his idol some of which he himself records and which would have driven any other man away in indignation. None the less he was good-hearted, and the other members of Johnson's circle, though they were often vexed by him and admitted him to 'The Club' only under virtual compulsion by Johnson, seem on the whole, in the upshot, to have liked him.

Certainly it is only by force of real genius of some sort, never by a mere lucky chance, that a man achieves the acknowledged masterpiece in any line of work. Boswell's genius, one is tempted to say, consists partly of his absorption in the worship of his hero; more largely, no doubt, in his inexhaustible devotion and patience. If the bulk of his book becomes tiresome to some readers, it nevertheless gives a picture of unrivalled fulness and life-likeness. Boswell aimed to be absolutely complete and truthful. When the excellent Hannah More entreated him to touch lightly on the less agreeable traits of his subject he replied flatly that he would not cut off Johnson's claws, nor make a tiger a cat to please anybody.

Edward Gibbon

The latter part of the eighteenth century produced not only the greatest of all biographies but also the history which can perhaps best claim the same rank, Edward Gibbon's 'Decline and Fall of the Roman Empire.' History of the modern sort, aiming at minute scientific accuracy through wide collection of materials and painstaking research, and at vivid reproduction of the life, situations and characters of the past, had scarcely existed anywhere, before Gibbon, since classical times.

The medieval chroniclers were mostly mere annalists, brief mechanical recorders of external events, and the few more philosophic historians of the sixteenth and seventeenth centuries do not attain the first rank. The way was partly prepared for Gibbon by two Scottish historians, his early contemporaries, the philosopher David Hume and the clergyman William Robertson, but they have little of his scientific conscientiousness. Gibbon, the son of a country gentleman in Surrey, was born in 1737. From Westminster School he passed at the age of fifteen to Oxford.

Ill-health and the wretched state of instruction at the university made his residence there, according to his own exaggerated account, largely unprofitable, but he remained for little more than a year; for, continuing the reading of theological works, in which he had become interested as a child, he was converted to Catholicism, and was hurried by his father to the care of a Protestant pastor in Lausanne, Switzerland. The pastor reconverted him in a year, but both conversions were merely intellectual, since Gibbon was of all men the most incapable of spiritual emotion. Later in life he became a philosophic sceptic. In Lausanne he fell in love with the girl who later actually married M. Necker, minister of finance under Louis XVI, and became the mother of the famous Mme. de Stael; but to Gibbon's father a foreign marriage was as impossible as a foreign religion, and the son, again, obediently yielded. He never again entertained the thought of marriage.

In his five years of study at Lausanne he worked

diligently and laid the broad foundation of the knowledge of Latin and Greek which was to be indispensable for his great work. His mature life, spent mostly on his ancestral estate in England and at a villa which he acquired in Lausanne, was as externally uneventful as that of most men of letters. He was for several years a captain in the English militia and later a member of Parliament and one of the Lords of Trade; all which positions were of course practically useful to him as a historian. He wrote a brief and interesting autobiography, which helps to reveal him as sincere and good-hearted, though cold and somewhat self-conceited, a rather formal man not of a large nature. He died in 1794.

His style possesses much of the same virtues and limitations as his substance. He has left it on record that he composed each paragraph mentally as a whole before committing any part of it to paper, balancing and reshaping until it fully satisfied his sense of unity and rhythm. Something of formality and ponderousness quickly becomes evident in his style, together with a rather mannered use of potential instead of direct indicative verb forms; how his style compares with Johnson's and how far it should be called pseudo-classical, are interesting questions to consider. One appreciative description of it may be quoted: 'The language of Gibbon never flags; he walks forever as to the clash of arms, under an imperial banner; a military music animates his magnificent descriptions of battles, of sieges, of panoramic scenes of antique civilization.' Burke was born in Dublin in 1729 of mixed English and Irish parentage. Both strains contributed very important elements to his nature.

As English we recognize his indomitable perseverance, practical good sense, and devotion to established principles;

as largely Irish his spontaneous enthusiasm, ardent emotion, and disinterested idealism. Always brilliant, in his earlier years he was also desultory and somewhat lawless. From Trinity College in Dublin he crossed over to London and studied law, which he soon abandoned. In 1756 he began his career as an author with 'A Vindication of Natural Society,' a skilful satire on the philosophic writings which Bolingbroke (the friend of Swift and Pope) had put forth after his political fall and which, while nominally expressing the deistic principles of natural religion, were virtually antagonistic to all religious faith.

Burke's 'Philosophical Inquiry into the Origin of our Ideas on the Sublime and Beautiful,' published the same year, and next in time after Dryden among important English treatises on esthetics, has lost all authority with the coming of the modern science of psychology, but it is at least sincere and interesting. Burke now formed his connection with Johnson and his circle. An unsatisfactory period as secretary to an official in Ireland proved prolog to the gift of a seat in Parliament from a Whig lord, and thus at the age of thirty-six Burke at last entered on the public life which was his proper sphere of action. Throughout his life, however, he continued to be involved in large debts and financial difficulties, the pressure of which on a less buoyant spirit would have been a very serious handicap. His most important discussions of American affairs are the 'Speech on American Taxation' (1774), the 'Speech on Conciliation with America' (1775), both delivered in Parliament while the controversy was bitter but before war had actually broken out, and 'A Letter to the Sheriffs of Bristol' (1777). Burke's plea was that although England had a theoretical constitutional right to tax the colonies it was impracticable to do so against their will, that the attempt was therefore useless and must lead to disaster, that measures of conciliation instead of force should be employed, and that the attempt to override the liberties of Englishmen in America, those liberties on which the greatness of England was founded, would establish a dangerous precedent for a similar course of action in the mother country itself.

The Romantic Movement

The reaction which was bound to accompany the triumph of Pseudo-classicism, as a reassertion of those instincts in human nature which Pseudo-classicism disregarded, took the form of a distinct Romantic Revival. Beginning just about as Pope's reputation was reaching its climax, and gathering momentum throughout the greater part of the eighteenth century, this movement eventually gained a predominance as complete as that which Pseudo-classicism had enjoyed, and became the chief force, not only in England but in all Western Europe, in the literature of the whole nineteenth century. The impulse was not confined to literature, but permeated all the life of the time. In the sphere of religion, especially, the second decade of the eighteenth century saw the awakening of the English church from lethargy by the great revival of John and Charles Wesley, whence, quite contrary to their original intention, sprang the Methodist denomination. In political life the French Revolution was a result of the same set of influences.

Romanticism showed itself partly in the supremacy of the Sentimental Comedy and in the great share taken by Sentimentalism in the development of the novel, of both of which we shall speak hereafter; but its fullest and most steadily progressive manifestation was in non-dramatic poetry.

Sailant Feature

Its main traits as they appear in the eighteenth century are as clearly marked as the contrasting ones of Pseudo-classicism, and we can enumerate them distinctly, though it must of course be understood that they appear in different authors in very different degrees and combinations.

1. There is a strong reassertion of the value of emotion, imagination, and enthusiasm. This naturally involves some reaction against the pseudo-classic, and also the true classic, regard for finished form.
2. There is, among the Romanticists, a general breaking away not only from the definite pseudo-classical principles, but from the whole idea of submission to fixed authority. Instead there is a spirit of independence and revolt, an insistence on the value of originality and the right of the individual to express himself in his own fashion.
3. The same passionate appreciation extends with the Romanticists to all full and rich beauty and everything grand and heroic.
4. There is a renewal of genuine appreciation and love for external Nature, not least for her large and great aspects, such as mountains and the sea. The contrast between the pseudo-classical and the romantic attitude in this respect is clearly illustrated, as has often been pointed out, by the difference between the impressions recorded by Addison and by the poet Gray in the presence of the Alps. Addison, discussing what he saw in Switzerland, gives most of his attention to the people and politics. One journey he describes as 'very troublesome,' adding: 'You can't imagine how I am pleased with the sight of a plain.' In the mountains he is conscious chiefly

of difficulty and danger, and the nearest approach to admiration which he indicates is 'an agreeable kind of horror.' Gray, on the other hand, speaks of the Grande Chartreuse as 'one of the most solemn, the most romantic, and the most astonishing scenes.... I do not remember to have gone ten paces without an exclamation that there was no restraining. Not a precipice, not a torrent, nor a cliff, but is pregnant with religion and poetry.'

5. This is naturally connected also with a love for the remote, the strange, and the unusual, for mystery, the supernatural, and everything that creates wonder. Especially, there is a great revival of interest in the Middle Ages, whose life seemed to the men of the eighteenth century, and indeed to a large extent really was, picturesque and by comparison varied and adventurous. In the eighteenth century this particular revival was called 'Gothic,' a name which the Pseudo-classicists, using it as a synonym for 'barbarous,' had applied to the Middle Ages and all their works, on the mistaken supposition that all the barbarians who overthrew the Roman Empire and founded the medieval states were Goths.
6. In contrast to the pseudo-classical preference for abstractions, there is, among the Romanticists, a devotion to concrete things, the details of Nature and of life. In expression, of course, this brings about a return to specific words and phraseology, in the desire to picture objects clearly and fully.
7. There is an increasing democratic feeling, a breaking away from the interest in artificial social life and a conviction that every human being is worthy of respect. Hence sprang the sentiment of universal

brotherhood and the interest in universal freedom, which finally extended even to the negroes and resulted in the abolition of slavery. But from the beginning there was a reawakening of interest in the life of the common people—an impulse which is not inconsistent with the love of the remote and unusual, but rather means the discovery of a neglected world of novelty at the very door of the educated and literary classes.

8. In poetic form, though the Romanticists did not completely abandon the pentameter couplet for a hundred years, they did energetically renounce any exclusive allegiance to it and returned to many other meters. Milton was one of their chief masters, and his example led to the revival of blank verse and of the octo-syllabic couplet. There was considerable use also of the Spenserian stanza, and development of a great variety of lyric stanza forms, though not in the prodigal profusion of the Elizabethan and Jacobean period.

James Thomson

At the age of twenty-five, Thomson, like many of his countrymen during his century and the previous one, came fortune-hunting to London, and the next year, 1726, while Pope was issuing his translation of 'The Odyssey,' he published a blank-verse poem of several hundred lines on 'Winter.' Its genuine though imperfect appreciation and description of Nature as she appears on the broad sweeps of the Scottish moors, combined with its novelty, gave it great success, and Thomson went on to write also of Summer, Spring and Autumn, publishing the whole work as 'The Seasons' in 1730. He was rewarded by the gift of sinecure offices from the government and did some further writing, including, probably, the patriotic lyric, 'Rule, Britannia,' and also pseudo-classical tragedies; but his only other poem of much importance is 'The Castle of Indolence' (a subject appropriate to his own good-natured, easy-going disposition), which appeared just before his death, in 1748. In it he employs Spenser's stanza, with real skill, but in a half-jesting fashion which the later eighteenth-century Romanticists also seem to have thought necessary when they adopted it, apparently as a sort of apology for reviving so old-fashioned a form.

'The Seasons' was received with enthusiasm not only in England but in France and Germany, and it gave an impulse for the writing of descriptive poetry which lasted for a generation; but Thomson's romantic achievement, though important, is tentative and incomplete, like that of all beginners. He described Nature from full and sympathetic first-hand observation, but there is still a certain stiffness about his manner, very different from the intimate and confident familiarity and power of spiritual interpretation which characterizes the great poets of three generations later. Indeed, the attempt to write several thousand lines of pure descriptive poetry was in itself ill-judged, since as the German critic Lessing later pointed out, poetry is the natural medium not for description but for narration; and Thomson himself virtually admitted this in part by resorting to long dedications and narrative episodes to fill out his scheme. Further, romantic as he was in spirit, he was not able to free himself from the pseudo-classical mannerisms; every page of his poem abounds with the old lifeless phraseology—'the finny tribes' for 'the fishes,' 'the vapoury whiteness' for 'the snow' or 'the hard-won treasures of the year' for 'the crops.' His blank verse, too, is comparatively clumsy—padded with unnecessary words and the lines largely end-stopped.

William Collins

There is marked progress in romantic feeling and power of expression as we pass from Thomson to his disciple, the frail lyric poet, William Collins. Collins, born at Chichester, was an undergraduate at Oxford when he published 'Persian Eclogues' in rimed couplets to which the warm feeling and free metrical treatment give much of romantic effect. In London three years later (1746) Collins put forth his significant work in a little volume of 'Odes.' Discouraged by lack of appreciation, always abnormally high-strung and neurasthenic, he gradually lapsed into insanity, and died at the age of thirty-seven. Collins' poems show most of the romantic traits and their impetuous emotion often expresses itself in the form of the false Pindaric ode which Cowley had introduced. His 'Ode on the Popular Superstitions of the Highlands,' further, was one of the earliest pieces of modern literature to return for inspiration to the store of medieval supernaturalism, in this case to Celtic supernaturalism. But Collins has also an exquisiteness of feeling which makes others of his pieces perfect examples of the true classical style. The two poems in 'Horatian' ode forms, that is in regular short stanzas, the 'Ode Written in the Year 1746' and the 'Ode to Evening' (unrimed), are particularly fine. With all this, Collins too was not able to escape altogether from pseudo-classicism. His subjects are often abstract—'The Passions,' 'Liberty,' and the like; his characters, too, in almost all his poems, are merely the old abstract personifications, Fear, Fancy, Spring, and many others; and his phraseology is often largely in the pseudo-classical fashion. His work illustrates, therefore, in an interesting way the conflict of poetic forces in his time and the influence of environment on a poet's mind. The true classic instinct and the romanticism are both his own; the pseudo-classicism belongs to the period.

Oliver Goldsmith

Next in order among the romantic poets after Gray, and more thoroughly romantic than Gray, was Oliver Goldsmith, though, with characteristic lack of the power of self-criticism, he supposed himself to be a loyal follower of Johnson and therefore a member of the opposite camp. Goldsmith, as every one knows, is one of the most attractive and lovable figures in English literature. Like Burke, of mixed English and Irish ancestry, the son of a poor country curate of the English Church in Ireland, he was born in 1728.

Awkward, sensitive, and tender-hearted, he suffered greatly in childhood from the unkindness of his fellows. As a poor student at the University of Dublin he was not more happy, and his lack of application delayed the gaining of his degree until two years after the regular time. The same Celtic desultoriness characterized all the rest of his life, though it could not thwart his genius. Rejected as a candidate for the ministry, he devoted three years to the nominal study of medicine at the Universities of Edinburgh and Leyden (in Holland). Next he spent a year on a tramping trip through Europe, making his way by playing the flute and begging. Then, gravitating naturally to London, he earned his living by working successively for a druggist, for the novelist-printer Samuel Richardson, as a teacher in a boys' school, and as a hack writer. At last at the age of thirty-two he achieved success with a series of periodical essays later entitled 'The Citizen of the World,' in which he criticized European politics and society with skill and insight. Bishop Percy now introduced him to Johnson, who from this time watched over him and saved him from the worst results of his irresponsibility. He was one of the original members of 'The Club.' In 1764 occurred the well-known and characteristic incident of the sale of 'The Vicar of Wakefield.' Arrested for debt at his landlady's instance, Goldsmith sent for Johnson and showed him the manuscript of the book. Johnson took it to a publisher, and though without much expectation of success asked and received L60 for it. It was published two years later. Meanwhile in 1764 appeared Goldsmith's descriptive poem, 'The Traveler,' based on his own experiences in Europe. Six years later it was followed by 'The Deserted Village,' which was received with the great enthusiasm that it merited. Such high achievement in two of the main divisions of literature was in itself remarkable, especially as Goldsmith was obliged to the end of his life to spend much of his time in hack writing, but in the later years of his short life he turned also with almost as good results to the drama (comedy). We must stop here for the few words of general summary which are all that the eighteenth century drama need receive in a brief survey like the present one.

During the first half of the century, as we have seen, an occasional pseudo-classical tragedy was written, none of them of any greater excellence than Addison's 'Cato' and Johnson's 'Irene'. The second quarter of the century was largely given over to farces and burlesques, which absorbed the early literary activity of the novelist Henry Fielding, until their attacks on Walpole's government led to a severe licensing act, which suppressed them. But the most distinctive and predominant forms of the middle and latter half of the century were, first, the Sentimental Comedy, whose origin may be roughly assigned to Steele, and, second, the domestic melodrama, which grew out of it. In the Sentimental Comedy the elements of mirth and romance which are the legitimate bases of comedy were largely subordinated to exaggerated pathos, and in the domestic melodrama the experiences of insignificant persons of the middle class were presented for sympathetic consideration in the same falsetto fashion.

Percy, Macpherson, and Chatterton

The appearance of Thomson's 'Winter' in 1726 is commonly taken as conveniently marking the beginning of the Romantic Movement. Another of its conspicuous dates is 1765, the year of the publication of the 'Reliques [pronounced Relics] of Ancient English Poetry' of the enthusiastic antiquarian Thomas (later Bishop) Percy. Percy drew from many sources, of which the most important was a manuscript volume, in which an anonymous seventeenth century collector had copied a large number of old poems and which Percy rescued just in the nick of time, as the maids in the house of one of his friends were beginning to use it as kindling for the fires.

His own book consisted of something less than two hundred very miscellaneous poems, ranging in date from the fourteenth century to his own day. Its real importance, however, lies in the fact that it contained a number of the old popular ballads. Neither Percy himself nor any one else in his time understood the real nature of these ballads and their essential difference from other poetry, and Percy sometimes tampered with the text and even filled out gaps with stanzas of his own, whose sentimental style is ludicrously inconsistent with the primitive vigor of the originals. But his book, which attained great popularity, marks the beginning of the special study of the ballads and played an important part in the revival of interest in medieval life.

Still greater interest was aroused at the time by the Ossianic poems of James Macpherson. From 1760 to 1763 Macpherson, then a young Highland Scots schoolmaster, published in rapid succession certain fragments of Gaelic verse and certain more extended works in poetical English prose which, he asserted, were part of the originals, discovered by himself, and translations, of the poems of the legendary Scottish bard Ossian, of the third Christian century. These productions won him substantial material rewards in the shape of high political offices throughout the rest of his long life. About the genuineness of the compositions, however, a violent controversy at once arose, and Dr. Johnson was one of the skeptics who vigorously denounced Macpherson as a shameless impostor.

The general conviction of scholars of the present day is that while Macpherson may have found some fragments of very ancient Gaelic verse in circulation among the Highlanders, he fabricated most of what he published. These works, however, 'Fingal' and the rest, certainly contributed to the Romantic Movement; and they are not only unique productions, but, in small quantities, still interesting. They can best be described as reflections of the misty scenes of Macpherson's native Highlands—vague impressionistic glimpses, succeeding one another in purposeless repetition, of bands of marching warriors whose weapons intermittently flash and clang through the fog, and of heroic women, white-armed and with flowing hair, exhorting the heroes to the combat or lamenting their fall. A very minor figure, but one of the most pathetic in the history of English literature, is that of Thomas Chatterton. While he was a boy in Bristol, Chatterton's imagination was possessed by the medieval buildings of the city, and when some old documents fell into his hands he formed the idea of composing similar works in both verse and prose and passing them off as medieval productions which he had discovered. To his imaginary author he gave the name of Thomas Rowley. Entirely successful in deceiving his fellow-townsmen, and filled with a great ambition, Chatterton went to London, where, failing to secure patronage, he committed suicide as the only resource against the begging to which his proud spirit could not submit. This was in 1770, and he was still only eighteen years old. Chatterton's work must be viewed under several aspects. His imitation of the medieval language was necessarily very imperfect and could mislead no one to-day; from this point of view the poems have no permanent significance. The moral side of his action need not be seriously weighed, as Chatterton never reached the age of responsibility and if he had lived would soon have passed from forgery to genuine work.

William Cowper

Equally pathetic is the figure of William Cowper, whose much longer life (1731-1800) and far larger literary production give him a more important actual place than can be claimed for Chatterton, though his natural ability was far less and his significance to-day is chiefly historical. Cowper's career, also, was largely frustrated by the same physical weaknesses which had ruined Collins, present in the later poet in still more distressing degree. Cowper is clearly a transition poet, sharing largely, in a very mild fashion, in some of the main romantic impulses, but largely pseudo-classical in his manner of thought and expression.

His life may be briefly summarized. Morbid timidity and equally morbid religious introspection, aggravated by disappointments in love, prevented him as a young man from accepting a very comfortable clerkship in the House of Lords and drove him into intermittent insanity, which closed more darkly about him in his later years. He lived the greater part of his mature life in the household of a Mrs. Unwin, a widow for whom he had a deep affection and whom only his mental affliction prevented him from marrying.

A long residence in the wretched village of Olney, where he forced himself to cooperate in all phases of religious work with the village clergyman, the stern enthusiast John Newton, produced their joint collection of 'Olney Hymns,' many of which deservedly remain among the most popular in our church song-books; but it inevitably increased Cowper's disorder.

Notably, after this he resigned himself to a perfectly simple life, occupied with the writing of poetry, the care of pets, gardening, and carpentry. The bulk of his work consists of long moralizing poems, prosy, prolix, often trivial, and to-day largely unreadable. Same of them are in the rimed couplet and others in blank verse. His blank-verse translation of Homer, published in 1791, is more notable, and 'Alexander Selkirk' and the humorous doggerel 'John Gilpin' are famous; but his most significant poems are a few lyrics and descriptive pieces in which he speaks out his deepest feelings with the utmost pathetic or tragic power.

In the expression of different moods of almost intolerable sadness 'On the Receipt of My Mother's Picture' and 'To Mary' (Mrs. Unwin) can scarcely be surpassed, and 'The Castaway' is final as the restrained utterance of morbid religious despair. Even in his long poems, in his minutely loving treatment of Nature he is the most direct precursor of Wordsworth, and he is one of the earliest outspoken opponents of slavery and cruelty to animals. How unsuited in all respects his delicate and sensitive nature was to the harsh experiences of actual life is suggested by Mrs. Browning with vehement sympathy in her poem, 'Cowper's Grave.'

William Blake

Still another utterly unworldly and frankly abnormal poet, though of a still different temperament, was William

Blake (1757-1827), who in many respects is one of the most extreme of all romanticists. Blake, the son of a London retail shopkeeper, received scarcely any book education, but at fourteen he was apprenticed to an engraver, who stimulated his imagination by setting him to work at making drawings in Westminster Abbey and other old churches. His training was completed by study at the Royal Academy of Arts, and for the rest of his life he supported himself, in poverty, with the aid of a devoted wife, by keeping a print-and-engraving shop. Among his own engravings the best known is the famous picture of Chaucer's Canterbury Pilgrims, which is not altogether free from the weird strangeness that distinguished most of his work in all lines. For in spite of his commonplace exterior life Blake was a thorough mystic to whom the angels and spirits that he beheld in trances were at least as real as the material world. When his younger brother died he declared that he saw the released soul mount through the ceiling, clapping its hands in joy. The bulk of his writing consists of a series of 'prophetic books' in verse and prose, works, in part, of genius, but of unbalanced genius, and virtually unintelligible. His lyric poems, some of them composed when he was no more than thirteen years old, are unlike anything else anywhere, and some of them are of the highest quality. Their controlling trait is childlikeness; for Blake remained all his life one of those children of whom is the Kingdom of Heaven. One of their commonest notes is that of childlike delight in the mysterious joy and beauty of the world, a delight sometimes touched, it is true, as in 'The Tiger,' with a maturer consciousness of the wonderful and terrible power behind all the beauty. Blake has intense indignation also for all cruelty and everything which he takes for cruelty, including the shutting up of children in school away from the happy life of out-of-doors. These are the chief sentiments of 'Songs of Innocence.' In 'Songs of Experience' the shadow of relentless fact falls somewhat more perceptibly across the page, though the prevailing ideas are the same. Blake's significant product is very small, but it deserves much greater reputation than it has actually attained. One characteristic external fact should be added.

Robert Burns

Burns, the oldest of the seven children of two sturdy Scotch peasants of the best type, was born in 1759 in Ayrshire, just beyond the northwest border of England. In spite of extreme poverty, the father joined with some of his neighbors in securing the services of a teacher for their children, and the household possessed a few good books, including Shakespeare and Pope, whose influence on the future poet was great. But the lot of the family was unusually hard. The father's health failed early and from childhocd the boys were obliged to do men's work in the field. Robert later declared, probably with some bitter exaggeration, that his life had combined 'the cheerless gloom of a hermit with the unceasing moil of a galley slave.' His genius, however, like his exuberant spirit, could not be crushed out. His mother had familiarized him from the beginning with the songs and ballads of which the country was full, and though he is said at first to have had so little ear for music that he could scarcely distinguish one tune from another, he soon began to compose songs (words) of his own as he followed the plough. In the greatness of his later success his debt to the current body of song and music should not be overlooked. He is only the last of a long succession of rural Scottish song-writers; he composed his own songs to accompany popular airs; and many of them are directly based on fragments of earlier songs. None the less his work rises immeasurably above all that had gone before it. The story of Burns' mature life is the pathetic one of a very vigorous nature in which genius, essential manliness, and good impulses struggled against and were finally overcome by violent passions, aggravated by the bitterness of poverty and repeated disappointments. His first effort, at eighteen, to better his condition, by the study of surveying at a neighboring town, resulted chiefly in throwing him into contact with bad companions; a venture in the business of flax-dressing ended in disaster; and the same ill-fortune attended the several successive attempts which he made at general farming. He became unfortunately embroiled also with the Church, which (the Presbyterian denomination) exercised a very strict control in Scotland. Compelled to do public penance for some of his offenses, his keen wit could not fail to be struck by the inconsistency between the rigid doctrines and the lives of some of the men who were proceeding against him; and he commemorated the feud in his series of overwhelming but painfully flippant satires.

Eighteenth Century the Novel

We have traced the literary production of the eighteenth century in many different forms, but it still remains to speak of one of the most important, the novel, which in the modern meaning of the word had its origin not long before 1750. Springing at that time into apparently sudden popularity, it replaced the drama as the predominant form of literature and has continued such ever since. The reasons are not hard to discover. The drama is naturally the most popular literary form in periods like the Elizabethan when the ability (or inclination) to read is not general, when men are dominated by the zest for action, and when cities have become sufficiently large to keep the theaters well filled. It is also the natural form in such a period as that of the Restoration, when literary life centers about a frivolous upper class who demand an easy and social form of entertainment.

But the condition is very different when, as in the eighteenth and still more in the nineteenth century, the habit of reading, and some recognition of its educating influence, had spread throughout almost all classes and throughout the country, creating a public far too large, too scattered, and too varied to gain access to the London and provincial theaters or to find all their needs supplied by a somewhat artificial literary form. The novel, on the other hand, gives a much fuller portrayal of life than does the drama, and allows the much more detailed analysis of characters and situations which the modern mind has come more and more to demand. The novel, which for our present purpose must be taken to include the romance, is, of course, only a particular and highly developed kind of long story, one of the latest members of the family of fiction, or the larger family of narrative, in prose and verse. The medieval romances, for example, included most of the elements of the novel, even, sometimes, psychological analysis; but the romances usually lacked the unity, the complex and careful structure, the thorough portrayal of character, and the serious attention to the real problems of life which in a general way distinguish the modern novel. Much the same is true of the Elizabethan 'novels,' which, besides, were generally short as well as of small intellectual and ethical caliber. During the Restoration period and a little later there began to appear several kinds of works which perhaps looked more definitely toward the later novel. Bunyan's religious allegories may likely enough have had a real influence on it, and there were a few English tales and romances of chivalry, and a few more realistic pieces of fiction. The habit of journal writing and the letters about London life sent by some persons in the city to their friends in the country should also be mentioned. The De Coverly papers in 'The Spectator' approach distinctly toward the novel. They give real presentation of both characters and setting (social life) and lack only connected treatment of the story (of Sir Roger). Defoe's fictions, picaresque tales of adventure, come still closer, but lack the deeper artistic and moral purpose and treatment suggested a moment ago.

Samuel Richardson

Born in 1689, in Derbyshire, Richardson early gave proof of his special endowments by delighting his childish companions with stories, and, a little later, by becoming the composer of the love letters of various young women. His command of language and an insistent tendency to moralize seemed to mark him out for the ministry, but his father was unable to pay for the necessary education and apprenticed him to a London printer. Possessed of great fidelity and all the quieter virtues, he rose steadily and became in time the prosperous head of his own printing house, a model citizen, and the father of a large family of children. Before he reached middle life he was a valetudinarian. His household gradually became a constant visiting place for a number of young ladies toward whom he adopted a fatherly attitude and who without knowing it were helping him to prepare for his artistic success. When he was not quite fifty his great reputation among his acquaintances as a letter-writer led some publishers to invite him to prepare a series of 'Familiar [that is, Friendly] Letters' as models for inexperienced young people. Complying, Richardson discovered the possibilities of the letter form as a means of telling stories, and hence proceeded to write his first novel, 'Pamela, or Virtue Rewarded,' which was published in 1740. It attained enormous success, which he followed up by writing his masterpiece, 'Clarissa Harlowe' (1747-8), and then 'The History of Sir Charles Grandison' (1753). He spent his latter years, as has been aptly said, in a sort of perpetual tea-party, surrounded by bevies of admiring ladies, and largely occupied with a vast feminine correspondence, chiefly concerning his novels. He died of apoplexy in 1761.

Henry Fielding

Fielding was born of an aristocratic family in Somersetshire in 1707. At Eton School and the University of Leyden (in Holland) he won distinction, but at the age of twenty he found himself, a vigorous young man with instincts for fine society, stranded in London without any tangible means of support. He turned to the drama and during the next dozen years produced many careless and ephemeral farces, burlesques, and light plays, which, however, were not without value as preparation for his novels. Meanwhile he had other activities—spent the money which his wife brought him at marriage in an extravagant experiment as gentleman-farmer; studied law and was admitted to the bar; and conducted various literary periodicals. His attacks on the government in his plays helped to produce the severe licensing act which put an end to his dramatic work and that of many other light playwrights. When Richardson's 'Pamela' appeared Fielding was disgusted with what seemed to him its hypocritical silliness, and in vigorous artistic indignation he proceeded to write 'The History of Joseph Andrews,' representing Joseph as the brother of Pamela and as a serving-man, honest, like her, in difficult circumstances. Beginning in a spirit of sheer burlesque, Fielding soon became interested in his characters, and in the actual result produced a rough but masterful picture of contemporary life. The coarse Parson Trulliber and the admirable Parson Adams are among the famous characters of fiction. But even in the later part of the book Fielding did not altogether abandon his ridicule of Richardson. He introduced among the characters the 'Squire B——' of 'Pamela,' only filling out the blank by calling him 'Squire Booby,' and taking pains to make him correspondingly ridiculous.

The chief characteristics of Fielding's nature and novels, mostly directly opposite or complementary to those of Richardson, are these:

1. His structure is that of the rambling picaresque story of adventure, not lacking, in his case, in definite progress toward a clearly-designed end, but admitting many digressions and many really irrelevant elements. The number of his characters, especially in 'Tom Jones,' is enormous. Indeed, the usual conception of a novel in his day, as the word 'History,' which was generally included in the title, indicates, was that of the complete story of the life of the hero or heroine, at least up to the time of marriage. It is virtually the old idea of the chronicle-history play. Fielding himself repeatedly speaks of his masterpiece as an 'epic.'
2. He is a broad realist, giving to his romantic actions a very prominent background of actual contemporary life. The portrayal is very illuminating; we learn from Fielding a great deal, almost everything, one is inclined to say, about conditions in both country and city in his time—about the state of travel, country inns, city jails, and many other things; but with his vigorous masculine nature he makes

abundant use of the coarser facts of life and character which a finer art avoids. However, he is extremely human and sympathetic; in view of their large and generous naturalness the defects of his character and works are at least pardonable.

3. His point of view is primarily humorous. He avowedly imitates the manner of Cervantes in 'Don Quixote' and repeatedly insists that he is writing a mock - epic. His very genuine and clear-sighted indignation at social abuses expresses itself through his omnipresent irony and satire, and however serious the situations he almost always keeps the ridiculous side in sight. He offends some modern readers by refusing to take his art in any aspect over-seriously; especially, he constantly asserts and exercises his 'right' to break off his story and chat quizzically about questions of art or conduct in a whole chapter at a time.
4. His knowledge of character, that of a generous-hearted man of the world, is sound but not subtile, and is deeper in the case of men than of women, especially in the case of men who resemble himself. Tom Jones is virtually Henry Fielding in his youth and is thoroughly lifelike, but Squire Allworthy, intended as an example of benevolent perfection, is no less of a pale abstraction than Sir Charles Grandison. The women, cleverly as their typical feminine traits are brought out, are really viewed only from without.

The Other Sentimentalists and Realists

Richardson and Fielding set in motion two currents, of sentimentalism and realism, respectively, which flowed vigorously in the novel during the next generation, and indeed (since they are of the essence of life), have continued, with various modifications, down to our own time. Of the succeeding realists the most important is Tobias Smollett, a Scottish ex-physician of violent and brutal nature, who began to produce his picaresque stories of adventure during the lifetime of Fielding. He made ferociously unqualified attacks on the statesmen of his day, and in spite of much power, the coarseness of his works renders them now almost unreadable. But he performed one definite service; in 'Roderick Random,' drawing on his early experiences as a ship's surgeon, he inaugurated the out-and-out sea story, that is the story which takes place not, like 'Robinson Crusoe,' in small part, but mainly, on board ship. Prominent, on the other hand, among the sentimentalists is Laurence Sterne, who, inappropriately enough, was a clergyman, the author of 'Tristram Shandy.' This book is quite unlike anything else ever written. Sterne published it in nine successive volumes during almost as many years, and he made a point of almost complete formlessness and every sort of whimsicality. The hero is not born until the third volume, the story mostly relates to other people and things, pages are left blank to be filled out by the reader—no grotesque device or sudden trick can be too fantastic for Sterne. But he has the gift of delicate pathos and humor, and certain episodes in the book are justly famous, such as the one where Uncle Toby carefully puts a fly out of the window, refusing to 'hurt a hair of its head,' on the ground that 'the world surely is wide enough to hold both thee and me.' The best of all the sentimental stories is Goldsmith's 'Vicar of Wakefield' (1766), of which we have already spoken.

Historical and 'Gothic' Romances

Stories which purported to reproduce the life of the

Past were not unknown in England in the seventeenth century, but the real beginning of the historical novel and romance belongs to the later part of the eighteenth century. The extravagance of romantic writers at that time, further, created a sort of subspecies called in its day and since the 'Gothic' romance. These 'Gothic' stories are nominally located in the Middle Ages, but their main object is not to give an accurate picture of medieval life, but to arouse terror in the reader, by means of a fantastic apparatus of gloomy castles, somber villains, distressed and sentimental heroines, and supernatural mystery. The form was inaugurated by Horace Walpole, the son of the former Prime Minister, who built near Twickenham (Pope's home) a pseudo-medieval house which he named Strawberry Hill, where he posed as a center of the medieval revival. Walpole's 'Castle of 'Otranto,' published in 1764, is an utterly absurd little story, but its novelty at the time, and the author's prestige, gave it a great vogue.

The really best 'Gothic' romances are the long ones written by Mrs. Ann Radcliffe in the last decade of the century, of which 'The Mysteries of Udolpho,' in particular, was popular for two generations. Mrs. Radcliffe's books overflow with sentimentality, but display real power, especially in imaginative description. Of the more truly historical romances the best were the 'Thaddeus of Warsaw' and 'Scottish Chiefs' of Miss Jane Porter, which appeared in the first decade of the nineteenth century.

Still another sort of novel was that which began to be written in the latter part of the century with the object of exposing some particular abuse in society. The first representatives of the class aimed, imitating the French sentimentalist Rousseau, to improve education, and in accordance with the sentimental Revolutionary misconception which held that all sin and sorrow result from the corruptions of civilization, often held up the primitive savage as a model of all the kindly virtues. The most important of the novels of purpose, however, were more thorough-going attacks on society composed by radical revolutionists, and the least forgotten is the 'Caleb Williams' of William Godwin (1794), which is intended to demonstrate that class-distinctions result in hopeless moral confusion and disaster.

The most permanent results of the latter part of the century in fiction were attained by three women who introduced and successively continued the novel which depicts, from the woman's point of view, with delicate satire, and at first in the hope of accomplishing some reform, or at least of showing the beauty of virtue and morality, the contemporary manners of well-to-do 'society.' The first of these authoresses was Miss Frances Burney, who later became Madame D'Arblay, but is generally referred to familiarly as Fanny Burney.

The unassuming daughter of a talented and much-esteemed musician, acquainted in her own home with many persons of distinction, such as Garrick and Sir Joshua Reynolds, and given from girlhood to the private writing of stories and of a since famous Diary, Miss Burney composed her 'Evelina' in leisure intervals during a number of years, and published it when she was twenty-five, in 1778. It recounts, in the Richardsonian letter form, the experiences of a country girl of good breeding and ideally fine character who is introduced into the life of London high society, is incidentally brought into contact with disagreeable people of various types, and soon achieves a great triumph by being acknowledged as the daughter of a repentant and wealthy man of fashion and by marrying an impossibly perfect young gentleman, also of great wealth. Structure and substance in 'Evelina' are alike somewhat amateurish in comparison with the novels of the next century; but it does manifest, together with some lack of knowledge of the real world, genuine understanding of the core, at least, of many sorts of character; it presents artificial society life with a light and pleasing touch; and it brought into the novel a welcome atmosphere of womanly purity and delicacy. 'Evelina' was received with great applause and Miss Burney wrote other books, but they are without importance.

Miss Edgeworth

Much more voluminous and varied was the work of Miss Burney's successor, Maria Edgeworth, who devoted a great part of her long life (1767-1849) to active benevolence and to attendance on her father, an eccentric and pedantic English gentleman who lived mostly on his estate in Ireland and who exercised the privilege of revising or otherwise meddling with most of her books. In the majority of her works Miss Edgeworth followed Miss Burney, writing of the experiences of young ladies in fashionable London life. In these novels her purpose was more obviously moral than Miss Burney's—she aimed to make clear the folly of frivolity and dissipation; and she also wrote moral tales for children which though they now seem old-fashioned were long and widely popular.

Since she had a first-hand knowledge of both Ireland and England, she laid the scenes of some of her books partly in both countries, thereby creating what was later called 'the international novel.' Her most distinctive achievement, however, was the introduction of the real Irishman (as distinct from the humorous caricature) into fiction. Scott testified that it was her example that suggested to him the similar portrayal of Scottish character and life.

Jane Austen

Much the greatest of this trio of authoresses is the last, Jane Austen, who perhaps belongs as much to the nineteenth century as the eighteenth. The daughter of a clergyman, she past an absolutely uneventful life of forty-two years (1775-1817) in various villages and towns in Southern England. She had finished her masterpiece, 'Pride and Prejudice,' at the age of twenty-two, but was unable for more than a dozen years to find a publisher for this and her other earlier works. When at last they were brought out she resumed her writing, but the total number of her novels is only six. Her field, also, is more limited than that of any other great English novelist; for she deliberately restricted herself, with excellent judgment, to portraying what she knew at first-hand, namely the life of the well-to-do classes of her own 'provincial' region. Moreover, her theme is always love; desirable marriage for themselves or their children seems to be the single object of almost all her characters; and she always conducts her heroine successfully to this goal. Her artistic achievement, like herself, is so well-bred and unobtrusive that a hasty reader may easily fail to appreciate it. Her understanding of character is almost perfect, her sense for structure and dramatic scenes (quiet ones) equally good, and her quiet and delightful humor and irony all-pervasive. Scott, with customary generosity, praised her 'power of rendering ordinary things and characters interesting from the truth of her portrayal,' in favorable contrast with his own facility in 'the Big Bow-Wow strain.'

Nevertheless the assertion of some present-day critics that she is the greatest of all English authoresses is certainly extravagant. Her novels, though masterly in their own field and style, do not have the fulness of description or the elaboration of action which add beauty and power to most later ones, and her lack of a sense for the greater issues of life denies her legitimate comparison with such a writer as George Eliot.

8

Later Eighteenth Century Literature

It is pertinent to note that the later eighteenth century there had been some periodicals devoted to literary criticism, but they were mere unauthoritative booksellers' organs, and it was left for the new reviews to inaugurate literary journalism of the modern serious type. 'The Edinburgh Review,' suggested and first conducted, in 1802, by the witty clergyman and reformer Sydney Smith, passed at once to the hands of Francis (later Lord) Jeffrey, a Scots lawyer who continued to edit it for nearly thirty years. Its politics were strongly liberal, and to oppose it the Tory '*Quarterly Review*' was founded in 1808, under the editorship of the satirist William Gifford and with the cooperation of Sir Walter Scott, who withdrew for the purpose from his connection with the 'Edinburgh.' These reviews were followed by other high-class periodicals, such as 'Blackwood's Magazine,' and most of the group have maintained their importance to till date

Samuel Taylor Coleridge

Born in Devonshire in 1772, the youngest of the many children of a self-made clergyman and schoolmaster, he was a precocious and abnormal child, then as always a fantastic dreamer, despised by other boys and unable to mingle with them. After the death of his father he was sent to Christ's Hospital, the 'Blue-Coat' charity school in London, where he spent nine lonely years in the manner briefly described in an essay of Charles Lamb, where Coleridge appears under a thin disguise.

The very strict discipline was no doubt of much value in giving firmness and definite direction to his irregular nature, and the range of his studies, both in literature and in other fields, was very wide. Through the aid of scholarships and of contributions from his brothers he entered Cambridge in 1791, just after Wordsworth had left the University; but here his most striking exploit was a brief escapade of running away and enlisting in a cavalry troop. Meeting Southey, then a student at Oxford, he drew him into a plan for a 'Pantisocracy' (a society where all should be equal), a community of twelve young couples to be founded in some 'delightful part of the new back settlements' of America on the principles of communistic cooperation in all lines, broad mental culture, and complete freedom of opinion.

Naturally, this plan never past beyond the dream stage. Coleridge left the University in 1794 without a degree, tormented by a disappointment in love. He had already begun to publish poetry and newspaper prose, and he now attempted lecturing. He and Southey married two sisters, whom Byron in a later attack on Southey somewhat inaccurately described as 'milliners of Bath'; and Coleridge settled near Bristol. After characteristically varied and unsuccessful efforts at conducting a periodical, newspaper writing, and preaching as a Unitarian (a creed which was then considered by most Englishmen disreputable and which Coleridge later abandoned), he moved with his wife in 1797 to Nether Stowey in Somersetshire. Expressly in order to be near him, Wordsworth and his sister Dorothy soon leased the neighboring manor-house of Alfoxden, and there followed the memorable year of intellectual and emotional stimulus when Coleridge's genius suddenly expanded into short-lived but wonderful activity and he wrote most of his few great poems, *'The Ancient Mariner,' 'Kubla Khan,'* and the First Part of *'Christabel.'* 'The Ancient Mariner' was planned by Coleridge and Wordsworth on one of their frequent rambles, and was to have been written in collaboration; but as it proceeded, Wordsworth found his manner so different from that of Coleridge that he withdrew altogether from the undertaking. The final result of the incident, however, was the publication in 1798 of 'Lyrical Ballads,' which included of Coleridge's work only this one poem, but of Wordsworth's several of his most characteristic ones. Coleridge afterwards explained that the plan of the volume contemplated two complementary sorts of poems.

He was to present supernatural or romantic characters, yet investing them with human interest and semblance of truth; while Wordsworth was to add the charm of novelty to everyday things and to suggest their kinship to the supernatural, arousing readers from their accustomed blindness to the loveliness and wonders of the world around us. No better description could be given of the poetic spirit and the whole poetic work of the two men. Like some other epoch-marking books, 'Lyrical Ballads' attracted little attention. Shortly after its publication Coleridge and the Wordsworths sailed for Germany, where for the greater part of a year Coleridge worked hard, if irregularly, at the language, literature, and philosophy. As a poet Coleridge's first great distinction is that which we have already pointed out, namely that he gives wonderfully subtile and appealing expression to the Romantic sense for the strange and the supernatural, and indeed for all that the word 'Romance' connotes at the present day. He accomplishes this result partly through his power of suggesting the real unity of the inner and outer worlds, partly through his skill, resting in a large degree on vivid impressionistic description, in making strange scenes appear actual, in securing from the reader what he himself called 'that willing suspension of disbelief which constitutes poetic faith.' Almost every one has felt the weird charm of *'The Ancient Mariner,'* where all the unearthly story centers about a moral and religious idea, and where we are dazzled by a constant succession of such pictures as these: In the second place, Coleridge is one of the greatest English masters of exquisite verbal melody, with its tributary devices of alliteration and haunting onomatopoeia. In this respect especially his influence on subsequent English poetry has been incalculable.

The details of his method students should observe for themselves in their study of the poems, but one particular matter should be mentioned. In 'Christabel' and to a somewhat less degree in 'The Ancient Mariner' Coleridge departed as far as possible from eighteenth century tradition by greatly varying the number of syllables in the lines, while keeping a regular number of stresses. Though this practice, as we have seen, was customary in Old English poetry and in the popular ballads, it was supposed by Coleridge and his contemporaries to be a new discovery, and it proved highly suggestive to other romantic poets. From hearing 'Christabel' read (from manuscript) Scott caught the idea for the free-and-easy meter of his poetical romances. With a better body and will Coleridge might have been one of the supreme English poets; as it is, he has left a small number of very great poems and has proved one of the most powerful influences on later English poetry.

William Wordsworth (1770-1850)

Noted poet, William Wordsworth was born in 1770 in Cumberland, in the 'Lake Region,' which, with its bold and varied mountains as well as its group of charming lakes, is the most picturesque part of England proper. He had the benefit of all the available formal education, partly at home, partly at a 'grammar' school a few miles away, but his genius was formed chiefly by the influence of Nature, and, in a qualified degree, by that of the simple peasant people of the region. Already as a boy, though normal and active, he began to be sensitive to the Divine Power in Nature which in his mature years he was to express with deeper sympathy than any poet before him. Early left an orphan, at seventeen he was sent by his uncles to Cambridge University. Here also the things which most appealed to him were rather the new revelations of men and life than the formal studies, and indeed the torpid instruction of the time offered little to any thoughtful student. On leaving Cambridge he was uncertain as to his life-work. He said that he did not feel himself 'good enough' for the Church, he was not drawn toward law, and though he fancied that he had capacity for a military career, he felt that 'if he were ordered to the West Indies his talents would not save him from the yellow fever.'

At first, therefore, he spent nearly a year in London in apparent idleness, an intensely interested though detached spectator of the city life, but more especially absorbed in his mystical consciousness of its underlying current of spiritual being. After this he crossed to France to learn the language. The Revolution was then (1792) in its early stages, and in his 'Prelude' Wordsworth has left the finest existing statement of the exultant anticipations of a new world of social justice which the movement aroused in himself and other young

English liberals. When the Revolution past into the period of violent bloodshed he determined, with more enthusiasm than judgment, to put himself forward as a leader of the moderate Girondins. From the wholesale slaughter of this party a few months later he was saved through the stopping of his allowance by his more cautious uncles, which compelled him, after a year's absence, to return to England. Wordsworth's poetic inspiration, less fickle than that of Coleridge, continued with little abatement for a dozen years; but about 1815, as he himself states in his fine but pathetic poem 'Composed upon an Evening of Extraordinary Splendour,' it for the most part abandoned him.

He continued, however, to produce a great deal of verse, most of which his admirers would much prefer to have had unwritten. The plain Anglo-Saxon yeoman strain which was really the basis of his nature now asserted itself in the growing conservatism of ideas which marked the last forty years of his life. His early love of simplicity hardened into a rigid opposition not only to the materialistic modern industrial system but to all change—the Reform Bill, the reform of education, and in general all progressive political and social movements.

It was on this abandonment of his early liberal principles that Browning based his spirited lyric 'The Lost Leader.' During the first half or more of his mature life, until long after he had ceased to be a significant creative force, Wordsworth's poetry, for reasons which will shortly appear, had been met chiefly with ridicule or indifference, and he had been obliged to wait in patience while the slighter work first of Scott and then of Byron took the public by storm.

Little by little, however, he came to his own, and by

about 1830 he enjoyed with discerning readers that enthusiastic appreciation of which he is certain for all the future. The crowning mark of recognition came in 1843 when on the death of his friend Southey he was made Poet Laureate. The honor, however, had been so long delayed that it was largely barren. Ten years earlier his life had been darkened by the mental decay of his sister and the death of Coleridge; and other personal sorrows now came upon him. He died in 1850 at the age of eighty.

Wordsworth, as we have said, is the chief representative of some (especially one) of the most important principles in the Romantic Movement; but he is far more than a member of any movement; through his supreme poetic expression of some of the greatest spiritual ideals he belongs among the five or six greatest English poets. First, he is the profoundest interpreter of Nature in all poetry. His feeling for Nature has two aspects.

He is keenly sensitive, and in a more delicately discriminating way than any of his predecessors, to all the external beauty and glory of Nature, especially inanimate Nature—of mountains, woods and fields, streams and flowers, in all their infinitely varied aspects. A wonderfully joyous and intimate sympathy with them is one of his controlling impulses. But his feeling goes beyond the mere physical and emotional delight of Chaucer and the Elizabethans; for him Nature is a direct manifestation of the Divine Power, which seems to him to be everywhere immanent in her; and communion with her, the communion into which he enters as he walks and meditates among the mountains and moors, is to him communion with God.

He is literally in earnest even in his repeated assertion that from observation of Nature man may learn (doubtless by the proper attuning of his spirit) more of moral truth than from all the books and sages. To Wordsworth Nature is man's one great and sufficient teacher. It is for this reason that, unlike such poets as Keats and Tennyson, he so often views Nature in the large, giving us broad landscapes and sublime aspects. Of this mystical semi-pantheistic Nature-religion his 'Lines composed above Tintern Abbey' are the noblest expression in literature.

All this explains why Wordsworth considered his function as a poet a sacred thing and how his intensely moral temperament found complete satisfaction in his art. It explains also, in part, the limitation of his poetic genius. Nature indeed did not continue to be to him, as he himself says that it was in his boyhood, absolutely 'all in all'; but he always remained largely absorbed in the contemplation and interpretation of it and never manifested, except in a few comparatively short and exceptional poems, real narrative or dramatic power. The variety of Wordsworth's poetry deserves special mention; in addition to his short lyric and narrative poems of Nature and the spiritual life several kinds stand out distinctly. A very few poems, the noble 'Ode to Duty,' 'Laodamia,' and 'Dion,' are classical in inspiration and show the finely severe repression and finish of classic style. Among his many hundreds of sonnets is a very notable group inspired by the struggle of England against Napoleon. Wordsworth was the first English poet after Milton who used the sonnet powerfully and he proves himself a worthy successor of Milton.

The great bulk of his work, finally, is made up of his long poems in blank-verse. 'The Prelude,' written during the years 1799-1805, though not published until after his death, is the record of the development of his poet's mind, not an outwardly stirring poem, but a unique and invaluable piece of spiritual autobiography. Wordsworth intended to make this only an introduction to another work of enormous length which was to have presented his views of Man, Nature, and Society. Of this plan he completed two detached parts, namely the fragmentary 'Recluse' and 'The Excursion,' which latter contains some fine passages, but for the most part is uninspired. Wordsworth, more than any other great English poet, is a poet for mature and thoughtful appreciation; except for a very small part of his work many readers must gradually acquire the taste for him.

Robert Southey

Robert Southey (1774-1843), a voluminous writer of verse and prose who from his friendship with Wordsworth and Coleridge has been associated with them as third in what has been inaptly called 'The Lake School' of poets, was thought in his own day to be their equal; but time has relegated him to comparative obscurity. An insatiate reader and admirable man, he wrote partly from irrepressible instinct and partly to support his own family and at times, as we have seen, that of Coleridge. An ardent liberal in youth, he, more quickly than Wordsworth, lapsed into conservatism, whence resulted his appointment as Poet Laureate in 1813 and the unremitting hostility of Lord Byron.

His rather fantastic epics, composed with great facility and much real spirit, are almost forgotten; he is remembered chiefly by three or four short poems—'The Battle of Blenheim,' 'My days among the dead are past,' 'The Old Man's Comforts' (You are old, Father William,' wittily parodied by 'Lewis Carroll' in 'Alice in Wonderland')—and by his excellent short prose 'Life of Nelson.'

Walter Scott

Scott, is personally one of the most delightful figures in

English literature, and he is probably the most famous of all the Scotsmen who have ever lived. He was descended from an ancient Border fighting clan, some of whose pillaging heroes he was to celebrate in his poetry, but he himself was born, in 1771, in Edinburgh, the son of an attorney of a privileged, though not the highest, class. In spite of some serious sicknesses, one of which left him permanently lame, he was always a very active boy, more distinguished at school for play and fighting than for devotion to study. But his unconscious training for literature began very early; in his childhood his love of poetry was stimulated by his mother, and he always spent much time in roaming about the country and picking up old ballads and traditional lore.

Loyalty to his father led him to devote six years of hard work to the uncongenial study of the law, and at twenty he was admitted to the Edinburgh bar as an advocate. Though his geniality and high-spirited brilliancy made him a social favorite he never secured much professional practice; but after a few years he was appointed permanent Sheriff of Selkirk, a county a little to the south of Edinburgh, near the English Border.

Later, in 1806, he was also made one of the Principal Clerks of Session, a subordinate but responsible office with a handsome salary which entailed steady attendance and work at the metropolitan law court in Edinburgh during half of each year. His instinct for literary production was first stimulated by the German Romantic poets. In 1796 he translated Burger's fiery and melodramatic ballad 'Lenore,' and a little later wrote some vigorous though hasty ballads of his own. In 1802-1803 he published 'Minstrelsy of the Scottish Border,' a collection of Scottish ballads and songs, which he carefully annotated. He went on in 1805, when he was thirty-four, to his first original verse-romance, 'The

Lay of the Last Minstrel.' Carelessly constructed and written, this poem was nevertheless the most spirited reproduction of the life of feudal chivalry which the Romantic Movement had yet brought forth, and its popularity was immediate and enormous. Always writing with the greatest facility, though in brief hours snatched from his other occupations, Scott followed up 'The Lay' during the next ten years with the much superior 'Marmion,' 'The Lady of the Lake,' and other verse-romances, most of which greatly increased both his reputation and his income.

In 1813 he declined the offer of the Poet Laureateship, then considered a position of no great dignity for a successful man, but secured the appointment of Southey, who was his friend. In 1811 he moved from the comparatively modest country house which he had been occupying to the estate of Abbotsford, where he proceeded to fulfill his ambition of building a great mansion and making himself a sort of feudal chieftain. To this project he devoted for years a large part of the previously unprecedented profits from his writings.

For a dozen years before, it should be added, his inexhaustible energy had found further occupation in connection with a troop of horse which he had helped to organize on the threat of a French invasion and of which he acted as quartermaster, training in barracks, and at times drilling for hours before breakfast. The amount and variety of his literary work was much greater than is understood by most of his admirers today.

He contributed largely, in succession, to the 'Edinburgh' and 'Quarterly' reviews, and having become a secret partner in the printing firm of the Ballantyne brothers, two of his school friends, exerted himself not only in the affairs of the company but in vast editorial labors of his own, which included among other things voluminously annotated editions of Dryden and Swift. His productivity is the more astonishing because after his removal to Abbotsford he gave a great part of his time not only to his family but also to the entertainment of the throngs of visitors who pressed upon him in almost continuous crowds. The explanation is to be found partly in his phenomenally vigorous constitution, which enabled him to live and work with little sleep; though in the end he paid heavily for this indiscretion. Scott's long poems, the best of them, are the chief examples in English of dashing verse romances of adventure and love. They are hastily done, as we have said, and there is no attempt at subtilty of characterization or at any moral or philosophical meaning; nevertheless the reader's interest in the vigorous and picturesque action is maintained throughout at the highest pitch.

Furthermore, they contain much finely sympathetic description of Scottish scenery, impressionistic, but poured out with enthusiasm. Scott's numerous lyrics are similarly stirring or moving expressions of the primal emotions, and some of them are charmingly musical. The qualities of the novels, which represent the culmination of Romantic historical fiction, are much the same. Through his bold and active historical imagination Scott vivifies the past magnificently; without doubt, the great majority of English readers know English history chiefly through his works. His dramatic power, also, at its best, is superb; in his great scenes and crises he is masterly as narrator and describer. In the presentation of the characters there is often much of the same superficiality as in the poems, but there is much also of the highest skill.

The novels may be roughly divided into three classes: first those, like 'Ivanhoe,' whose scene is laid in the twelfth or thirteenth century; second those, like 'Kenilworth,' which are located in the fifteenth or sixteenth; and third, those belonging to England and Scotland of the seventeenth and eighteenth. In the earlier ones sheer romance predominates and the hero and heroine are likely to be more or less conventional paragons, respectively, of courage and tender charm; but in the later ones Scott largely portrays the life and people which he himself knew; and he knew them through and through. His Scottish characters in particular, often especially the secondary ones, are delightfully realistic portraits of a great variety of types. Mary Queen of Scots in 'The Abbot' and Caleb Balderstone in 'The Bride of Lammermoor' are equally convincing in their essential but very personal humanity. Descriptions of scenery are correspondingly fuller in the novels than in the poems and are equally useful for atmosphere and background.

Lord Byron (1788-1824)

Byron (George Gordon Byron) expresses mainly the spirit of individual revolt, revolt against all existing institutions and standards. This was largely a matter of his own personal temperament, but the influence of the time also had a share in it, the time when the apparent failure of the French Revolution had thrown the pronounced liberals back upon their own resources in bitter dissatisfaction with the existing state of society.

Byron was born in 1788. His father, the violent and worthless descendant of a line of violent and worthless nobles, was just then using up the money which the poet's mother had brought him, and soon abandoned her. She in turn was wildly passionate and uncontrolled, and in bringing up her son indulged alternately in fits of genuine tenderness and capricious outbursts of mad rage and unkindness. Byron suffered also from another serious handicap; he was born with deformed feet, so that throughout life he walked clumsily—a galling irritation to his sensitive pride. In childhood his poetic instincts were stimulated by summers spent among the scenery of his mother's native Scottish Highlands. At the age of ten, on the death of his great-uncle, he succeeded to the peerage as Lord Byron, but for many years he continued to be heavily in debt, partly because of lavish extravagance, which was one expression of his inherited reckless wilfulness. Throughout his life he was obliged to make the most heroic efforts to keep in check another inherited tendency, to corpulence; he generally restricted his diet almost entirely to such meager fare as potatoes and soda-water, though he often broke out also into periods of unlimited self-indulgence.

From Harrow School he passed to Trinity College, Cambridge, where Macaulay and Tennyson were to be among his successors. Aspiring to be an athlete, he made himself respected as a fighter, despite his deformity, by his strength of arm, and he was always a powerful swimmer. Deliberately aiming also at the reputation of a debauchee, he lived wildly, though now as later probably not altogether so wickedly as he represented. After three years of irregular attendance at the University his rank secured him the degree of M. A., in 1808. He had already begun to publish verse, and when 'The Edinburgh Review' ridiculed his very juvenile 'Hours of Idleness' he added an attack on Jeffrey to a slashing criticism of contemporary poets which he had already written in rimed couplets (he always professed the highest admiration for Pope's poetry), and published the piece as 'English Bards and Scotch Reviewers.'

He was now settled at his inherited estate of Newstead Abbey (one of the religious foundations given to members of the nobility by Henry VIII when he confiscated them from the Church), and had made his appearance in his hereditary place in the House of Lords; but following his instinct for excitement and for doing the expensively conspicuous thing he next spent two years on a European tour, through Spain, Greece, and Turkey. In Greece he traveled, as was necessary, with a large native guard, and he allowed reports to become current that he passed through a succession of romantic and reckless adventures. The first literary result of his journey was the publication in 1812 of the first two cantos of 'Childe Harold's Pilgrimage.' This began as the record of the wanderings of Childe Harold, a dissipated young noble who was clearly intended to represent the author himself; but Byron soon dropped this figure as a useless impediment in the series of descriptions of Spain and Greece of which the first two cantos consist. He soon abandoned also the attempt to secure an archaic effect by the occasional use of Spenserian words, but he wrote throughout in Spenser's stanza, which he used with much power.

The public received the poem with the greatest enthusiasm; Byron summed up the case in his well-known comment: 'I awoke one morning and found myself famous.' In fact, 'Childe Harold' is the best of all Byron's works, though the third and fourth cantos, published some years later, and dealing with Belgium, the battle of Waterloo, and central Europe, are superior to the first two. Its excellence consists chiefly in the fact that while it is primarily a descriptive poem, its pictures, dramatically and finely vivid in themselves, are permeated with intense emotion and often serve only as introductions to passionate rhapsodies, so that the effect is largely lyrical. Though Byron always remained awkward in company he now became the idol of the world of fashion. He followed up his first literary success by publishing during the next four years his brief and vigorous metrical romances, most of them Eastern in setting, 'The Giaour' (pronounced by Byron 'Jower'), 'The Bride of Abydos,' 'The Corsair,' 'Lara,' 'The Siege of Corinth,' and 'Parisina.'

These were composed not only with remarkable facility but in the utmost haste, sometimes a whole poem in only a few days and sometimes in odds and ends of time snatched from social diversions.

As such, the results are only too clearly apparent; the meter is often slovenly, the narrative structure highly defective, and the characterization superficial or flatly inconsistent. In other respects the poems are thoroughly characteristic of their author. In each of them stands out one dominating figure, the hero, a desperate and terrible adventurer, characterized by Byron himself as possessing 'one virtue and a thousand crimes,' merciless and vindictive to his enemies, tremblingly obeyed by his followers, manifesting human tenderness only toward his mistress (a delicate romantic creature to whom he is utterly devoted in the approved romantic-sentimental fashion), and above all inscrutably enveloped in a cloud of pretentious romantic melancholy and mystery.

Like Childe Harold, this impossible and grandiose figure of many incarnations was well understood by every one to be meant for a picture of Byron himself, who thus posed for and received in full measure the horrified admiration of the public. But in spite of all this melodramatic clap-trap the romances, like 'Childe Harold,' are filled with the tremendous Byronic passion, which, as in 'Childe Harold,' lends great power alike to their narrative and their description. Byron now made a strangely ill-judged marriage with a Miss Milbanke, a woman of the fashionable world but of strict and perhaps even prudish moral principles. After a year she left him, and 'society,' with characteristic inconsistency, turned on him in a frenzy of superficial indignation.

He shortly (1816) fled from England, never to return, both his colossal vanity and his truer sensitive self stung by the injustice to fury against the hypocrisy and conventionalities of English life, which, in fact, he had always despised. He spent the following seven years as a wanderer over Italy and central Europe. He often lived scandalously; sometimes he was with the far more fine-spirited Shelley; and he sometimes furnished money to the Italians who were conducting the agitation against their tyrannical foreign governments.

Their defiant handling of Old Testament material and therefore of Christian theology was shocking to most respectable Englishmen and led Southey to characterize Byron as the founder of the 'Satanic School' of English poetry. More significant is the longest and chief of his satires, 'Don Juan,' [Footnote: Byron entirely anglicized the second word and pronounced it in two syllables—Ju-an.] on which he wrote intermittently for years as the mood took him. It is ostensibly the narrative of the adventures of a young Spaniard, but as a story it rambles on formlessly without approaching an end, and its real purpose is to serve as an utterly cynical indictment of mankind, the institutions of society, and accepted moral principles. Byron often points the cynicism by lapsing into brilliant doggerel, but his double nature appears in the occasional intermingling of tender and beautiful passages.

Byron's fiery spirit was rapidly burning itself out. In his uncontrolled zest for new sensations he finally tired of poetry, and in 1823 he accepted the invitation of the European committee in charge to become a leader of the Greek revolt against Turkish oppression. He sailed to the Greek camp at the malarial town of Missolonghi, where he showed qualities of leadership but died of fever after a few months, in 1824, before he had time to accomplish anything. It is hard to form a consistent judgment of so inconsistent a being as Byron. At the core of his nature there was certainly much genuine goodness—generosity, sympathy, and true feeling. However much we may discount his sacrifice of his life in the cause of a foreign people, his love of political freedom and his hatred of tyranny were thoroughly and passionately sincere, as is repeatedly evident in such poems as the sonnet on 'Chillon,' 'The Prisoner of Chillon,' and the 'Ode on Venice.' On the other hand his violent contempt for social and religious hypocrisy had as much of personal bitterness as of disinterested principle; and his persistent quest of notoriety, the absence of moderation in his attacks on religious and moral standards, his lack of self-control, and his indulgence in all the vices of the worser part of the titled and wealthy class require no comment. Whatever allowances charity may demand on the score of tainted heredity, his character was far too violent and too shallow to approach to greatness.

His poetry has also an elemental sweep and grandeur. The majesty of Nature, especially of the mountains and the ocean, stirs him to feeling which often results in superb stanzas, like the well-known ones at the end of 'Childe Harold' beginning 'Roll on, thou deep and dark blue Ocean, roll'! Too often, however, Byron's passion and facility of expression issue in bombast and crude rhetoric.

Percy Bysshe Shelley (1792-1832)

Shelley, born in 1792, belonged to a family of Sussex country gentry; a baronetcy bestowed on his grandfather during the poet's youth passed from his father after his own death to his descendants. Matthew Arnold has remarked that while most of the members of any aristocracy are naturally conservative, confirmed advocates of the system under which they enjoy great privileges, any one of them who happens to be endowed with radical ideas is likely to carry these to an extreme. In Shelley's case this general tendency was strengthened by reaction against the benighted Toryism of his father and by most of the experiences of his life from the very outset. At Eton his hatred of tyranny was fiercely aroused by the fagging system and the other brutalities of an English school; he broke into open revolt and became known as 'mad Shelley,' and his schoolfellows delighted in driving him into paroxysms of rage.

Already at Eton he read and accepted the doctrines of the French pre-Revolutionary philosophers and their English interpreter William Godwin. He came to believe not only that human nature is essentially good, but that if left to itself it can be implicitly trusted; that sin and misery are merely the results of the injustice springing from the institutions of society, chief of which are organized government, formal religion, law, and formal marriage; and that the one essential thing is to bring about a condition where these institutions can be abolished and where all men may be allowed to follow their own inclinations. The great advance which has been made since Shelley's time in the knowledge of history and the social sciences throws a pitiless light on the absurdity of this theory, showing that social institutions, terribly imperfect as they are, are by no means chiefly bad but rather represent the slow gains of thousands of years of painful progress; none the less the theory was bound to appeal irresistibly to such an impulsive and inexperienced idealism as that of Shelley.

It was really, of course, not so much against social

institutions themselves that Shelley revolted as against their abuses, which were still more flagrantly apparent in his time than in ours. When he repudiated Christianity and declared himself an atheist, what he actually had in mind was the perverted parody of religion mainly offered by the Church of his time; and, as some one has observed, when he pronounced for love without marriage it was because of the tragedies that he had seen in marriages without love. Much must be ascribed also to his sheer radicalism—the instinct to fly violently against whatever was conventionally accepted and violently to flaunt his adherence to whatever was banned. In 1810 Shelley entered Oxford, especially exasperated by parental interference with his first boyish love, and already the author of some crude prose-romances and poetry.

In the university he devoted his time chiefly to investigating subjects not included or permitted in the curriculum, especially chemistry; and after a few months, having written a pamphlet on 'The Necessity of Atheism' and sent it with conscientious zeal to the heads of the colleges, he was expelled. Still a few months later, being then nineteen years old, he allowed himself to be led, admittedly only through pity, into a marriage with a certain Harriet Westbrook, a frivolous and commonplace schoolgirl of sixteen. For the remaining ten years of his short life he, like Byron, was a wanderer, sometimes in straits for money, though always supported, after some time generously enough, by his father.

At first he tried the career of a professional agitator; going to Ireland he attempted to arouse the people against English tyranny by such devices as scattering copies of addresses from his window in Dublin or launching them in bottles in the Bristol Channel; but he was soon obliged to flee the country. Some of Shelley's shorter poems are purely poetic expressions of poetic emotion, but by far the greater part are documents (generally beautiful also as poetry) in his attack on existing customs and cruelties. Matthew Arnold, paraphrasing Joubert's description of Plato, has characterized him as 'a beautiful and ineffectual angel, beating in the void his luminous wings in vain.' This is largely true, but it overlooks the sound general basis and the definite actual results which belong to his work, as to that of every great idealist. On the artistic side the most conspicuous thing in his poetry is the ecstatic aspiration for Beauty and the magnificent embodiment of it. Shelley is the poetic disciple, but a thoroughly original disciple, of Coleridge. His esthetic passion is partly sensuous, and he often abandons himself to it with romantic unrestraint. His 'lyrical cry,' of which Matthew Arnold has spoken, is the demand, which will not be denied, for beauty that will satisfy his whole being. Sensations, indeed, he must always have, agreeable ones if possible, or in default of them, painful ones; this explains his occasional touches of repulsive morbidness.

But the repulsive strain is exceptional. No other poetry is crowded in the same way as his with pictures glorious and delicate in form, light, and color, or is more musically palpitating with the delight which they create. To Shelley as a follower of Plato, however, the beauty of the senses is only a manifestation of ideal Beauty, the spiritual force which appears in other forms as Intellect and Love; and Intellect and Love as well are equal objects of his unbounded devotion. Hence his sensuousness is touched with a real spiritual quality. In his poetic emotion, as in his social ambitions, Shelley is constantly yearning for the unattainable. One of our best critics has observed: 'He never shows his full power in dealing separately with intellectual or moral or physical beauty. His appropriate sphere is swift sensibility, the intersecting line between the sensuous and the intellectual or moral. Mere sensation is too literal for him, mere feeling too blind and dumb, mere thought too cold.... Wordsworth is always exulting in the fulness of Nature, Shelley is always chasing its falling stars.' (R.H. Hutton).

The contrast, here hinted at, between Shelley's view of Nature and that of Wordsworth, is extreme and entirely characteristic; the same is true, also, when we compare Shelley and Byron. Shelley's excitable sensuousness produces in him in the presence of Nature a very different attitude from that of Wordsworth's philosophic Christian-mysticism. For the sensuousness of Shelley gets the upper hand of his somewhat shadowy Platonism, and he creates out of Nature mainly an ethereal world of delicate and rapidly shifting sights and sounds and sensations. And while he is not unresponsive to the majestic greatness of Nature in her vast forms and vistas, he is never impelled, like Byron, to claim with them the kinship of a haughty elemental spirit.

No doubt, he wrote not like Shakespeare or Pope, for Londoners sitting in a theatre or a coffee-house, intelligence's vivid enough but definitely embodied in a definite society, able to fly, but also able to sit; he wrote, or rather he sang, to his own soul, to other spirit-sparks of the fire of Liberty scattered over the dark earth, to spirits in the air, to the boundless spirit of Nature or Freedom or Love.

John Keats (1795-1821)

John Keats was born in London in 1795, the first son of a livery-stable keeper. Romantic emotion and passionateness were among his chief traits from the start; but he was equally distinguished by a generous spirit, physical vigor At boarding-school, however, he turned from headstrong play to enthusiastic reading of Spenser and other great English and Latin poets and of dictionaries of Greek and Roman mythology and life. An orphan at fourteen, the mismanagement of his guardians kept him always in financial difficulties, and he was taken from school and apprenticed to a suburban surgeon.

After five years of study and hospital practice the call of poetry proved too strong, and he abandoned his profession to revel in Spenser, Shakespeare, and the Italian epic authors. He now became an enthusiastic disciple of the literary and political radical, Leigh Hunt, in whose home at Hampstead he spent much time. Hunt was a great poetic stimulus to Keats, but he is largely responsible for the flippant jauntiness and formlessness of Keats' earlier poetry, and the connection brought on Keats from the outset the relentless hostility of the literacy critics, who had dubbed Hunt and his friends 'The Cockney [i.e., Vulgar] School of Poetry.'

A few months later, in 1821, he died at Rome, at the age of twenty-five. His tombstone, in a neglected corner of the Protestant cemetery just outside the city wall, bears among other words those which in bitterness of spirit he himself had dictated: 'Here lies one whose name was writ in water.' But, in fact, not only had he created more great poetry than was ever achieved by any other man at so early an age, but probably no other influence was to prove so great as his on the poets of the next generation.

His poetry can be assessed best as follows:

1. Keats is, as we have implied, the great apostle of full though not unhealthy enjoyment of external Beauty, the beauty of the senses. He once said: 'I feel sure I should write, from the mere yearning

and tenderness I have for the beautiful, even if my night's labors should be burnt every morning and no eye ever rest upon them.' His use of beauty in his poetry is marked at first by passionate Romantic abandonment and always by lavish Romantic richness. This passion was partly stimulated in him by other poets, largely by the Italians, and especially by Spenser, from one of whose minor poems Keats chose the motto for his first volume: 'What more felicity can fall to creature than to enjoy delight with liberty?' Shelley's enthusiasm for Beauty, as we have seen, is somewhat similar to that of Keats. But for both Spenser and Shelley, in different fashions, external Beauty is only the outer garment of the Platonic spiritual Beauty, while to Keats in his poetry it is, in appearance at least, almost everything. He once exclaimed, even, 'Oh for a life of sensations rather than of thoughts!' Notable in his poetry is the absence of any moral purpose and of any interest in present-day life and character, particularly the absence of the democratic feeling which had figured so largely in most of his Romantic predecessors. These facts must not be over-emphasized, however. His famous final phrasing of the great poetic idea—'Beauty is truth, truth beauty'—itself shows consciousness of realities below the surface, and the inference which is sometimes hastily drawn that he was personally a fiberless dreamer is as far as possible from the truth. In fact he was always vigorous and normal, as well as sensitive; he was always devoted to outdoor life; and his very attractive letters, from which his nature can best be judged, are not only overflowing with unpretentious and cordial human feeling but testify that he was not really unaware of specific social and moral issues. Indeed, occasional passages in his poems indicate that he intended to deal with these issues in other poems when he should feel his powers adequately matured. Whether, had he lived, he would have proved capable of handling them significantly is one of the questions which must be left to conjecture, like the other question whether his power of style would have further developed.

2. Keats is one of the supreme masters of poetic expression, expression the most beautiful, apt, vivid, condensed, and imaginatively suggestive.

3. Keats never attained dramatic or narrative power or skill in the presentation of individual character. In place of these elements he has the lyric gift of rendering moods. Aside from ecstatic delight, these are mostly moods of pensiveness, languor, or romantic sadness, like the one so magically suggested in the 'Ode to a Nightingale,' of Ruth standing lonely and 'in tears amid the alien corn.'

4. Conspicuous in Keats is his spiritual kinship with the ancient Greeks. He assimilated with eager delight all the riches of the Greek imagination, even though he never learned the language and was dependent on the dull mediums of dictionaries and translations. It is not only that his recognition of the permanently significant and beautiful embodiment of the central facts of life in the Greek stories led him to select some of them as the subjects for several of his most important poems; but his whole feeling, notably his feeling for Nature, seems almost precisely that of the Greeks, especially, perhaps, of the earlier generations among whom their mythology took

> shape. To him also Nature appears alive with divinities. Walking through the woods he almost expects to catch glimpses of hamadryads peering from their trees, nymphs rising from the fountains, and startled fauns with shaggy skins and cloven feet scurrying away among the bushes.

Notably, in his later poetry, also, the deeper force of the Greek spirit led him from his early Romantic formlessness to the achievement of the most exquisite classical perfection of form and finish. His Romantic glow and emotion never fade or cool, but such poems as the Odes to the Nightingale and to a Grecian Urn, and the fragment of 'Hyperion,' are absolutely flawless and satisfying in structure and expression.

9

The Nineteenth Century English Literature

It is pertinent to note that in English different epochs are named after contemporary reigning queen/king. As such in the most common parlance, nineteenth century in English literature is known as Victorian Era.

Remarkably, the last completed period of English literature, almost coincident in extent with the reign of the queen whose name it bears (Victoria, queen 1837-1901), stands nearly beside The Elizabethan period in the significance and interest of its work. The Elizabethan literature to be sure, in its imaginative and spiritual enthusiasm, is the expression of a period more profoundly great than the Victorian; but the Victorian literature speaks for an age which witnessed incomparably greater changes than any that had gone before in all the conditions of life—material comforts, scientific knowledge, and, absolutely speaking, in intellectual and spiritual enlightenment.

Moreover, to twentieth century students the Victorian literature makes a specially strong appeal because it is in part the literature of our own time and its ideas and point of view are in large measure ours.

As major revolutionary development before the accession of Queen Victoria the 'industrial revolution,' the vast development of manufacturing made possible in the latter part of the eighteenth century by the introduction of coal and the steam engine, had rendered England the richest nation in the world, and the movement continued with steadily accelerating momentum throughout the period. Hand in hand with it went the increase of population from less than thirteen millions in England in 1825 to nearly three times as many at the end of the period.

The introduction of the steam railway and the steamship, at the beginning of the period, in place of the lumbering stagecoach and the sailing vessel, broke up the old stagnant and stationary habits of life and increased the amount of travel at least a thousand times. The discovery of the electric telegraph in 1844 brought almost every important part of Europe, and eventually of the world, nearer to every town dweller than the nearest county had been in the eighteenth century; and the development of the modern newspaper out of the few feeble sheets of 1825 (dailies and weeklies in London, only weeklies elsewhere), carried full accounts of the doings of the whole world, in place of long-delayed fragmentary rumors, to every door within a few hours.

No less striking was the progress in public health and the increase in human happiness due to the enormous advance in the sciences of medicine, surgery, and hygiene. Indeed these sciences in their modern form virtually began with the discovery of the facts of bacteriology about 1860, and the use of antiseptics fifteen years later, and not much earlier began the effective opposition to the frightful epidemics which had formerly been supposed to be dependent only on the will of Providence.

Political and social progress, though less astonishing, was substantial. In 1830 England, nominally a monarchy, was in reality a plutocracy of about a hundred thousand men—landed nobles, gentry, and wealthy merchants—whose privileges dated back to fifteenth century conditions. The first Reform Bill, of 1832, forced on Parliament by popular pressure, extended the right of voting to men of the 'middle class,' and the subsequent bills of 1867 and 1885 made it universal for men.

Meanwhile the House of Commons slowly asserted itself against the hereditary House of Lords, and thus England became perhaps the most truly democratic of the great nations of the world. At the beginning of the period the social condition of the great body of the population was extremely bad. Laborers in factories and mines and on farms were largely in a state of virtual though not nominal slavery, living, many of them, in unspeakable moral and physical conditions. Little by little improvement came, partly by the passage of laws, partly by the growth of trades-unions. The substitution in the middle of the century of free-trade for protection through the passage of the 'Corn-Laws' afforded much relief by lowering the price of food. Socialism, taking shape as a definite movement in the middle of the century, became one to be reckoned with before its close, though the majority of the more well-to-do classes failed to understand even then the growing necessity for far-reaching economic and social changes.

Humanitarian consciousness, however, gained greatly during the period. The middle and upper classes awoke to some extent to their duty to the poor, and sympathetic benevolent effort, both organized and informal, increased very largely in amount and intelligence. Popular education, too, which in 1830 had no connection with the State and was in every respect very incomplete, was developed and finally made compulsory as regards the rudiments. Still more permanently significant, perhaps, was the transformation of the former conceptions of the nature and meaning of the world and life, through the discoveries of science. Geology and astronomy now gradually compelled all thinking people to realize the unthinkable duration of the cosmic processes and the comparative littleness of our earth in the vast extent of the universe.

Absolutely revolutionary for almost all lines if thought was the gradual adoption by almost all thinkers of the theory of Evolution, which, partly formulated by Lamarck early in the century, received definite statement in 1859 in Charles Darwin's 'Origin of Species.' The great modification in the externals of religious belief thus brought about was confirmed also by the growth of the science of historical criticism. While all the new influences were manifesting themselves in Victorian literature they did not, of course, supersede the great general inherited tendencies.

This literature is in the main romantic. On the social side this should be evident; the Victorian social humanitarianism is merely the developed form of the eighteenth century romantic democratic impulse. On the esthetic side the romantic traits are also present, though not so aggressively as in the previous period; with romantic vigor the Victorian literature often combines exquisite classical finish; indeed, it is so eclectic and composite that all the definite older terms take on new and less sharply contrasting meanings when applied to it. So long a period naturally falls into sub-divisions; during its middle part in particular, progress and triumphant romanticism, not yet largely attacked by scientific scepticism, had created a prevailing atmosphere of somewhat passive sentiment and optimism both in society and in literature which has given to the adjective 'mid-Victorian' a very definite denotation.

The adjective and its period are commonly spoken of with contempt in our own day by those persons who pride themselves on their complete sophistication and superiority to all intellectual and emotional weakness.

Lord Macaulay

Thomas Babington Macaulay, represents in the fullest degree the Victorian vigor and delight in material progress, but is quite untouched by the Victorian spiritual striving. The descendant of Scottish ministers and English Quakers, Macaulay was born in 1800. His father was a tireless and devoted member of the group of London anti-slavery workers (Claphamites), and was Secretary of the company which conducted Sierra Leone (the African state for enfranchised negroes); he had also made a private fortune in African trade.

From his very babyhood the son displayed almost incredible intellectual precocity and power of memory. His voracious reading began at the age of three, when he 'for the most part lay on the rug before the fire, with his book on the floor, and a piece of bread-and-butter in his hand.' Once, in his fifth year, when a servant had spilled an urn of hot coffee over his legs, he replied to the distressed inquiries of the lady of the house, 'Thank you, madam, the agony is abated.' Least noteworthy among Macaulay's works are his poems, of which the 'Lays of Ancient Rome' are chief. Here his purpose is to embody his conception of the heroic historical ballads which must have been current among the early Romans as among the medieval English—to recreate these ballads for modern readers. For this sort of verse Macaulay's temperament was precisely adapted, and the 'Lays' present the simple characters, scenes, and ideals of the early Roman republican period with a sympathetic vividness and in stirring rhythms which give them an unlimited appeal to boys. None the less the 'Lays' really make nothing else so clear as that in the true sense of the word Macaulay was not at all a poet.

They show absolutely nothing of the finer feeling which adds so much, for example, to the descriptions in Scott's somewhat similar romances, and they are separated by all the breadth of the world from the realm of delicate sensation and imagination to which Spenser and Keats and all the genuine poets are native-born. But the power of Macaulay's prose works, as no critic has failed to note, rests on his genius as an orator. For oratory he was rarely endowed. The composition of a speech was for him a matter of a few hours; with almost preternatural mental activity he organized and sifted the material, commonly as he paced up and down his garden or his room; then, the whole ready, nearly verbatim, in his mind, he would pass to the House of Commons to hold his colleagues spell-bound during several hours of fervid eloquence.

Gladstone testified that the announcement of Macaulay's intention to speak was 'like a trumpet call to fill the benches.' The great qualities, then, of his essays and his 'History' are those which give success to the best sort of popular oratory—dramatic vividness and clearness, positiveness, and vigorous, movement and interest. He realizes characters and situations, on the external side, completely, and conveys his impression to his readers with scarcely any diminution of force. Of expository structure he is almost as great a master as Burke, though in his essays and 'History' the more concrete nature of his material makes him prevailingly a narrator. He sees and presents his subjects as wholes, enlivening them with realistic details and pictures, but keeping the subordinate parts subordinate and disposing of the less important events in rapid summaries.

Of clear and trenchant, though metallic, narrative and expository style he is a master. His sentences, whether long or short, are always lucid; he knows the full value of a short sentence suddenly snapped out after a prolonged period; and no other writer has ever made such' frequent and striking (though somewhat monotonous) use of deliberate oratorical balance of clauses and strong antithesis, or more illuminating use of vivid resumes.

The best of his essays, like those on the Earl of Chatham and on the two men who won India for England, Clive and Warren Hastings, are models of the comparatively brief comprehensive dissertation of the form employed by Johnson in his 'Lives of the Poets.' Macaulay, however, manifests the, defects even of his virtues. His positiveness, fascinating and effective as it is for an uncritical reader, carries with it extreme self-confidençe and dogmatism, which render him violently intolerant of any interpretations of characters and events except those that he has formed, and formed sometimes hastily and with prejudice. The very clearness and brilliancy of his style are often obtained at the expense of real truth; for the force of his sweeping statements and his balanced antitheses often requires much heightening or even distortion of the facts; in making each event and each character stand out in the plainest outline he has often stripped it of its background of qualifying circumstances.

These specific limitations, it will be evident, are outgrowths of his great underlying deficiency—the deficiency in spiritual feeling and insight. Macaulay is a masterly limner of the external side of life, but he is scarcely conscious of the interior world in which the finer spirits live and work out their destinies. Carlyle's description of his appearance is significant: 'I noticed the homely Norse features that you find everywhere in the Western Isles, and I thought to myself, "Well, any one can see that you are an honest, good sort of fellow, made out of oatmeal."

Macaulay's eminently clear, rapid, and practical mind comprehended fully and respected whatever could be seen and understood by the intellect; things of more subtle nature he generally disbelieved in or dismissed with contempt. In dealing with complex or subtle characters he cannot reveal the deeper spiritual motives from which their action sprang; and in his view of history he does not include the underlying and controlling spiritual forces. Macaulay was the most brilliant of those whom the Germans have named Philistines, the people for whom life consists of material things; specifically he was the representative of the great body of middle-class early-Victorian liberals, enthusiastically convinced that in the triumphs of the Liberal party, of democracy, and of mechanical invention, the millennium was being rapidly realized.

Macaulay wrote a fatal indictment of himself when in praising Bacon as the father of modern science he depreciated Plato, the idealist. Plato's philosophy, said Macaulay, 'began in words and ended in words,' and he added that 'an acre in Middlesex is better than a peerage in Utopia.' In his literary and personal essays, therefore, such as the famous ones on Milton and Bacon, which belong early in his career, all his immense reading did not suffice to produce sympathetic and sensitive judgments; there is often more pretentiousness of style than significance of interpretation. In later life he himself frankly expressed regret that he had ever written these essays.

Thomas Carlyle

Thomas Carlyle was born in 1795 in the village of Ecclefechan, just across the line from England, and not far from Burns' county of Ayr. His fierce, intolerant, melancholy, and inwardly sensitive spirit, together with his poverty, rendered him miserable throughout his school days, though he secured, through his father's sympathy, a sound elementary education. He tramped on foot the ninety miles from Ecclefechan to Edinburgh University, and remained there for four years; but among the subjects of study he cared only for mathematics, and he left at the age of seventeen without receiving a degree.

From this time for many years his life was a painful struggle, a struggle to earn his living, to make a place in the world, and to find himself in the midst of his spiritual doubts and the physical distress caused by lifelong dyspepsia and insomnia. For some years and in various places he taught school and received private pupils, for very meager wages, latterly in Edinburgh, where he also did literary hack-work.

He had planned at first to be a minister, but the unorthodoxy of his opinions rendered this impossible; and he also studied law only to abandon it. His first important work, a 'Life of Schiller,' was published in 1825, and in 1826 he was married to Miss Jane Welsh. She was a brilliant but quiet woman, of social station higher than his; for some years he had been acting as counselor in her reading and intellectual development.

No marriage in English Literature has been more discussed, a result, primarily, of the publication by Carlyle's friend and literary executor, the historian J. A. Froude, of Carlyle's autobiographical Reminiscences and Letters. After

Mrs. Carlyle's death Carlyle blamed himself bitterly for inconsiderateness toward her, and it is certain that his erratic and irritable temper, partly exasperated by long disappointment and by constant physical misery, that his peasant-bred lack of delicacy, and his absorption in his work, made a perpetual and vexatious strain on Mrs. Carlyle's forbearance throughout the forty years of their life together.

The evidence, however, does not show that the marriage was on the whole really unfortunate or indeed that it was not mainly a happy one. Carlyle also wrote the first of his chief works, 'Sartor Resartus,' for which, in 1833-4, he finally secured publication, in 'Fraser's Magazine,' to the astonishment and indignation of most of the readers. The title means 'The Tailor Retailored,' and the book purports to be an account of the life of a certain mysterious German, Professor Teufelsdrockh (pronounced Toyfelsdreck) and of a book of his on The Philosophy of Clothes. Of course this is allegorical, and Teufelsdrockh is really Carlyle, who, sheltering himself under the disguise, and accepting only editorial responsibility, is enabled to narrate his own spiritual struggles and to enunciate his deepest convictions, sometimes, when they are likely to offend his readers, with a pretense of disapproval.

The Clothes metaphor (borrowed from Swift) sets forth the central mystical or spiritual principle toward which German philosophy had helped Carlyle, the idea, namely, that all material things, including all the customs and forms of society, such as government and formalized religion, are merely the comparatively insignificant garments of the spiritual reality and the spiritual life on which men should center their attention. Even Time and Space and the whole material world are only the shadows of the true Reality, the spiritual Being that cannot perish. Carlyle has learned to repudiate, and he would have others repudiate, 'The Everlasting No,' the materialistic attitude of unfaith in God and the spiritual world, and he proclaims 'The Everlasting Yea,' wherein are affirmed, the significance of life as a means of developing character and the necessity of accepting life and its requirements with manly self-reliance and moral energy. 'Seek not Happiness,' Carlyle cries, 'but Blessedness. Love not pleasure; love God.' This is the central purport of the book.

In the second place and as a natural corollary Carlyle vigorously denounces, throughout, all shams and hypocrisies, the results of inert or dishonest adherence to outgrown ideas or customs. He attacks, for instance, all empty ostentation; war, as both foolish and wicked; and the existing condition of society with its terrible contrast between the rich and the poor. Again, he urges still a third of the doctrines which were to prove most characteristic of him, that Gospel of Work which had been proclaimed so forcibly, from different premises, five hundred years before by those other uncompromising Puritans, the authors of 'Piers Plowman.' In courageous work, Carlyle declares, work whether physical or mental, lies the way of salvation not only for pampered idlers but for sincere souls who are perplexed and wearied with over-much meditation on the mysteries of the universe, 'Be no, longer a Chaos,' he urges, 'but a World, or even Worldkin. Produce! Produce! Were it but the pitifullest infinitesimal, fraction of a Product, produce it, in God's name! 'Tis the utmost thou hast in thee: out with it, then. Up, up! Whatsoever thy hand findeth to do, do it with thy whole might. Work while it is called Today; for the Night cometh, wherein no man can work.'

Remarkably, of his most striking eccentricities is the

remarkable style which he deliberately invented for 'Sartor Resartus' and used thenceforth in all his writings (though not always in so extreme a form). Some of the specific peculiarities of this style are taken over, with exaggeration, from German usage; some are Biblical or other archaisms; others spring mainly from Carlyle's own amazing mind.

His purpose in employing, in the denunciation of shams and insincerities, a form itself so far removed from directness and simplicity was in part, evidently, to shock people into attention; but after all, the style expresses appropriately his genuine sense of the incoherence and irony of life, his belief that truth can be attained only by agonizing effort, and his contempt for intellectual and spiritual commonplaceness. Carlyle was a strange combination of greatness and narrowness. Like Macaulay, he was exasperatingly blind and bigoted in regard to the things in which he had no personal interest, though the spheres of their respective enthusiasms and antipathies were altogether different.

Carlyle viewed pleasure and merely esthetic art with the contempt of the Scottish Covenanting fanatics, refusing even to read poetry like that of Keats; and his insistence on moral meanings led him to equal intolerance of such story-tellers as Scott. In his hostility to the materialistic tendencies so often deduced from modern science he dismissed Darwin's 'Origin of Species' with the exclamation that it showed up the capricious stupidity of mankind and that he never could read a page of it or would waste the least thought upon it.

John Ruskin

It is pertinent to note that among the other great Victorian writers the most obvious disciple of Carlyle in his opposition to the materialism of modern life is John Ruskin. Ruskin's parents were Scotch, but his father, a man of artistic tastes, was established as a wine-merchant in London and had amassed a fortune before the boy's birth in 1819. The atmosphere of the household was sternly Puritan, and Ruskin was brought up under rigid discipline, especially by his mother, who gave him most of his early education.

He read, wrote, and drew precociously; his knowledge of the Bible, in which his mother's training was relentlessly thorough, of Scott, Pope, and Homer, dates from his fifth or sixth year. His career as a writer began immediately after he left the University. It falls naturally into two parts, the first of about twenty years, when he was concerned almost altogether with Art, chiefly Painting and Architecture; and the second somewhat longer, when he was intensely absorbed in the problems of society and strenuously working as a social reformer.

From the outset, however, he was actuated by an ardent didactic purpose; he wrote of Art in order to awake men's spiritual natures to a joyful delight in the Beautiful and thus to lead, them to God, its Author. The particular external direction of Ruskin's work in Art was given, as usual, more or less by accident. His own practice in water-color drawing led him as a mere youth to a devoted admiration for the landscape paintings of the contemporary artist J.M.W. Turner. Turner, a romantic revolutionist against the eighteenth century theory of the grand style, was then little appreciated; and when Ruskin left the University he began, with characteristic enthusiasm, an article on 'Modern Painters,' designed to demonstrate Turner's superiority to all possible rivals. Even the first part of this work expanded itself into a volume, published in 1843, when Ruskin was only twenty-four; and at intervals during the next seventeen years he issued four additional volumes, the result of prolonged study both of Nature and of almost all the great paintings in Europe.

The completed book is a discursive treatise, the various volumes necessarily written from more or less different view-points, on many of the main aspects, general and technical, of all art, literary as well as pictorial. For Ruskin held, and brilliantly demonstrated, that the underlying principles of all the Fine Arts are identical, and 'Modern Painters' contains some of the most famous and suggestive passages of general literary criticism ever written, for example those on The Pathetic Fallacy and The Grand Style.

Still further, to Ruskin morality and religion are inseparable from Art, so that he deals searchingly, if incidentally, with those subjects as well. Among his fundamental principles are the ideas that a beneficent God has created the world and its beauty directly for man's use and pleasure; that all true art and all true life are service of God and should be filled with a spirit of reverence; that art should reveal truth; and that really great and good art can spring only from noble natures and a sound national life.

In the intervals of this work Ruskin published others less comprehensive, two of which are of the first importance. *'The Seven Lamps of Architecture'* argues that great art, as the supreme expression of life, is the result of seven moral and religious principles, Sacrifice, Truth, Power, and the like. *'The Stones of Venice'* is an, impassioned exposition of the beauty of Venetian Gothic architecture, and here as always Ruskin expresses his vehement preference for the Gothic art of the Middle Ages as contrasted with the less original and as it seems to him less sincere style of the Renaissance. The publication of the last volume of *'Modern*

Painters' in 1860 roughly marks the end of Ruskin's first period. Several influences had by this time begun to sadden him. More than ten years before, with his usual filial meekness, he had obeyed his parents in marrying a lady who proved uncongenial and who after a few years was divorced from him.

Meanwhile acquaintance with Carlyle had combined with experience to convince him of the comparative ineffectualness of mere art-criticism as a social and religious force. He had come to feel with increasing indignation that the modern industrial system, the materialistic political economy founded on it, and the whole modern organization of society reduce the mass of men to a state of intellectual, social, and religious squalor and blindness, and that while they continue in this condition it is of little use to talk to them about Beauty.

He believed that some of the first steps in the necessary redemptive process must be the education of the poor and a return to what he conceived (certainly with much exaggeration) to have been the conditions of medieval labor, when each craftsman was not a mere machine but an intelligent and original artistic creator; but the underlying essential was to free industry from the spirit of selfish money-getting and permeate it with Christian sympathy and respect for man as man. The ugliness of modern life in its wretched city tenements and its hideous factories Ruskin would have utterly destroyed, substituting such a beautiful background (attractive homes and surroundings) as would help to develop spiritual beauty. With his customary vigor Ruskin proceeded henceforth to devote himself to the enunciation, and so far as possible the realization of these beliefs, first by delivering lectures and writing books. He was met, like all reformers, with a storm of protest, but most of his ideas gradually became the accepted principles of social theory.

Among his works dealing with these subjects may be named 'Unto This Last,' 'Munera Pulveris' (The Rewards of the Dust—an attack on materialistic political economy), and 'Fors Clavigera' (Fortune the Key-Bearer), the latter a series of letters to workingmen extending over many years. To 1865 belongs his most widely-read book, 'Sesame and Lilies,' three lectures on the spiritual meaning of great literature in contrast to materialism, the glory of womanhood, and the mysterious significance of life. All this activity had not caused Ruskin altogether to abandon the teaching of art to the members of the more well-to-do classes, and beginning in 1870 he held for three or four triennial terms the newly-established professorship of Art at Oxford and gave to it much hard labor. But this interest was now clearly secondary in his mind. Ruskin's temper was always romantically high-strung, excitable, and irritable. His intense moral fervor, his multifarious activities, and his disappointments were also constant strains on his nervous force. In 1872, further, he was rejected in marriage by a young girl for whom he had formed a deep attachment and who on her death-bed, three years later, refused, with strange cruelty, to see him. In 1878 his health temporarily failed, and a few years later he retired to the home, 'Brantwood,' at Coniston in the Lake Region, which he had bought on the death of his mother. Ruskin took his last breath in 1900.

Matthew Arnold

As a poet Arnold is generally admitted to rank among the Victorians next after Tennyson and Browning. The criticism, partly true, that he was not designed by Nature to be a poet but made himself one by hard work rests on his intensely, and at the outset coldly, intellectual and moral temperament. He himself, in modified Puritan spirit, defined poetry as a criticism of life; his mind was philosophic; and in his own verse, inspired by Greek poetry, by Goethe and Wordsworth, he realized his definition. In his work, therefore, delicate melody and sensuous beauty were at first much less conspicuous than a high moral sense, though after the first the elements of external beauty greatly developed, often to the finest effect. In form and spirit his poetry is one of the very best later reflections of that of Greece, dominated by thought, dignified, and polished with the utmost care. 'Sohrab and Rustum,' his most ambitious and greatest single poem, is a very close and admirable imitation of 'The Iliad.'

Yet, as the almost intolerable pathos of 'Sohrab and Rustum' witnesses, Arnold is not by any means deficient, any more than the Greek poets were, in emotion. He affords, in fact, a striking example of classical form and spirit united with the deep, self-conscious, meditative feeling of modern Romanticism. In substance Arnold's poetry is the expression of his long and tragic spiritual struggle. To him religion, understood as a reverent devotion to Divine things, was the most important element in life, and his love of pure truth was absolute; but he held that modern knowledge had entirely disproved the whole dogmatic and doctrinal scheme of historic Christianity and that a new spiritual revelation was necessary. To his Romantic nature, however, mere knowledge and mere modern science, which their followers were so confidently exalting, appeared by no means adequate to the purpose; rather they seemed to him largely futile, because they did not stimulate the emotions and so minister to the spiritual life.

Further, the restless stirrings of his age, beginning to

arouse itself from the social lethargy of centuries, appeared to him pitifully unintelligent and devoid of results. He found all modern life, as he says in 'The Scholar-Gypsy,' a 'strange disease,' in which men hurry wildly about in a mad activity which they mistake for achievement. In Romantic melancholy he looked wistfully back by contrast to periods when 'life was fresh and young' and could express itself vigorously and with no torturing introspection.

The exaggerated pessimism in this part of his outcry is explained by his own statement, that he lived in a transition time, when the old faith was (as he held) dead, and the new one (partly realized in our own generation) as yet 'powerless to be born.' Arnold's poetry, therefore, is to be viewed as largely the expression, monotonous but often poignantly beautiful, of a temporary mood of questioning protest. But if his conclusion is not positive, it is at least not weakly despairing.

Each man, he insists, should diligently preserve and guard in intellectual and moral integrity the fortress of his own soul, into which, when necessary, he can retire in serene and stoical resignation, determined to endure and to 'see life steadily and see it whole.' Unless the man himself proves traitor, the littlenesses of life are powerless to conquer him. In fact, the invincible courage of the thoroughly disciplined spirit in the midst of doubt and external discouragement has never been, more nobly expressed than by Arnold in such poems as 'Palladium' and 'The Last Word.' For the cure of these evils Arnold's proposed remedy was Culture, which he defined as a knowledge of the best that has been thought and done in the world and a desire to make the best ideas prevail. Evidently this Culture is not a mere knowledge of books, unrelated to the rest of life. It has indeed for its basis a very wide range of knowledge, acquired by intellectual processes, but this knowledge alone Arnold readily admitted to be 'machinery.'

The real purpose and main part of Culture is the training, broadening, and refining of the whole spirit, including the emotions as well as the intellect, into sympathy with all the highest ideals, and therefore into inward peace and satisfaction. Thus Culture is not indolently selfish, but is forever exerting itself to 'make the best ideas'—which Arnold also defined as 'reason and the will, of God'—'prevail.' Arnold felt strongly that a main obstacle to Culture was religious narrowness.

He held that the English people had been too much occupied with the 'Hebraic' ideal of the Old Testament, the interest in morality or right conduct, and though he agreed that this properly makes three quarters of life, he insisted that it should be joined with the Hellenic (Greek) ideal of a perfectly rounded nature. He found the essence of Hellenism expressed in a phrase which he took from Swift, 'Sweetness and Light,' interpreting Sweetness to mean the love of Beauty, material and spiritual, and Light, unbiased intelligence; and he urged that these forces be allowed to have the freest play.

He vigorously attacked the Dissenting denominations, because he believed them to be a conspicuous embodiment of Philistine lack of Sweetness and Light, with an unlovely insistence on unimportant external details and a fatal blindness to the meaning of real beauty and real spirituality. Though he himself was without a theological creed, he was, and held that every Englishman should be, a devoted adherent of the English Church, as a beautiful, dignified, and national expression of essential religion, and therefore a very important influence for Culture. Arnold's doctrine, of course, was not perfectly comprehensive nor free from prejudices; but none could be essentially more useful for his generation or ours.

We may readily grant that it is, in one sense or another, a doctrine for chosen spirits, but if history makes anything clear it is that chosen spirits are the necessary instruments of all progress and therefore the chief hope of society. The differences between Arnold's teaching and that of his two great contemporaries are probably now clear. All three are occupied with the pressing necessity of regenerating society. Carlyle would accomplish this end by means of great individual characters inspired by confidence in the spiritual life and dominating their times by moral strength; Ruskin would accomplish it by humanizing social conditions and spiritualizing and refining all men's natures through devotion to the principles of moral Right and esthetic Beauty; Arnold would leaven the crude mass of society, so far as possible, by permeating it with all the myriad influences of spiritual, moral, and esthetic culture.

All three, of course, like every enlightened reformer, are aiming at ideal conditions which can be actually realized only in the distant future. Arnold's style is one of the most charming features of his work. Clear, direct, and elegant, it reflects most attractively his own high breeding; but it is also eminently forceful, and marked by very skilful emphasis and reiteration. One of his favorite devices is a pretense of great humility, which is only a shelter from which he shoots forth incessant and pitiless volleys of ironical raillery, light and innocent in appearance, but irresistible in aim and penetrating power.

Lord Alfred Tennyson

It is pertinent to note that in poetry, apart from the drama, the Victorian period is the greatest in English literature. Its most representative, though not its greatest, poet is Alfred Tennyson. Tennyson, the fourth of a large family of children, was born in Somersby, Lincolnshire, in 1809. That year, as it happened, is distinguished by the birth of a large number of eminent men, among them Gladstone, Darwin, and Lincoln. Tennyson's father was a clergyman, holding his appointments from a member of the landed gentry; his mother was peculiarly gentle and benevolent. From childhood the poet, though physically strong, was moody and given to solitary dreaming; from early childhood also he composed poetry, and when he was seventeen he and one of his elder brothers brought out a volume of verse, immature, but of distinct poetic feeling and promise.

The next year they entered Trinity College, Cambridge, where Tennyson, too reserved for public prominence, nevertheless developed greatly through association with a gifted group of students. Called home by the fatal illness of his father shortly before his four year's were completed, he decided, as Milton had done, and as Browning was even then doing, to devote himself to his art; but, like Milton, he equipped himself, now and throughout his life, by hard and systematic study of many of the chief branches of knowledge, including the sciences. His next twenty years were filled with difficulty and sorrow.

Two volumes of poems which he published in 1830 and 1832 were greeted by the critics with their usual harshness, which deeply wounded his sensitive spirit and checked his further publication for ten years; though the second of these volumes contains some pieces which, in their later, revised, form, are among his chief lyric triumphs. In 1833 his warm friend Arthur Hallam, a young man of extraordinary promise, who was engaged, moreover, to one of Tennyson's sisters, died suddenly without warning. Tennyson's grief, at first overwhelming, was long a main factor in his life and during many years found slow artistic expression in 'In Memoriam' and other poems. A few years later came another deep sorrow.

Tennyson formed an engagement of marriage with Miss Emily Sellwood, but his lack of worldly prospects led her relatives to cancel it. Always a lover of the sea, he soon took up his residence in the Isle of Wight. His production of poetry was steady, and its variety great. The largest of all his single achievements was the famous series of 'Idylls of the King,' which formed a part of his occupation for many years. In much of his later work there is a marked change from his earlier elaborate decorativeness to a style of vigorous strength. At the age of sixty-five, fearful that he had not yet done enough to insure his fame, he gave a remarkable demonstration of poetic vitality by striking out into the to him new field of poetic drama.

His important works here are the three tragedies in which he aimed to complete the series of Shakespeare's chronicle-history plays; but he lacked the power of dramatic action, and the result is rather three fine poems than successful plays. In 1883, after having twice refused a baronetcy, he, to the regret of his more democratic friends, accepted a peerage (barony). Tennyson disliked external show, but he was always intensely loyal to the institutions of England, he felt that literature was being honored in his person, and he was willing to secure a position of honor for his son, who had long rendered him devoted service. He died quietly in 1892, at the age of eighty-three, and was buried in Westminster Abbey beside Browning, who had found a resting-place there three years earlier. His personal character, despite some youthful morbidness, was unusually delightful, marked by courage, honesty, sympathy, and straightforward manliness.

An Assessment of his Poetry

Now a few words about poetry and poetic style.

1. The variety of his poetic forms is probably greater than that of any other English poet. In summary catalogue may be named: lyrics, both delicate and stirring; ballads; romantic dreams and fancies; descriptive poems; sentimental reveries, and idyls; long narratives, in which he displays perfect narrative skill; delightfully realistic character-sketches, some of them in dialect; dramas; and meditative poems, long and short, on religious, ethical, and social questions. In almost all these forms he has produced numerous masterpieces.

2. Most characteristic, perhaps, is his exquisite artistry (in which he learned much from Keats). His appreciation for sensuous beauty, especially color, is acute; his command of poetic phraseology is unsurpassed; he suggests shades of, feeling and elusive aspiration with, marvelously subtile power; his descriptions are magnificently beautiful, often with much detail; and his melody is often the perfection of sweetness. Add the truth and tenderness of his emotion, and it results that he is one of the finest and most moving of lyric poets. Nor is all this beauty vague and unsubstantial. Not only was he the most careful of English poets, revising his works with almost unprecedented pains, but his scientific habit of mind insists on the greatest accuracy; in his allusions to Nature he often introduces scientific facts in a way thitherto unparalleled, and sometimes even only doubtfully poetic. The influence of the classic literatures on his style and expression was great; no poet combines more harmoniously classic perfection and romantic feeling.

3. His chief deficiency is in the dramatic quality. No one can present more finely than he moods (often carefully set in a harmoniously appropriate background of external nature) or characters in stationary position; and there is splendid spirit in his narrative passages of vigorous action. Nevertheless his genius and the atmosphere of his poems are generally dreamy, romantic, and aloof from actual life. A brilliant critic has caustically observed that he 'withdraws from the turmoil of the real universe into the fortress of his own mind, and beats the enemy in toy battles with toy soldiers.' He never succeeded in presenting to the satisfaction of most good critics a vigorous man in vigorous action.

4. The ideas of his poetry are noble and on the whole clear. He was an independent thinker, though not an innovator, a conservative liberal, and was so widely popular because he expressed in frank but reverent fashion the moderately advanced convictions of his time. His social ideals, in which he is intensely interested, are those of Victorian humanitarianism. He hopes ardently for a steady amelioration of the condition of the masses, proceeding toward a time when all men shall have real opportunity for full development; and freedom is one of his chief watchwords. But with typical English conservatism he believes that progress must be gradual, and that it should be controlled by order, loyalty, and reverence. Like a true Englishman, also, he is sure that the institutions of England are the best in the world, so that he is a strong supporter of the monarchy and the hereditary aristocracy.

In religion, his inherited belief, rooted in his deepest fibers, early found itself confronted by the discoveries of modern science, which at first seemed to him to proclaim that the universe is much what it seemed to the young Carlyle, a remorseless monster, 'red in tooth and claw,' scarcely thinkable as the work of a Christian God who cares for man. Tennyson was too sincere to evade the issue, and after years of inner struggle he arrived at a positive faith in the central principles of Christianity, broadly interpreted, though it was avowedly a faith based on instinct and emotional need rather than on unassailable reasoning. His somewhat timid disposition, moreover, never allowed him to enunciate his conclusions with anything like the buoyant aggressiveness of his contemporary, Robert Browning. How greatly science had influenced his point of view appears in the conception which is central in his later poetry, namely that the forces of the universe are governed by unchanging Law, through which God works. The best final expression of his spirit is the lyric 'Crossing the Bar,' which every one knows and which at his own request is printed last in all editions of his works.

Elizabeth Barrett Browning and Robert Browning

Robert Browning was born in a London suburb in 1812 (the same year with Dickens), of very mixed ancestry, which may partly explain the very diverse traits in his nature and poetry. His father, a man of artistic and cultured tastes, held a subordinate though honorable position in the Bank of England. The son inherited a strong instinct for all the fine arts, and though he composed verses before he could write, seemed for years more likely to become a musician than a poet. His formal schooling was irregular, but he early began to acquire from his father's large and strangely-assorted library the vast fund of information which astonishes the reader of his poetry, and he too lived a healthy out-of-door life.

His parents being Dissenters, the universities were not open to him, and when he was seventeen his father somewhat reluctantly consented to his own unhesitating choice of poetry as a profession. For seventeen years more he continued in his father's home, living a normal life among his friends, writing continuously, and gradually acquiring a reputation among some good critics, but making very little impression on the public. Some of his best short poems date from these years, such as 'My Last Duchess' and 'The Bishop Orders His Tomb'; but his chief effort went into a series of seven or eight poetic dramas, of which 'Pippa Passes' is best known and least dramatic. They are noble poetry, but display in marked degree the psychological subtilety which in part of his poetry demands unusually close attention from the reader.

In one of the pieces in her volumes of 1844 Elizabeth Barrett mentioned Browning, among other poets, with generous praise. This led to a correspondence between the two, and soon to a courtship, in which Browning's earnestness finally overcame Miss Barrett's scrupulous hesitation to lay upon him (as she felt) the burden of her invalidism. Indeed her invalidism at last helped to turn the scales in Browning's favor, for the physicians had declared that Miss Barrett's life depended on removal to a warmer climate, but to this her father, a well-intentioned but strangely selfish man, absolutely refused to consent.

The record of the courtship is given in Mrs. Browning's 'Sonnets from the Portuguese' (a whimsical title, suggested by Mrs. Browning's childhood nickname, 'The Little Portuguese'), which is one of the finest of English sonnet-sequences. The marriage, necessarily clandestine, took place in 1846; Mrs. Browning's father thenceforth treated her as one dead, but the removal from her morbid surroundings largely restored her health for the remaining fifteen years of her life. During these fifteen years the two poets resided chiefly in various cities of Italy, with a nominal home in

Florence, and Mrs. Browning had an inherited income which sufficed for their support until their poetry became profitable.

Their chief works during this period were Mrs. Browning's 'Aurora Leigh' (1856), a long 'poetic novel' in blank verse dealing with the relative claims of Art and Social Service and with woman's place in the world; and Browning's most important single publication, his two volumes of 'Men and Women' (1855), containing fifty poems, many of them among his very best. Mrs. Browning was passionately interested in the Italian struggle for independence against Austrian tyranny, and her sudden death in 1861 seems to have been hastened by that of the Italian statesman Cavour.

Browning, at first inconsolable, soon returned with his son to London, where he again made his home, for the rest of his life. Henceforth he published much poetry, for the most part long pieces of subtile psychological and spiritual analysis. In 1868-9 he brought out his characteristic masterpiece, 'The Ring and the Book,' a huge psychological epic, which proved the tardy turning point in his reputation. People might not understand the poem, but they could not disregard it, the author became famous, almost popular, and a Browning cult arose, marked by the spread of Browning societies in both England and America.

Browning enjoyed his success for twenty years and died quietly in 1889 at the home of his son in Venice. Browning earnestly reciprocated his wife's loyal devotion and seemed really to believe, as he often insisted, that her poetry was of a higher order than his own. Her achievement, indeed, was generally overestimated, in her own day and later, but it is now recognized that she is scarcely a really great artist. Her intense emotion, her fine Christian idealism, and her very wide reading give her real power; her womanly tenderness is admirable; and the breadth of her interests and sometimes the clearness of her judgment are notable; but her secluded life of ill-health rendered her often sentimental, high-strung, and even hysterical. She has in her the impulses and material of great poetry, but circumstances and her temperament combined to deny her the patient self-discipline necessary for the best results. She writes vehemently to assert the often-neglected rights of women and children or to denounce negro slavery and all oppression; and sometimes, as when in 'The Cry of the Children' she revealed the hideousness of child-labor in the factories, she is genuine and irresistible; but more frequently she produces highly romantic or mystical imaginary narrations (often in medieval settings). She not seldom mistakes enthusiasm or indignation for artistic inspiration, and she is repeatedly and inexcusably careless in meter and rime. Perhaps her most satisfactory poems, aside from those above mentioned, are 'The Vision of Poets' and 'The Rime of the Duchess May.'

Salient features of her poetry can be summarised as follows:

1. Browning is the most thoroughly vigorous and dramatic of all great poets who employ other forms than the actual drama. Of his hundreds of poems the great majority set before the reader a glimpse of actual life and human personalities—an action, a situation, characters, or a character—in the clearest and most vivid possible way. Sometimes the poem is a ringing narration of a fine exploit, like 'How They Brought the Good News'; sometimes it is quieter and more reflective. Whatever the style, however, in the great majority of cases Browning employs the form which without having actually invented it he developed into an instrument of thitherto unsuspected power, namely

the dramatic monolog in which a character discusses his situation or life or some central part or incident, of it, under circumstances which reveal with wonderful completeness its significance and his own essential character. To portray and interpret life in this way, to give his readers a sudden vivid understanding of its main forces and conditions in representative moments, may be called the first obvious purpose, or perhaps rather instinct, of Browning and his poetry. The dramatic economy of space which he generally attains in his monologs is marvelous. In 'My Last Duchess' sixty lines suffice to etch into our memories with incredible completeness and clearness two striking characters, an interesting situation, and the whole of a life's tragedy.

2. Despite his power over external details it is in the human characters, as the really significant and permanent elements of life, that Browning is chiefly interested; indeed he once declared directly that the only thing that seemed to him worth while was the study of souls. The number and range of characters that he has portrayed are unprecedented, and so are the keenness, intenseness, and subtilety of the analysis. Andrea del Sarto, Fra Lippo Lippi, Cleon, Karshish, Balaustion, and many scores of others, make of his poems a great gallery of portraits unsurpassed in interest by those of any author whatever except Shakespeare. It is little qualification of his achievement to add that all his persons are somewhat colored by his own personality and point of view, or that in his later poetry he often splits hairs very ingeniously in his effort to understand and present sympathetically the motives of all characters, even the worst. These are merely some of the secondary aspects of his peculiar genius. Browning's favorite heroes and heroines, it should be added, are men and women much like himself, of strong will and decisive power of action, able to take the

lead vigorously and unconventionally and to play controlling parts in the drama of life.

3. The frequent comparative difficulty of Browning's poetry arises in large part first from the subtilety of his thought and second from the obscurity of his subject-matter and his fondness for out-of-the-way characters. It is increased by his disregard of the difference between his own extraordinary mental power and agility on the one hand and on the other the capacity of the average person, a disregard which leads him to take much for granted that most readers are obliged to study out with no small amount of labor. Moreover Browning was hasty in composition, corrected his work little, if at all, and was downright careless in such details as sentence structure. But the difficulty arising from these various eccentricities occurs chiefly in his longer poems, and often serves mainly as a mental stimulus. Equally striking, perhaps, is his frequent grotesqueness in choice of subject and in treatment, which seems to result chiefly from his wish to portray the world as it actually is, keeping in close touch with genuine everyday reality; partly also from his instinct to break away from placid and fiberless conventionality.

4. Browning is decidedly one of those who hold the poet to be a teacher, and much, indeed most, of his poetry is occupied rather directly with the questions of religion and the deeper meanings of life. Taken all together, that is, his poetry constitutes a very extended statement of his philosophy of life. The foundation of his whole theory is a confident and aggressive optimism. He believes, partly on the basis of intellectual reasoning, but mainly on what seems to him the convincing testimony of instinct, that the universe is controlled by a loving God, who has made life primarily a thing of happiness for man. Man should accept

life with gratitude and enjoy to the full all its possibilities. Evil exists only to demonstrate the value of Good and to develop character, which can be produced only by hard and sincere struggle. Unlike Tennyson, therefore, Browning has full confidence in present reality—he believes that life on earth is predominantly good. Nevertheless earthly life is evidently incomplete in itself, and the central law of existence is Progress, which gives assurance of a future life where man may develop the spiritual nature which on earth seems to have its beginning and distinguishes man from the brutes. This future life, however, is probably not one but many, a long succession of lives, the earlier ones not so very different, perhaps, from the present one on earth; and even the worst souls, commencing the next life, perhaps, as a result of their failure here, at a spiritual stage lower than the present one, must ultimately pass through all stages of the spiritual process, and come to stand with all the others near the perfection of God himself.

This whole theory, which, because later thought has largely adopted it from Browning, seems much less original to-day than when he first propounded it, is stated and reiterated in his poems with a dynamic idealizing power which, whether or not one assents to it in details, renders it magnificently stimulating. It is rather fully expressed as a whole, in two of Browning's best known and finest poems, 'Rabbi ben Ezra,' and 'Abt Vogler.' Some critics, it should be added, however, feel that Browning is too often and too insistently a teacher in his poetry and that his art would have gained if he had introduced his philosophy much more incidentally.

5. In his social theory Browning differs not only from Tennyson but from the prevailing thought of his age, differs in that his emphasis is individualistic. Like all the

other Victorians he dwells on the importance of individual devotion to the service of others, but he believes that the chief results of such effort must be in the development of the individual's character, not greatly in the actual betterment of the world. The world, indeed, as it appears to him, is a place of probation and we cannot expect ever to make it over very radically; the important thing is that the individual soul shall use it to help him on his 'lone way' to heaven. Browning, accordingly, takes almost no interest in the specific social and political questions of his day, a fact which certainly will not operate against the permanence of his fame.

More detrimental, no doubt, aside from the actual faults which we have mentioned, will be his rather extravagant Romanticism—the vehemence of his passion and his insistence on the supreme value of emotion.

Rossetti and the Pre-Raphaelite Movement

Many of the secondary Victorian poets must here be passed by, but several of them are too important to be dismissed without at least brief notice. The middle of the century is marked by a new Romantic impulse, the Pre-Raphaelite Movement, which begins with Dante Gabriel Rossetti. Rossetti was born in London in 1828. His father was an Italian, a liberal refugee from the outrageous government of Naples, and his mother was also half Italian. The household, though poor, was a center for other Italian exiles, but this early and tempestuous political atmosphere created in the poet, by reaction, a lifelong aversion for politics. His desultory education was mostly in the lines of painting and the Italian and English poets. His own practice in poetry began as early as is usual with poets, and before he was nineteen, by a special inspiration, he wrote his best and most famous poem, 'The Blessed Damosel.' In the school of the Royal Academy of Painting, in 1848, he met William Holman Hunt and John E. Millais, and the three formed the Pre-Raphaelite Brotherhood, in which Rossetti, whose disposition throughout his life was extremely self-assertive, or even domineering, took the lead. The purpose of the Brotherhood was to restore to painting and literature the qualities which the three enthusiasts found in the fifteenth century Italian painters, those who just preceded Raphael. Rossetti and his friends did not decry the noble idealism of Raphael himself, but they felt that in trying to follow his grand style the art of their own time had become too abstract and conventional. They wished to renew emphasis on serious emotion, imagination, individuality, and fidelity to truth; and in doing so they gave special attention to elaboration of details in a fashion distinctly reminiscent of medievalism. Their work had much, also, of medieval mysticism and symbolism. Besides painting pictures they published a very short-lived periodical, 'The Germ,' containing both literary material and drawings. Ruskin, now arriving at fame and influence, wrote vigorously in their favor, and though the Brotherhood did not last long as an organization, it has exerted a great influence on subsequent painting.

Rossetti's impulses were generous, but his habits were eccentric and selfish, and his life unfortunate. His engagement with Miss Eleanor Siddal, a milliner's apprentice (whose face appears in many of his pictures), was prolonged by his lack of means for nine years; further, he was an agnostic, while she held a simple religious faith, and she was carrying on a losing struggle with tuberculosis. Sixteen months after their marriage she died, and on a morbid impulse of remorse for inconsiderateness in his treatment of her Rossetti buried his poems, still unpublished, in her coffin. After some years, however, he was persuaded to disinter and publish them. Meanwhile he had formed friendships with the slightly younger artists William Morris and Edward Burne-Jones, and they established a company for the manufacture of furniture and other articles, to be made beautiful as well as useful, and thus to aid in spreading the esthetic sense among the English people. After some years Rossetti and Burne-Jones withdrew from the enterprise, leaving it to Morris.

Rossetti continued all his life to produce both poetry and paintings. His pictures are among the best and most gorgeous products of recent romantic art—'Dante's Dream,' 'Beata Beatrix,' 'The Blessed Damosel,' and many others. During his later years he earned a large income, and he lived in a large house in Cheyne Row, Chelsea (near Carlyle), where for a while, as long as his irregular habits permitted, the novelist George Meredith and the poet Swinburne were also inmates. He gradually grew more morbid, and became a rather pitiful victim of insomnia, the drug chloral, and spiritualistic delusions about his wife. He died in 1882.

Remarkably, Rossetti's poetry is absolutely unlike that of any other English poet, and the difference is clearly due in large part to his Italian race and his painter's instinct. He has, in the didactic sense, absolutely no religious, moral, or social interests; he is an artist almost purely for art's sake, writing to give beautiful embodiment to moods, experiences, and striking moments. If it is true of Tennyson, however, that he stands aloof from actual life, this is far truer of Rossetti. His world is a vague and languid region of enchantment, full of whispering winds, indistinct forms of personified abstractions, and the murmur of hidden streams; its landscape sometimes bright, sometimes shadowy, but always delicate, exquisitely arranged for luxurious decorative effect.

In his ballad-romances, to be sure, such as, 'The King's Tragedy,' there is much dramatic vigor; yet there is still more of medieval weirdness. Rossetti, like Dante, has much of spiritual mysticism, and his interest centers in the inner rather than the outer life; but his method, that of a painter and a southern Italian, is always highly sensuous. His melody is superb and depends partly on a highly Latinized vocabulary, archaic pronunciations, and a delicate genius in sound-modulation, the effect being heightened also by frequent alliteration and masterly use of refrains. 'Sister Helen,' obviously influenced by the popular ballad 'Edward, Edward,' derives much of its tremendous tragic power from the refrain, and in the use of this device is perhaps the most effective poem in the world. Rossetti is especially facile also with the sonnet.

William Morris

William Morris, a man of remarkable versatility and tremendous energy, which expressed themselves in poetry and many other ways, was the son of a prosperous banker, and was born in London in 1834. At Oxford in 1853-55 he became interested in medieval life and art, was stimulated by the poetry of Mrs. Browning and Tennyson, became a friend of Burne-Jones, wrote verse and prose, and was a member of a group called 'The Brotherhood,' while a little later published for a year a monthly magazine not unlike 'The Germ.' He apprenticed himself to an architect, but at the same time also practised several decorative arts, such as woodcarving, illuminating manuscripts, and designing furniture, stained glass and embroidery. Together with Burne-Jones, moreover, he became an enthusiastic pupil of Rossetti in painting. His first volume of verse, 'The Defence of Guinevere and Other Poems,' put forth in 1858, shows the influence of Rossetti and Pre-Raphaelitism, but it mainly gives vivid presentation to the spirit of fourteenth-century French chivalry.

In 1861 came the foundation of the decorative-art firm of Morris and Co., which after some years grew into a large business, continued to be Morris' main occupation to the end of his life, and has exercised a great influence, both in England and elsewhere, on the beautifying of the surroundings of domestic life. Meanwhile Morris had turned to the writing of long narrative poems, which he composed with remarkable fluency. The most important is the series of versions of Greek and Norse myths and legends which appeared in 1868-70 as 'The Earthly Paradise.' Shortly after this he became especially interested in Icelandic literature and published versions of some of its stories; notably one of the Siegfried tale, 'Sigurd the Volsung.' In the decade from 1880 to 1890 he devoted most of his energy to work for the Socialist party, of which he became a leader. His ideals were largely identical with those of Ruskin; in particular he wished to restore (or create) in the lives of workingmen conditions which should make of each of them an independent artist. The practical result of his experience was bitter disappointment, he was deposed from his leadership, finally abandoned the party, and returned to art and literature.

Charles Swinburne

Born in 1837 into a wealthy family, the son of an admiral, Charles Swinburne devoted himself throughout his life wholly to poetry, and his career was almost altogether devoid of external incident. After passing through Eton and Oxford he began as author at twenty-three by publishing two plays imitative of Shakespeare. Five years later he put forth 'Atalanta in Calydon,' a tragedy not only drawn from

Greek heroic legend, but composed in the ancient Greek manner, with long dialogs and choruses.

These two volumes express the two intensely vigorous forces which were strangely combined in his nature; for while no man has ever been a more violent romanticist than Swinburne, yet, as one critic has said, 'All the romantic riot in his blood clamored for Greek severity and Greek restraint.' During the next fifteen years he was partly occupied with a huge poetic trilogy in blank verse on Mary Queen of Scots, and from time to time he wrote other dramas and much prose criticism, the latter largely in praise of the Elizabethan dramatists and always wildly extravagant in tone. He produced also some long narrative poems, of which the chief is 'Tristram of Lyonesse.' His chief importance, however, is as a lyric poet, and his lyric production was large. His earlier poems in this category are for the most part highly objectionable in substance or sentiment, but he gradually worked into a better vein. He was a friend of George Meredith, Burne-Jones, Morris, Rossetti (to whom he loyally devoted himself for years), and the painter Whistler. He died in 1909. Swinburne carried his radicalism into all lines. Though an ardently patriotic Englishman, he was an extreme republican; and many of his poems are dedicated to the cause of Italian independence or to liberty in general.

The significance of his thought, however, is less than that of any other English poet who can in any sense be called great; his poetry is notable chiefly for its artistry, especially for its magnificent melody. Indeed, it has been cleverly said that he offers us an elaborate service of gold and silver, but with little on it except salt and pepper. In his case, however, the mere external beauty and power often seem their own complete and satisfying justification.

His command of different meters is marvelous; he uses twice as many as Browning, who is perhaps second to him in this respect, and his most characteristic ones are those of gloriously rapid anapestic lines with complicated rime-schemes. Others of his distinctive traits are lavish alliteration, rich sensuousness, grandiose vagueness of thought and expression, a great sweep of imagination, and a corresponding love of vastness and desolation. He makes much decorative use of Biblical imagery and of vague abstract personifications—in general creates an atmosphere similar to that of Rossetti.

Now we shall introduce you to some other Victorian poets.

Among the other Victorian poets, three, at least, must be mentioned. Arthur Hugh Clough (1819-1861), tutor at Oxford and later examiner in the government education office, expresses the spiritual doubt and struggle of the period in noble poems similar to those of Matthew Arnold, whose fine elegy 'Thyrsis' commemorates him. Edward Fitzgerald (1809-1883), Irish by birth, an eccentric though kind-hearted recluse, and a friend of Tennyson, is known solely for his masterly paraphrase (1859) of some of the Quatrains of the skeptical eleventh-century Persian astronomer-poet Omar Khayyam. The similarity of temper between the medieval oriental scholar and the questioning phase of the Victorian period is striking (though the spirit of Fitzgerald's verse is no doubt as much his own as Omar's), and no poetry is more poignantly beautiful than the best of this. Christina Rossetti (1830-94), the sister of Dante Gabriel Rossetti, lived in London with her mother in the greatest seclusion, occupied with an ascetic devotion to the English Church, with her poetry, and with the composition, secondarily, of prose articles and short stories. Her poetry is limited almost entirely to the lyrical expression of her spiritual experiences, much of it is explicitly religious, and all of it is religious in feeling. It is tinged with the Pre-Raphaelite mystic medievalism; and a quiet and most affecting sadness is its dominant trait; but the power and beauty of a certain small part of it perhaps entitle her to be called the chief of English poetesses.

Charles Dickens

The most popular of all English novelists, Charles Dickens, was born in 1812, the son of an unpractical and improvident government navy clerk whom, with questionable taste, he later caricatured in 'David Copperfield' as Mr. Micawber. The future novelist's schooling was slight and irregular, but as a boy he read much fiction, especially seventeenth and eighteenth century authors, whose influence is apparent in the picaresque lack of structure of his own works. From childhood also he showed the passion for the drama and the theater which resulted from the excitably dramatic quality of his own temperament and which always continued to be the second moving force of his life.

When he was ten years old his father was imprisoned for debt (like Micawber, in the Marshalsea prison), and he was put to work in the cellar of a London shoe-blacking factory. On his proud and sensitive disposition this humiliation, though it lasted only a few months, inflicted a wound which never thoroughly healed; years after he was famous he would cross the street to avoid the smell from an altogether different blacking factory, with its reminder 'of what he once was.'

To this experience, also, may evidently be traced no small part of the intense sympathy with the oppressed poor, especially with helpless children, which is so prominent in his novels. Obliged from the age of fifteen to earn his own living, for the most part, he was for a while a clerk in a London lawyer's office, where he observed all sorts and conditions of people with characteristic keenness. Still more valuable was his five or six years' experience in the very congenial and very active work of a newspaper reporter, where his special department was political affairs. This led up naturally to his permanent work. The successful series of lively 'Sketches by Boz' dealing with people and scenes about London was preliminary to 'The Pickwick Papers,' which made the author famous at the age of twenty-four. During the remaining thirty-three years of his life Dickens produced novels at the rate of rather more than one in two years. He composed slowly and carefully but did not revise greatly, and generally published by monthly installments in periodicals which, latterly, he himself established and edited. Next after 'The Pickwick Papers' came 'Oliver Twist,' and 'David Copperfield' ten years later. Of the others, 'Martin Chuzzlewit,' 'Dombey and Son,' 'Bleak House,' and 'A Tale of Two Cities,' are among the best. For some years Dickens also published an annual Christmas story, of which the first two, 'A Christmas Carol' and 'The Chimes,' rank highest. Dickens' magnificent emotional power is not balanced, however, by a corresponding intellectual quality; in his work, as in his temperament and bearing, emotion is always in danger of running to excess. One of his great elements of strength is his sense of humor, which has created an almost unlimited number of delightful scenes and characters; but it very generally becomes riotous and so ends in sheer farce and caricature, as the names of many of the characters suggest at the outset. Indeed Dickens has been rightly designated a grotesque novelist—the greatest of all grotesque novelists. Similarly his pathos is often exaggerated until it passes into mawkish sentimentality, so that his humbly-bred heroines, for example, are made to act and talk with all the poise and certainty which can really spring only from wide experience and broad education. Dickens' zeal for reform, also, sometimes outruns his judgment or knowledge and leads him to assault evils that had actually been abolished long before he wrote.

No other English author has approached Dickens in the number of characters whom he has created; his twenty novels present literally thousands of persons, almost all thoroughly human, except for the limitations that we have already noted. Their range is of course very great, though it never extends successfully into the 'upper' social classes. For Dickens was violently prejudiced against the nobility and against all persons of high social standing, and when he attempted to introduce them created only pitifully wooden automatons. For the actual English gentleman we must pass by his Sir Leicester Dedlocks and his Mr. Veneerings to novelists of a very different viewpoint, such as Thackeray and Meredith. Dickens' inexhaustible fertility in characters and scenes is a main cause of the rather extravagant lack of unity which is another conspicuous feature of his books. He usually made a good preliminary general plan and proceeded on the whole with firm movement and strong suspense. But he always introduces many characters and sub-actions not necessary to the main story, and develops them quite beyond their real artistic importance.

Not without influence here was the necessity of filling a specified number of serial instalments, each of a definite number of pages, and each requiring a striking situation at the end. Moreover, Dickens often follows the eighteenth-century picaresque habit of tracing the histories of his heroes from birth to marriage. In most respects, however,

Dickens' art improved as he proceeded. The love element, it should be noted, as what we have already said implies, plays a smaller part than usual among the various aspects of life which his books present. Not least striking among Dickens' traits is his power of description. His observation is very quick and keen, though not fine; his sense for the characteristic features, whether of scenes in Nature or of human personality and appearance, is unerring; and he has never had a superior in picturing and conveying the atmosphere both of interiors and of all kinds of scenes of human life. London, where most of his novels are wholly or chiefly located, has in him its chief and most comprehensive portrayer.

William M. Thackeray

Thackeray, the son of an East India Company official, was born at Kolkata (India) in 1811. His father died while he was a child and he was taken to England for his education; he was a student in the Charterhouse School and then for a year at Cambridge. Next, on the Continent, he studied drawing, and though his unmethodical and somewhat idle habits prevented him from ever really mastering the technique of the art, his real knack for it enabled him later on to illustrate his own books in a semi-grotesque but effective fashion. Desultory study of the law was interrupted when he came of age by the inheritance of a comfortable fortune, which he managed to lose within a year or two by gambling, speculations, and an unsuccessful effort at carrying on a newspaper. Real application to newspaper and magazine writing secured him after four years a place on 'Eraser's Magazine,' and he was married. Not long after, his wife became insane, but his warm affection for his daughters gave him throughout his life genuine domestic happiness.

For ten years Thackeray's production was mainly in the line of satirical humorous and picaresque fiction, none of it of the first rank. During this period he chiefly attacked current vices, snobbishness, and sentimentality, which latter quality, Thackeray's special aversion, he found rampant in contemporary life and literature, including the novels of Dickens. The appearance of his masterpiece, 'Vanity Fair' (the allegorical title taken from a famous incident in 'Pilgrim's Progress'), in 'Fraser's Magazine' in 1847-8 (the year before Dickens' 'David Copperfield') brought him sudden fame and made him a social lion. Within the next ten years he produced his other important novels, of which the best are 'Pendennis,' 'Henry Esmond,' and 'The Newcomes,' and also his charming essays (first delivered as lectures) on the eighteenth century in England, namely 'English Humorists,' and 'The Four Georges.' All his novels except 'Henry Esmond' were published serially, and he generally delayed composing each instalment until the latest possible moment, working reluctantly except under the stress of immediate compulsion. He was for three years, at its commencement, editor of 'The Cornhill Magazine.' He died in 1863 at the age of fifty-two, of heart failure.

Now we will introduce you to some other middle and later Victorian novelists.

Several of the other novelists of the mid-century and later produced work which in a period of less prolific and less highly developed art would have secured them high distinction. Charles Kingsley (1819-1875) spent most of his life, by his own self-renouncing choice, as curate and rector of the little Hampshire parish of Eversley, though for some years he also held the professorship of history at Cambridge. An aggressive Protestant, he drifted in his later years into the controversy with Cardinal Newman which opened the way for Newman's 'Apologia.' From the outset, Kingsley was an enthusiastic worker with F. D. Maurice in the Christian Socialist movement which aimed at the betterment of the conditions of life among the working classes. 'Alton Locke' and 'Yeast,' published in 1849, were powerful but reasonable and very influential expressions of his convictions—fervid arguments in the form of fiction against existing social injustices. His most famous books are 'Hypatia' (1853), a novel dealing with the Church in its conflict with Greek philosophy in fifth-century Alexandria, and 'Westward Ho!' (1855) which presents with sympathetic largeness of manner the adventurous side of Elizabethan life. His brief 'Andromeda' is one of the best English poems in the classical dactylic hexameter.

Charles Reade (1814-1884), a man of dramatic disposition somewhat similar to that of Dickens (though Reade had a University education and was admitted to the bar), divided his interest and fiery energies between the drama and the novel. But while his plays were of such doubtful quality that he generally had to pay for having them acted, his novels were often strong and successful. Personally he was fervently evangelical, and like Dickens he was often inspired to write by indignation at social wrongs. His 'Hard Cash' (1863), which attacks private insane asylums, is powerful; but his most important work is 'The Cloister and the Hearth' (1861), one of the most informing and vivid of all historical novels, with the father of Erasmus for its hero.

No novelist can, be more thrilling and picturesque than Reade, but he lacks restraint and is often highly sensational and melodramatic. Altogether different is the method of Anthony Trollope (1815-1882) in his fifty novels. Trollope, long a traveling employe in the post-office service, was a man of very assertive and somewhat commonplace nature. Partly a disciple of Thackeray, he went beyond Thackeray's example in the refusal to take his art altogether seriously as an art; rather, he treated it as a form of business, sneering at the idea of special inspiration, and holding himself rigidly to a mechanical schedule of composition—a definite and unvarying number of pages in a specified number of hours on each of his working days. The result is not so disastrous as might have been expected; his novels have no small degree of truth and interest.

The most notable are the half dozen which deal with ecclesiastical life in his imaginary county of Barsetshire, beginning with 'The Warden' and 'Barchester Towers.' His 'Autobiography' furnishes in some of its chapters one of the noteworthy existing discussions of the writer's art by a member of the profession.

Richard Blackmore (1825-1900), first a lawyer, later manager of a market-garden, was the author of numerous novels, but will be remembered only for 'Lorna Doone' (1869), a charming reproduction of Devonshire country life assigned to the romantic setting of the time of James II. Its simple-minded and gigantic hero John Ridd is certainly one of the permanent figures of English fiction.

Walter Pater (1839-1894), an Oxford Fellow, also represents distinctly the spirit of unworldliness, which in his case led to a personal aloofness from active life. He was the master of a delicately-finished, somewhat over-fastidious, style, which he employed in essays on the Renaissance and other historical and artistic topics and in a spiritual romance, 'Marius the Epicurean' (1885). No less noteworthy than 'John Inglesant,' and better constructed, this latter is placed in the reign of the Roman Emperor Marcus Aurelius, but its atmosphere is only in part historically authentic.

Joseph H. Shorthouse (1834-1903), a Birmingham chemical manufacturer, but a man of very fine nature, is likewise to be mentioned for a single book, 'John Inglesant' (1881). Located in the middle of the seventeenth century, when the strife of religious and political parties afforded material especially available for the author's purpose, this is a spiritual romance, a High Churchman's assertion of the supremacy of the inner over the outer life. From this point of view it is one of the most significant of English novels, and though much of it is philosophical and though it is not free from technical faults, parts of it attain the extreme limit of absorbing narrative interest.

George Meredith (1828-1910)

George Meredith holds an unquestioned place in the highest rank of novelists. In time he is partly contemporary with George Eliot, as he began to publish a little earlier than she. But he long outlived her and continued to write to the end of his life; and his recognition was long delayed; so that he may properly be placed in the group of later Victorian novelists. His long life was devoid of external incident; he was long a newspaper writer and afterward literary reader for a publishing house; he spent his later years quietly in Surrey, enjoying the friendship of Swinburne and other men of letters. Among novelists he occupies something the same place which Browning, a person of very different temperament and ideas, holds among poets. He writes only for intelligent and thoughtful people and aims to interpret the deeper things of life and character, not disregarding dramatic external incident, but using it as only one of the means to his main purpose.

His style is brilliant, epigrammatic, and subtile; and he prefers to imply many things rather than to state them directly. All this makes large, perhaps sometimes too large, demands on the reader's attention, but there is, of course, corresponding stimulation. Meredith's general attitude toward life is the fine one of serene philosophic confidence, the attitude in general of men like Shakespeare and Goethe. He despises sentimentality, admires chiefly the qualities of quiet strength and good breeding which are exemplified among the best members of the English aristocracy; and in all his interpretation is very largely influenced by modern science.

His virile courage and optimism are as pronounced as those of Browning; he wrote a noteworthy 'Essay on Comedy' and oftentimes insists on emphasizing the comic rather than the tragic aspect of things, though he can also be powerful in tragedy; and his enthusiasms for the beauty of the world and for the romance of youthful love are delightful. He may perhaps best be approached through 'Evan Harrington' (1861) and 'The Ordeal of Richard Feverel' (1859). 'The Egoist' (1879) and 'Diana of the Crossways' (1885) are among his other strongest books. In his earlier years he wrote a considerable body of verse, which shows much the same qualities as his prose.

Thomas Hardy

In Thomas Hardy the pessimistic interpretation of modern science is expressed frankly and fully, with much the same pitiless consistency that distinguishes contemporary European writers such as Zola. Mr. Hardy early turned to literature from architecture and he has lived a secluded life in southern England, the ancient Wessex, which he makes the scene of all his novels. His knowledge of life is sure and his technique in all respects masterly. He has preferred to deal chiefly with persons in the middle and poorer classes of society because, like Wordsworth, though with very different emphasis, he feels that in their experiences the real facts of life stand out most truly. His deliberate theory is a sheer fatalism—that human character and action are the inevitable result of laws of heredity and environment over which man has no control. 'The Return of the Native' (1878) and 'Far from the Madding Crowd' (1874) are among his best novels, though the sensational frankness of 'Tess of the D'Urbervilles' (1891) has given it greater reputation.

Robert Stevenson

Robert Louis Stevenson (1850-1894), the first of the rather prominent group of recent Scotch writers of fiction, is as different as possible from Hardy. Destined for the career of civil engineer and lighthouse builder in which his father and grandfather were distinguished, he proved unfitted for it by lack both of inclination and of health, and the profession of law for which he later prepared himself was no more congenial. From boyhood he, like Scott, studied human nature with keen delight in rambles about the country, and unlike Scott he was incessantly practising writing merely for the perfection of his style. As an author he won his place rather slowly; and his whole mature life was a wonderfully courageous and persistent struggle against the sickness which generally prevented him from working more than two or three hours a day and often kept him for months in bed unable even to speak. A trip to California in an emigrant train in 1879-1880 brought him to death's door but accomplished its purpose, his marriage to an American lady, Mrs. Osbourne, whom he had previously met in artist circles in France. He first secured a popular success with the boys' pirate story, 'Treasure Island,' in 1882. 'A Child's Garden of Verses' (1885) was at once accepted as one of the most irresistibly sympathetic of children's classics; and 'The Strange Case of Dr. Jekyll and Mr. Hyde' (1886), a unique and astonishingly powerful moral lesson in the form of a thrilling little romance which strangely anticipates the later discoveries of psychology, made in its different way a still stronger impression.

Stevenson produced, considering his disabilities, a remarkably large amount of work—essays, short stories, and romances—but the only others of his books which need here be mentioned are the four romances of Scotch life in the eighteenth century which belong to his later years; of these 'The Master of Ballantrae' and the fragmentary 'Weir of Hermiston' are the best. His letters, also, which, like his widely-circulated prayers, reveal his charming and heroic personality, are among the most interesting in the history of English Literature. R.L. Stevenson, in the midst of an age perhaps too intensely occupied with the deeper questions, stood for a return to the mere spirit of romance, and for occasional reading he furnishes delightful recreation. In the last analysis, however, his general lack of serious significance condemns him at most to a secondary position.

At his best his narrative technique (as in 'The Master of Ballantrae') is perfect; his portrayal of men (he almost never attempted women) is equally certain; his style has no superior in English; and his delicate sensibility and keenness of observation render him a master of description. But in his attitude toward life he never reached full maturity (perhaps because of the supreme effort of will necessary for the maintenance of his cheerfulness); not only did he retain to the end a boyish zest for mere adventure, but it is sometimes adventure of a melodramatic and unnecessarily disagreeable kind, and in his novels and short stories he offers virtually no interpretation of the world.

No recent English prose writer has exercised a wider influence than he, but none is likely to suffer as time goes on a greater diminution of reputation.

Rudyard Kipling

The name which naturally closes the list of Victorian writers is that of Rudyard Kipling, though he belongs, perhaps, as much to the twentieth century as to the one preceding. The son of a professor of architecture and sculpture in the University of Bombay, India, he was born in that city in 1865. Educated in England in the United Services College (for officers in the army and navy), he returned at the age of seventeen to India. Kipling is the representative of the vigorous life of action as led by manly and efficient men, and of the spirit of English imperialism. His poem "The White Man's Burden" sums up his imperialism—the creed that it is the duty of the higher races to civilize the lower ones with a strong hand; and he never doubts that the greater part of this obligation rests at present upon England—a theory, certainly, to which history lends much support.

Kipling is endowed with the keenest power of observation, with the most genuine and most democratic human sympathies, and with splendid dramatic force. Consequently he has made a unique contribution to literature in his portrayals, in both prose and verse, of the English common soldier and of English army life on the frontiers of the Empire. On the other hand his verse is generally altogether devoid of the finer qualities of poetry. 'Danny Deever,' 'Pharaoh and the Sergeant,' 'Fuzzy Wuzzy,' 'The Ballad of East and West,' 'The Last Chantey,' 'Mulholland's Contract,' and many others, are splendidly stirring, but their colloquialism and general realism put them on a very different level from the work of the great masters who express the deeper truths in forms of permanent beauty. At times, however, Kipling too gives voice to religious feelings, of a simple sort, in an impressive fashion, as in 'McAndrews' Hymn,' 'The Recessional,' and 'When earth's last picture is painted.' His sweeping rhythms and his grandiose forms of expression, suggestive of the vast spaces of ocean and plain and of inter-stellar space with which he delights to deal, have been very widely copied by minor verse-writers. His very vivid and active imagination enables him not only to humanize animal life with remarkable success, as in the prose 'Jungle-Books,' but to range finely in the realms of the mysterious, as in the short stories 'They' and 'The Brushwood Boy.' Of short-stories he is the most powerful recent writer, as witness 'The Man Who Would Be King,' 'The Man Who Was,' 'Without Benefit of Clergy,' and 'Wee Willie Winkie'; though with all the frankness of modern realism he sometimes leads us into scenes of extreme physical horror. With longer stories he is generally less successful; 'Kim,' however, has much power.

10

Modern Phase

The Twentieth Century

Beginning as early as the latter part of the eighteenth century literary production, thanks largely to the tremendous increase of education and of newspapers and magazines, has steadily grown, until now it has reached bewildering volume and complexity, in which the old principles are partly merged together and the new tendencies, for contemporary observers, at least, scarcely stand out with decisive distinctness. Most significant to-day, perhaps, are the spirit of independence, now carried in some respects beyond the farthest previous Romantic limits, and the realistic impulse, in which the former impulses of democracy and humanitarianism play a large part. Facts not to be disregarded are the steady advance of the short story, beginning early in the Victorian period or before, to a position of almost chief prominence with the novel; and the rise of American literature to a position approaching equality with that of England. Of single authors none have yet certainly achieved places of the first rank, but two or three may be named.

Mr. William De Morgan, by profession a manufacturer of artistic pottery, has astonished the world by beginning to publish at the age of sixty-five a series of novels which show no small amount of Thackeray's power combined with too large a share of Thackeray's diffuseness.

Mr. Alfred Noyes (born 1880) is a refreshingly true lyric poet and balladist, and Mr. John Masefield has daringly enlarged the field of poetry by frank but very sincere treatment of extremely realistic subjects. But none of these authors can yet be termed great. About the future it is useless to prophesy, but the horrible war of 1914 is certain to exert for many years a controlling influence on the thought and literature of both England and the whole world, an influence which, it may be hoped, will ultimately prove stimulating and renovating.

Between the two wars, a revival of romanticism in poetry is associated with the work of W.H. (Wystan Hugh) Auden (1907-73), Louis MacNeice (1907-63) and Cecil Day-Lewis (1904-72). Auden seems to be a major figure on the poetic landscape, but is almost too contemporary to see in perspective. The Welsh poet, Dylan Thomas (1914-53) is notable for strange effects of language, alternating from extreme simplicity to massive overstatement.

Of poets who have achieved celebrity in the second half of the century, evaluation is even more difficult, but writers of note include the American Robert Lowell (1917-77), Philip Larkin (1922-1985), R.S. Thomas (1913-2000), Thom Gunn (1929-2004), Ted Hughes (1930-1998) and the 1995 Nobel laureate Seamus Heaney (b. 1939).

Notable Writers Outside Mainstream Movements

Any list of "important" names is bound to be uneven and selective. Identifying broad movements leads to the exclusion of those who do not easily fit into schematic outlines of history. Writers not referred to above, but highly regarded by some readers might include Laurence Sterne (1713-68), author of *Tristram Shandy*, R.L. Stevenson (1850-94) writer of *Kidnapped* and *The Strange Case of Dr. Jekyll and Mr. Hyde*, Oscar Wilde (1854-1900), author of *The Importance of Being Earnest*, and novelists such as Arnold Bennett (1867-1931), John Galsworthy (1867-1933) and the Americans F. Scott Fitzgerald (1896-1940), Ernest Hemingway (1898-1961), John Steinbeck (1902-68) and J.D. Salinger (b. 1919). Two works notable not just for their literary merit but for their articulation of the spirit of the age are Fitzgerald's *The Great Gatsby* and Salinger's *The Catcher in the Rye*. The American dramatist Arthur Miller (b. 1915) has received similar acclaim for his play *Death of a Salesman* (1949). Miller is more popular in the UK than his native country, and is familiar to many teachers and students because his work is so often set for study in examinations.

In recent times the novel has developed different genres such as the thriller, the whodunnit, the pot-boiler, the western and works of science-fiction, horror and the sex-and-shopping novel. Some of these may be brief fashions (the western seems to be dying) while others such as the detective story or science-fiction have survived for well over a century. As the dominant form of narrative in contemporary western popular culture, the novel may have given way to the feature film and television drama. But it has proved surprisingly resilient. As society alters, so the novel may reflect or define this change; many works may be written, but few of them will fulfil this defining rôle; those which seem to do so now, may not speak to later generations in the same way.

Bibliography

Alexander, Harriet, *American and British Poetry*. Athens, Ohio, 1984.

Bell, Inglis F. and Baird, Donald. *The English novel, 1578-1956; a checklist of twentieth-century criticism*. Denver, 1959.

Cevasco, G.A. *Three decadent poets: Ernest Dowson, John Gray, and Lionel Johnson: and annotated bibliography*. New York 1990.

Chielens, Edward E. *The literary journal in America to 1900*. Detroit, 1975.

Chielens, Edward E. *The literary journal in America, 1900-1950*. Detroit, 1977.

Cline, Gloria S. and Baker, Jeffrey A. *An index to criticisms of British and American poetry*. Metuchen, N.J., 1973.

Contemporary poets. James Vinson, ed. 2d ed. New York, 1975.

Deutsch, Babette. *Poetry handbook, a dictionary of terms*. 4th ed. New York, 1974.

Frank, Frederick S. *The first Gothics: a critical guide to the English Gothic novel*. New York, 1987.

Gerstenberger, Donna and Hendrick, George. *The American novel; a checklist of twentieth-century criticism*. Chicago, 1961-70. 2v.

Granger, Edith. *Index to poetry*. 6th ed. New York, 1973.

Granger's Index to poetry, 1970-1977, ed. by William F. Bernhardt. 8th rev. and enl. New York, 1986.

Jackson, J.R. de J. *Romantic poetry by women: a bibliography, 1770-1835*. Oxford, 1993.

Kuntz, Joseph M. *Poetry explication: a checklist of interpretation since 1925 of British and American poems, past and present*. New York, 1962.

Myers, Jack and Michael Simms. *Longman Dictionary and Handbook of Poetry*. New York, 1985.

New Princeton encyclopedia of poetry and poetics. Ed. by Alex Preminger. Princeton, 1993.

Palmegian, E. M. *Crime in Victorian Britain: an annotated bibliography from nineteenth-century British Magazines*. Westport, Ct, 1993.

Palmer, Helen H. and Dyson, Anne Jane. *English novel explication: criticisms to 1972*. Hamden, Conn., 1973. Suppl. 1: Hamden, Conn., 1976.

Robbins, John Albert, ed. *American literary manuscripts; a checklist*. 2d ed. Athens, Ga., 1977.

Rupert, James and John R. Leo. *Guide to American Poetry Explication* . Boston, 1989. v.1: Colonial and 19th century; v. 2: Modern and Contemporary.

Stanton, Michael N. *English literary journals, 1900-1950: a guide to information sources*. Detroit, 1982.

Topp, Chester W. *Victorian yellowbacks & paperbacks, 1849-1905*. Denver, 1993

Victorian periodicals: a guide to research. Ed. by J. Don Vann and Rosemary T. Van Arsdel. New York, 1978.

Vinson, James, ed. *Contemporary novelists*. 2d ed. London, 1976.

White, Robert B. *The English literary journal to 1900*. Detroit, 1977.

Index

●●●